100 *Great* JOURNEYS

100 *Great* JOURNEYS

CONSULTANT EDITOR: *Keith Lye*

ILEX

100 Great Journeys

First published in the UK in 2008 by

I L E X

The Old Candlemakers
West Street
Lewes
East Sussex BN7 2NZ
www.ilex-press.com

Copyright © 2008 The Ilex Press Limited

Publisher: Alastair Campbell
Creative Director: Peter Bridgewater
Managing Editor: Chris Gatcum
General Editor: Keith Lye
Art Director: Julie Weir
Designer: Graham Davis
Design Assistant: Emily Harbison

Cover images: © Alamy / Corbis

British Library Cataloguing-in-Publication Data
A catalogue record for this book is available from
the British Library.

ISBN 13: 978-1-905814-31-2
ISBN 10: 1-905814-31-3

Printed in Thailand

CONTENTS

People have always been curious about what lies beyond the horizon. In prehistoric times, our hunter-gatherer ancestors migrated from their homelands in Africa to eventually colonize every part of the world. Some were searching for food and water, while others wanted to find new homes, but what they had in common was the need to set out on a journey of exploration.

Beyond the horizon
The beauty of travel

Today, for those who have the time and the money, most travel is relatively comfortable and rapid. Instead of traveling by foot, on horseback, or in a horse-drawn carriage, people speed across continents by road and rail, while air transport has become commonplace, enabling us to reach remote and exotic places without much difficulty at all.

Road transport is popular in the Western world, not only as a means of getting from A to B, but as a comfortable way of exploring further afield. In the United States, where most people own cars, a single highway—such as Highway 61 or Route 66—can offer hundreds of miles of culture, history, and scenic interest, all from the comfort of an automobile and a stretch of paved road. The adventurous tourist can journey along more remote routes in far flung destinations, traveling along the Grand Trunk Road, which winds through the Khyber Pass, or recreating the dream of Cecil Rhodes and his route from Cairo to Cape Town.

Yet while the road is appealing, traveling by rail is often considered much more romantic, as exemplified by the Orient Express. Train passengers can view breath-taking landscapes in destinations as disparate as New Zealand, Canada, the Isthmus of Kra, and the frozen wastes of Siberia, all from the comfort of their personal compartment, a dining car, or a purpose-built observation deck.

But although traveling under power is convenient, some areas of outstanding natural beauty are always best seen on foot—or maybe on horseback—not least because the pollution and noise that accompany many forms of modern transport can damage fragile environments. Today, an increasing number of travelers realize that we all have a responsibility to help to protect the places that we come to enjoy, and a new word—*ecotourism*—has entered our vocabulary.

In the past, great journeys were invariably undertaken on foot or horseback, but while the mode of travel was limited, the reasons were not. Alexander the Great's conquests were inspired by military glory, while pioneers such as Marco Polo sought new trade routes. Others, such as the Forty-niners in North America, were motivated by nothing more than a personal lust for gold.

WELCOME TO
WA/SA BORDER VILLAGE
SOUTH POLE 6,619 km
1994 km
NEW
15,075
LONDON
BERLIN
16,025
17,204 km
PERTH
km
1320 km
WELLINGTON 4,738 km
HOBART 2,100 km
CAPE TOWN
15,558 km
SYDNEY
km
MOSCOW
15,913 km

> ## "To travel hopefully is a better thing than to arrive."
> *Robert Louis Stevenson*

From the 15th century, the discoveries made during the European Age of Exploration gradually filled in huge gaps in the world map. The opening up of the Americas and Africa by European explorers dramatically extended people's understanding of the the rich diversity of our planet, and exploration of the remote areas of the world continued for hundreds of years. Tragically, though, exploration and discovery had its darker side. The exploration and mapping of the coasts of Africa triggered the European slave trade, and following the explorers came colonizers. Contact with common diseases against which the indigenous peoples had no defence, together with territorial wars, often led to the decimation of local populations, not just in Africa, but with the Native Americans of North America, and other local cultures.

Almost as powerful a motive as exploration is religion, with many people undertaking journeys inspired by their chosen deity or spiritual leader. Followers of Christianity visit shrines containing holy relics, retracing medieval pilgrimage routes, or taking paths that lead to Jerusalem, or Rome. For Muslims, Mecca is the destination that all members of the faith should visit once in their lifetime, while others seek out the holy places trodden by great religious leaders, such as Buddha, or the Dalai Lama.

But while religion is a major source of inspiration, others fascinated by military history undertake long journeys to tramp across the sites of great battles or military emplacements, such as the Great Wall of China, or follow the routes of great military commanders, such as Simón Bolívar or Napoleon. The aftermath of war undoubtedly leads many to seek out battlefields often marked by huge cemeteries where loved ones or ancestors found their final resting place.

Travel has always included an element of excitement and adventure, a sense of facing the unknown, and perhaps a risk of danger. Some travelers relish physical and mental challenges; to climb the peaks of the world's highest mountains, or sail around the globe.

Antique world maps often contained large gaps, which the more imaginative cartographers populated with strange beasts. "Here be dragons!" was a caption that filled some of the empty spaces on

old maps. Although most of the world has now been mapped using aerial photography, and the fear of mythical beasts dispelled, that does not deter people from embarking on their own voyages of discovery. Many have no specific objective in mind, other than to experience the sheer joy and exhilaration of travel, reveling in the many incidental surprises they encounter on their way.

The journeys in this chapter have one overwhelming characteristic in common: they are all immensely, almost epically long, spanning—and in some cases bridging—continents. Yet these are not merely journeys through a vast variety of landscapes; they are journeys through history, and any one of them will take you deep into the heart and soul of the lands they cross.

HIT THE ROAD, JACK!
Riveting journeys by road

Route 66 and Highway 61—the first slanting across the United States from Chicago to Los Angeles, the other heading north from the Deep South to Canada—are vivid statements of the reality of 20th century America. They are roads of aspiration and desperation along which migrants traveled in times of plenty and poverty alike, seeking new lives and to escape economic deprivation, whether the result of the Depression or the social inequalities of the South. They fueled the birth of suburban California and carried the music of the South to cities in the north.

The Gringo Road, especially where it crosses Mexico and Central America, is also a great cultural highway, carrying

economic migrants north and US know-how south across the high deserts of Mexico and the tropical richness of Central America.

History on a still grander scale pervades the Silk Road across Asia and the majestic Grand Trunk Road, which slices its way across northern India, Pakistan, and Afghanistan. The Silk Road was the major axis of trade between the empires of the Old World and in the days of Mongol dominance, the crucial artery between Europe and the legendary riches of Cathay. Both the Hippie Trail, which lured Western baby boomers seeking mystical enlightenment to India, and the route followed by the extraordinary Peking—Paris automobile rally of 1907 can almost be said to be latter-day recreations of these crucial Eurasian routes of access.

Yet a permanent link between Cairo and Cape Town eluded even Cecil Rhodes, Britain's most visionary and ruthless imperialist. For the properly hardy, however, this is still a route that can be cautiously traveled. More practical are the routes across the Sahara wastes taken by the Paris–Dakar Rally—off-road racing at its most extreme.

ROUTE 66
The Main Street of America

To drive Route 66 is to see America. The Great Diagonal Road unites the fast-lane cities of Chicago and Los Angeles with small-town America, extending 2,485 miles (4,000 km) across grassy plains and desert. Established in 1926 as one of the original federal routes, it became the "road of opportunity" for migrants heading west from Oklahoma during the Dust Bowl years of the 1930s. Their plight along the "Mother Road" was immortalized in Steinbeck's greatest work, *The Grapes of Wrath*. Route 66 also provided a vital artery in World War II, and roadside services sprang up along its length, which soon adapted to the tourist trade as the route's popularity grew in the post-war years. Overtaken by four-lane interstates, it was officially decommissioned in 1985, with several sections now re-signed as "Historic Route 66," while other stretches are sadly no longer motorable.

Right: Los Angeles will forever be associated with the film industry, with tourists flocking to see the Hollywood sign, Grauman's Theater with its celebrity footprints, and the thrilling theme parks, such as Universal Studios. The locals love the city for its fine weather and the sandy beaches, while discerning visitors head to the Getty Center, home to one of the world's greatest art collections.

From Chicago to LA

Perched on the shores of Lake Michigan, Chicago has shrugged off its gangster past and now boasts iconic skyscrapers, a plethora of museums, and some of the best shopping in America. A hearty breakfast at Lou's Café sets travelers up for their journey south, across the Mississippi by the Chain of Rocks Bridge, to St Louis with its 632 ft (192 m) Gateway

Arch, reflecting the city's role as Gateway to the West. The expansive plains of Kansas, Oklahoma, and Texas are studded with small towns sporting outlandish motels, wacky drive-throughs, and iconic landmarks, such as the nose-diving cadillacs at Cadillac Ranch. In New Mexico, the Chaco Canyon has provided great insights into the 1,000-year-old beliefs and technology of the Ancient Pueblo Peoples, while the spectacular desert scenery of Arizona is punctured by the perfectly circular Meteor Crater, before the desert gives way to California, and the city of Los Angeles.

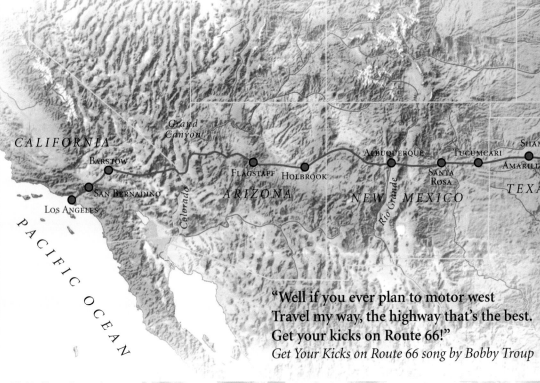

"Well if you ever plan to motor west
Travel my way, the highway that's the best.
Get your kicks on Route 66!"
Get Your Kicks on Route 66 song by Bobby Troup

Right: Chaco Canyon in New Mexico was a major cultural centre of the Anasazi people. Very little is known for certain about this advanced society, which had grand buildings containing over 100 rooms, and a network of roads leading 50 miles (80 km) to other centers.

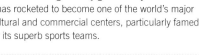

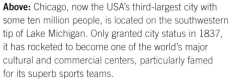

Above: Chicago, now the USA's third-largest city with some ten million people, is located on the southwestern tip of Lake Michigan. Only granted city status in 1837, it has rocketed to become one of the world's major cultural and commercial centers, particularly famed for its superb sports teams.

Above: The Gateway Arch in St Louis marks the start of the Lewis and Clark Trail, which together with Route 66, helped people to colonize the west. An interior tram takes visitors to the observation deck.

Left: Much older is Chain of Rocks Bridge, the key crossing point of the Mississippi, just north of St Louis. The curve in the bridge was intended to allow vessels to avoid the water intakes.

John Steinbeck

Born in 1902, John Steinbeck grew up in the Salinas Valley in California. After a short spell in New York in the late 1920s, struggling to become a writer, he returned to California. His first work, *The Cup of Gold* (1929), was a novel about pirate Henry Morgan, but his breakthrough came when he began to write from experience of the harsh world around him in Tortilla Flat. The San Francisco News then hired him to report on migrant workers escaping the Dust Bowl in the depression years of the 1930s. These experiences became the source for his finest works: the novella *Of Mice and Men* (1937) and the Pulitzer Prize-winning novel *The Grapes of Wrath* (1939). Despite criticism from some for the left-wing views portrayed in the novel, Hollywood converted the epic story to film the following year. It won him the Nobel Prize for Literature in 1962, six years before his death.

THE HIPPIE TRAIL TO KATHMANDU
The laid-back wanderings of the heady Sixties

In the 1960s, disaffected young hippies, seeking escape from consumerist Western culture, became enraptured by the spiritual and exotic Far East. Many set off in search of enlightenment—or cheap hash—in their psychedelic, beaten-up vans or hitching rides, with time being of no importance. A well-worn hippie trail sprang up, typically starting in Amsterdam or London and heading through Europe, Turkey, Iran, and India. The final destination for many was Kathmandu, which still has a road nicknamed Freak Street in memory of the busloads of hippies that disembarked there heading for its dope-filled dens. With rising Middle East tensions and Russia's 1979 invasion of Afghanistan, the route became less popular, but the ideals and dreams of this generation still live on.

Above: Amsterdam, the "Venice of the North," has flourished for some 700 years, but came to world prominence in the 17th century as a center for finance and diamonds, as well as for its art scene, with Rembrandt being based here. Later artists such as Vincent Van Gogh have added to this cultural heritage.

Overland to Kathmandu

From laissez-faire Amsterdam, with its world-class museums and infamous Red Light district and drug scene, hitch across Europe, taking time to savor a beer in Munich and mull over a coffee in Ljubljana. In the shadow of Istanbul's massive-domed Hagia Sophia, sample the baklava at the Pudding Shop, the first meeting point on the hippie trail. Wend your way through the Cappadoccia to Doğubeyazıt, nicknamed "Doggy Biscuit"

by travelers waiting for their Iranian visas. Tehran has Iran's finest palaces, while Esfahan is just the place for a *hookah* with the locals near vast Imam Square. A long haul across barren desert reaches war-torn Afghanistan, then it's on through the heart of India to reach "hippie nirvana" in Kathmandu. Have your fill of UNESCO World Heritage Sites, or just chill out in the place where the Himalayas reach the heavens.

"I had indeed learned how to cast off the evils of the world and the city, just as long as I had a decent pack on my back."
Jack Kerouac, The Dharma Bums

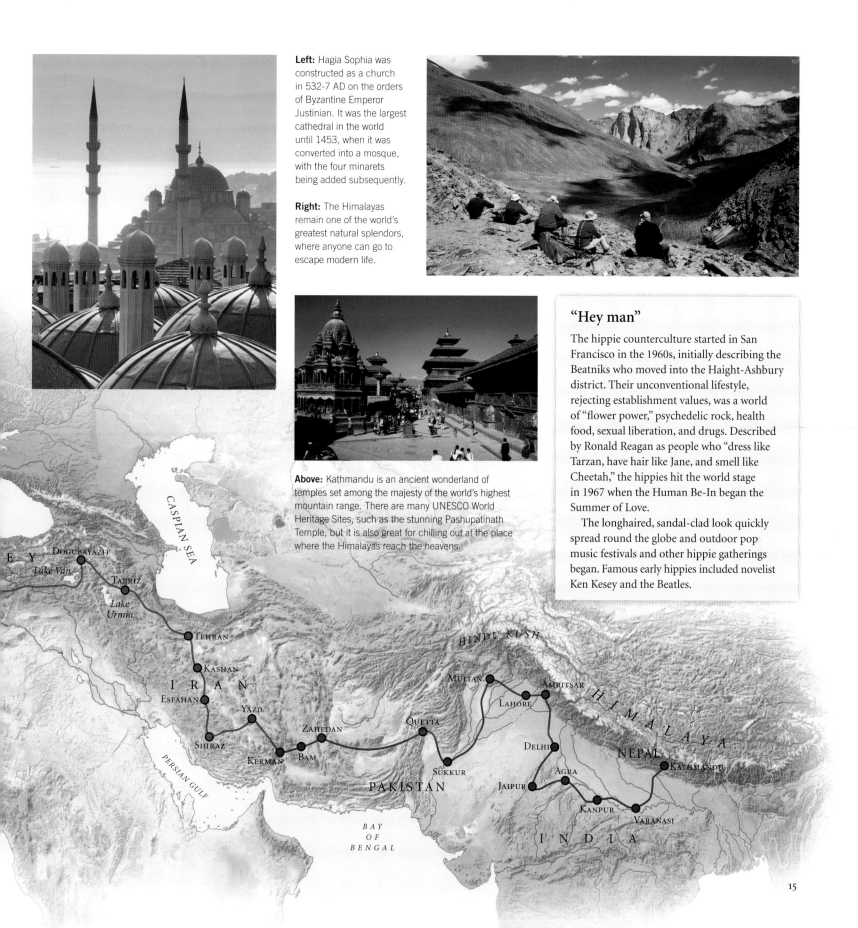

Left: Hagia Sophia was constructed as a church in 532-7 AD on the orders of Byzantine Emperor Justinian. It was the largest cathedral in the world until 1453, when it was converted into a mosque, with the four minarets being added subsequently.

Right: The Himalayas remain one of the world's greatest natural splendors, where anyone can go to escape modern life.

Above: Kathmandu is an ancient wonderland of temples set among the majesty of the world's highest mountain range. There are many UNESCO World Heritage Sites, such as the stunning Pashupatinath Temple, but it is also great for chilling out at the place where the Himalayas reach the heavens.

"Hey man"

The hippie counterculture started in San Francisco in the 1960s, initially describing the Beatniks who moved into the Haight-Ashbury district. Their unconventional lifestyle, rejecting establishment values, was a world of "flower power," psychedelic rock, health food, sexual liberation, and drugs. Described by Ronald Reagan as people who "dress like Tarzan, have hair like Jane, and smell like Cheetah," the hippies hit the world stage in 1967 when the Human Be-In began the Summer of Love.

The longhaired, sandal-clad look quickly spread round the globe and outdoor pop music festivals and other hippie gatherings began. Famous early hippies included novelist Ken Kesey and the Beatles.

THE GRAND TRUNK ROAD
From Kabul to Calcutta

Built in the 16th century by the Mughal ruler Sher Shah Suri (Sher Khan, 1540-1545) to link the scattered dominions he had conquered across northern India, the Grand Trunk Road is one of Asia's greatest highways, and traveling along it today remains an unforgettable journey. Over its rutted, but paved length—some 2,000 miles (3,200 km) across northern India and Pakistan from the mouth of the Ganges to the Khyber Pass—the modern traveler will experience the constant bustle of South Asia's colorful daily life. With the hair-raising driving that is commonplace in the Subcontinent, you will encounter a wide variety of traffic, from horses, bicycles, and laden buffalo carts, to rickshaws and ancient trucks hauling their loads to market.

The route of mutiny

The Grand Trunk Road makes its way through many of the centers of the British imperial crisis known as the Indian Mutiny, or Revolt (1857-59). Sparked off by a refusal by both Muslim and Hindu sepoys (hired soldiers) to use ammunition coated in animal fat, the revolt turned into a widespread uprising against British colonial rule. Cities like Lucknow were besieged and largely destroyed. Within two months, Delhi was in rebel hands and the revolt spread down the Ganges, attracting disillusioned local rulers and peasants alike. Although many Britons were massacred, regaining control was achieved with extreme brutality by British colonial forces.

Above: The Khyber Pass is the only viable link southwest from Afghanistan into South Asia. A remote and treacherous passage, it is one of the great corridors of history, being used by Alexander the Great, the Mughals and, disastrously, the British in their attempts to subdue Afghanistan during the 19th century.

Above: The Red Fort at the center of Old Delhi was not just a major military base, but lay at the heart of the capital's commerce. It formed a hub for travelers of all kinds: merchants, traders, pilgrims, and spies, for all of whom the Grand Trunk Road was a vital artery.

Calcutta to Kabul

Traveling westwards along its first 1,000 miles (1,600 km) or so, from the major port of Calcutta (Kolkota), across the sprawling plain of the Ganges and its tributaries, towards the national capital, New Delhi, the Grand Trunk Road follows the sacred river. It passes through major Hindu religious centers such as Patna and Varanasi (Benares), before reaching Muslim-influenced centers along the Yamuna, such as Allahabad, and arriving at the Mughal heartland of Rajasthan. Beyond the capital, the road begins its next 1,000 mile (1,600 km) trek, crossing the flat farmlands northwest of Delhi, skirting the foothills of the Himalayan range, and gradually winding its way to Lahore in Pakistan. From here it rises towards Islamabad and Peshawar before crossing the Khyber Pass to reach the remote Afghan capital of Kabul.

Above: Sher Khan was part of the Muslim Mughal dynasty, which ruled northern India from 1526-1857. The first stretch of paved highway joined his capital, Agra, with his home town of Sasaram, but was soon extended to the Mughal homelands.

Above: The palaces, mosques, and shrines of Rajasthan are masterpieces of Islamic architecture, including the exquisite Taj Mahal near Agra. Built by the emperor Shah Jahan in 1654 as a mausoleum for his wife, the white marbled building is one of many stunning Islamic edifices along the Grand Trunk Road.

HIMALAYA

LAHORE

PUNJAB

Ferozepore
(Firozpur)

RAJISTAN

Farrukhnagar

DELHI
Jhajjar
Delhi
Dadri
Meerut

NEPAL

FATEPUR SIKI   AGRA

Farrukhabad

Lucknow

Ajodyha   Fayzabad

Cawnpore
(Kanpur)

Singhbhaum
(Bihar)

ALLAHABAD   VARANASI

PATNA

I N D I A

BIHAR

BENGAL

KOLKATA
(CALCUTTA)

✗ Centers of
   Indian Mutiny

FIND OUT MORE
Kim
Rudyard Kipling

The Siege of Krishnapur
J. G. Farrell

Flashman
George Fraser

City of Djinns
William Dalrymple

Days and Nights on the Grand Trunk Road
Anthony Weller

"...such a river of life as nowhere else exists in the world."
Rudyard Kipling, Kim, 1901

HIGHWAY 61
The Blues Highway

Before 1991, US 61 ran for 1,714 miles (2,758 km) from New Orleans, Louisiana, in the south as far north as the Canadian border. In the days before the present interstate highway system, this route acted as a vital connection between north and south. The northern section was then shortened by 314 miles (505 km) to make a total of 1,400 miles (2,253 km), terminating in the city of Wyoming, Minnesota at the intersection of I-35. The present route is officially known as Highway 61, which bisects the American heartland, rolling through the southern states of Louisiana, Mississippi, Tennessee, Arkansas, Missouri, and northwards into Iowa, Wisconsin, and Minnesota. In some sections it is a four-lane highway, in others just two-lanes.

Bob Dylan and the Blues Highway

Running through the Mississippi Delta country famed for its blues musicians, Highway 61 is also referred to as the Blues Highway, and perhaps the closest link between the road and music comes through Bob Dylan. Born in Duluth, Minnesota, along the route of Highway 61, the eponymous stretch of asphalt inspired Dylan's first all-rock album of 1965, *Highway 61 Revisited*, and for the young musician, this seemingly never-ending road promised an escape from provincial Minnesota and the chance to fulfill his dreams.

Highway of history

Highway 61 is associated with a number of landmark events, such as the murder of Martin Luther King, Jr. at a motel just off the highway. A number of musicians who worked their way up and down the route were haunted by its magnitude, including Elvis Presley (in Memphis), the blues musician Robert Johnson (at Clarksdale he purportedly sold his soul to the devil to master the blues), and the blues singer Bessie Smith (who died here in an automobile accident).

> **"I never left home, but I know every inch of this highway."**
> *Pokey Jones, Highway 61 (movie)*

Above: New Orleans, named after Philippe II, Duc d'Orleans, is one of the oldest cities in the United States. It sits alongside the Mississippi river in southern Louisiana, and is famous for its jazz, cuisine, and annual Mardi Gras parade. Some parts of the city still bear the scars of Hurricane Katrina, which hit in 2005.

GULF OF MEXICO

THE GRINGO ROAD
The Pan-American Highway

Forming the longest highway in the world, the Pan-American Highway extends from Alaska to Chile, crossing 15 countries and a wide range of landscapes. The section from Mexico to Panama was built in World War II to provide a land link for supplying the US-controlled canal and passes great Mayan complexes and colonial cities, many ringed by volcanoes or set deep in the jungle. Foreigners or *gringos* entering this Spanish-speaking world will be disappointed as the asphalt disintegrates into gravel, sand, and potholes, before ending completely at Yaviza. It restarts 54 miles (87 km) later in Colombia.

Above: Aldous Huxley described Lake Atitlan as "Como with the addition of several immense volcanoes. It really is too much of a good thing." Ancient Teotihuacan reached its peak around the 2nd century AD, and its immense Pyramid of the Sun is one of the largest pyramids in the world.

Into the Hispanic Americas

From Mexico City, one of the world's largest cities, you head south for the great Mayan complexes of Palenque and Chichén Itza, before passing into Guatemala's highland region for some of the best sights of the Americas—the colorful market at Chichicastenango, Lake Atitlan framed by volcanoes, and the Spanish colonial gem, Antigua. The beauty of El Salvador, Honduras, and Nicaragua belies years of brutal civil war and the ravages of recent hurricanes and earthquakes. Costa Rica boasts more volcanoes, including the exceptionally active Arenal, and magnificent jungle, such as at Corcovado. At the 19th century engineering marvel of the Panama Canal, you can take a short boat ride from Caribbean to Pacific, or follow the route by train.

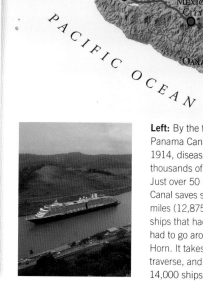

Left: By the time the Panama Canal opened in 1914, disease had killed thousands of workers. Just over 50 miles long, the Canal saves some 8,000 miles (12,875 km) for those ships that had previously had to go around Cape Horn. It takes nine hours to traverse, and handles some 14,000 ships each year.

THE PARIS—DAKAR RALLY
Across the Sahara

The Paris-Dakar Rally (officially now just the Dakar) was launched in 1979 and is the world's most grueling off-road rally. Its legendary toughness stems not just from the distances covered—typically between 5,500 and 8,000 miles (8,850—12,875 km) in about 17 days, with individual stages of up to 500 miles (805 km)—but from the harsh terrain. The bulk of the race is across the trackless wastes of the western Sahara, among the most inhospitable regions of the globe, with rocky scrubland alternating with sand dunes. On average, only one-third of the competitors make it to the finish. Since 1995, a number of cities have been used as the starting point, replacing Paris, but on all but four occasions the destination has been Dakar in Senegal.

Above and below: It is the hostility of the Sahara that appeals to devotees of the Paris—Dakar. For off-road racers this is the ultimate challenge: a brutally unforgiving and relentless trial that stretches men and machinery to their limits, and sometimes beyond.

Thierry Sabine

The Paris-Dakar was founded by a Frenchman, Thierry Sabine. In 1977, taking part in a motorbike race from the Ivory Coast to Nice, he became lost in the Libyan Desert. Though eventually rescued, the experience of his days of solitude made him determined to organize a rally through similarly hostile territory. If Paris was the logical starting point, Dakar in the former French colony of Senegal was as logical an end point. The race was a success from the start, but it has never been far from controversy. It has often been claimed that its environmental impact on some of the poorest counties in the world is negative, and despite increasingly sophisticated safety measures, 48 competitors have been killed to date. An unknown number of spectators, almost all in Africa, have also been killed. Sabine himself died in 1986 in a helicopter crash during the race that saw the deaths of all six on board.

Choose your vehicle

There are four categories of entrants: cars, motorbikes, quads, and trucks. The first two are further sub-divided into three categories, the last into four categories. In general, about 80% of the entrants are amateurs and it is here, unsurprisingly, that the rate of attrition is highest. Many vehicle manufacturers, principally European and Japanese, naturally see the Dakar as an ideal marketing opportunity. The most successful manufacturer, with a total of 12 wins in the car class, including seven in a row between 2001 and 2007, is Mitsubishi. The most successful French manufacturers are Citroën and Peugeot, each with four wins. Only one man has recorded four wins in the prestigious car class, Finland's Ari Vatanen, in 1987, 1989, 1990, and 1991.

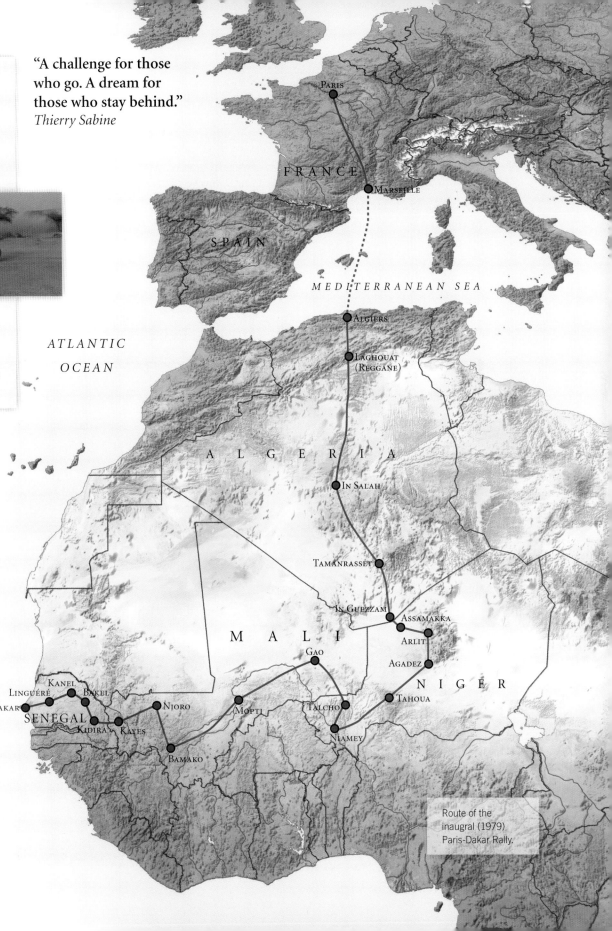

"A challenge for those who go. A dream for those who stay behind."
Thierry Sabine

Route of the inaugral (1979) Paris-Dakar Rally.

Paris or Bust
The Peking to Paris race of 1907

In 1907 the car was scarcely 20 years old, and those machines that existed were not just expensive, but underpowered, uncomfortable, and unreliable. Yet that year the French newspaper *Le Matin* came up with the audacious proposal of a car race from Paris to Peking—a distance of approximately 10,000 miles (16,095 km) over terrain that was not merely hostile, but actively impassable, and where the means of servicing such temperamental vehicles was non-existent. It was either brilliantly visionary or laughably absurd, but to the astonishment of those who mocked it, not only did five cars line up for the start, but four of those finished and a new era of motorized transport beckoned.

Prince Scipione Borghese

Although five cars started, 40 vehicles initially entered, a figure that inevitably represented wishful thinking on the part of most of the competitors. As their numbers dropped, *Le Matin* decided it would make more sense

to race from Peking to Paris, rather than the other way round, but when the scale of what it was proposing dawned, the paper had second thoughts and attempted to cancel the race.

It was largely thanks to an Italian, Prince Scipione Borghese, that the race went ahead. Borghese was by far the best funded and best prepared of the racers, and asserted that he would take part whatever the paper decided. *Le Matin* backed down, and at 8 am on June 10, 1907, the race began.

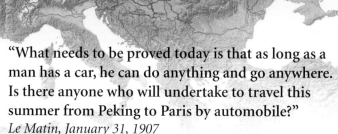

"What needs to be proved today is that as long as a man has a car, he can do anything and go anywhere. Is there anyone who will undertake to travel this summer from Peking to Paris by automobile?"
Le Matin, January 31, 1907

Left: On August 20, 1907, Prince Borghese's bright-red Itala 40 arrived in Paris to win the race. The Italian was 20 days ahead of the remaining three machines.

Right: There were two French cars in the race, both de Dion Boutons. With their small engines, the muddy conditions of the Urals in particular highlighted their weakness.

Left: It is hard to imagine any terrain less suited to the unreliable and rickety vehicles in the race than the wastes of Siberia.

Right: The Gobi Desert was the site of the only retirement: the woefully underpowered Contal tri-cycle of Frenchmen Auguste Pons and Octace Foucualt, who were eventually rescued by a Mongol caravan.

Off the beaten track

The most obvious difficulty facing the racers was that for the vast bulk of the race—which traversed China, Mongolia, Siberia, went across the Urals, and on into eastern Russia—there were no roads. Where tracks or trade routes existed, they were intended exclusively for carts drawn by beasts of burden or camel trains. The many mountains that had to be crossed were entirely beyond the capacity of all the vehicles, which could only be pushed or pulled by oxen, horses, or natives hastily press-ganged into service. Rivers and lakes meant perilous crossings on local craft, or daring ventures over rickety bridges that were never intended to carry anything as heavy as a petrol-driven vehicle. Ironically, the Gobi Desert provided much easier traveling, and despite the frequency with which the cars overheated a firm sandy surface allowed speeds approaching 60 mph.

FINE OUT MORE
Prince Borghese's Trail
Genevieve Obert

Peking to Paris
Luigi Barzini

Right: At 8 am on June 10 1907, the race began. Among the entrants was Charles Goddard, an itinerant Dutch circus worker who had never driven at all when he entered the race. Charming, cajoling, and penniless, he persuaded the Dutch car manufacturer Spyker to enter a car on his behalf. In Berlin, he was arrested for fraud.

RHODES' DREAM
Cairo to Cape Town

The "Scramble for Africa" saw almost all of the continent placed under direct European colonial rule in little more than 20 years after 1880. France, Portugal, Belgium, Germany, Italy, Spain, and Britain all sought to consolidate existing territories, and acquire new ones. Foremost among Britain's advocates of colonialism was Cecil Rhodes, a magnate, politician, and tireless imperialist. If in the end even he was unable to create a continuous belt of British-administered territories the length of Africa from Egypt in the north to Cape Town in the south, he was nonetheless directly responsible for the annexation of Northern and Southern Rhodesia, today respectively Zambia and Zimbabwe.

Right: Cecil Rhodes depicted in a contemporary cartoon as a modern-day Colossus of Rhodes. Although his proposed route was never built, his influence on the continent was still immense.

Cecil Rhodes

Rhodes was viewed with suspicion in British government circles; a reckless adventurer as likely to embarrass as to enrich the country. However, being one of the richest men in the world, for a penny-pinching government he had the great attraction of being prepared to finance his ventures himself. In addition, his strategic goal of linking all British African territories on a north—south axis chimed with the government's overriding goal of protecting the sea routes to India and the East. Further, any steps that could thwart the ambitions of Britain's most direct imperial rivals in Africa—Germany, Portugal, and France—naturally garnered support. Accordingly, in 1889 Rhodes was granted a charter by the British government to annexe those territories between the Limpopo river and the great lakes of central Africa.

> "I contend that we [the British] are the finest race in the world and that the more of the world we inhabit the better it is for the human race."
> *Cecil Rhodes*

By fair means or foul

Armed with his charter, Rhodes established the British South Africa Company to administer what he intended would form a vast extension of the British empire. Opposition from local African rulers was swept aside by a mixture of bribery, threat, and deceit. Seeking a mining concession from Lobengula, king of the Ndebele of Matabeleland (a concession crucial in persuading the British government to grant Rhodes his charter), he claimed that no more than 10 white men would ever be present in Matabeleland. It was also agreed that the British would have no right to permanent settlement in Matabeleland, a promise Rhodes never intended to keep.

Above and below: Across much of sub-Saharan Africa, transport has historically been an uncertain business. Huge distances, hostile terrain, political uncertainty, and poverty have conspired to hinder the development of all but the most basic transport infrastructure. For many Africans today, travel by foot remains the only option.

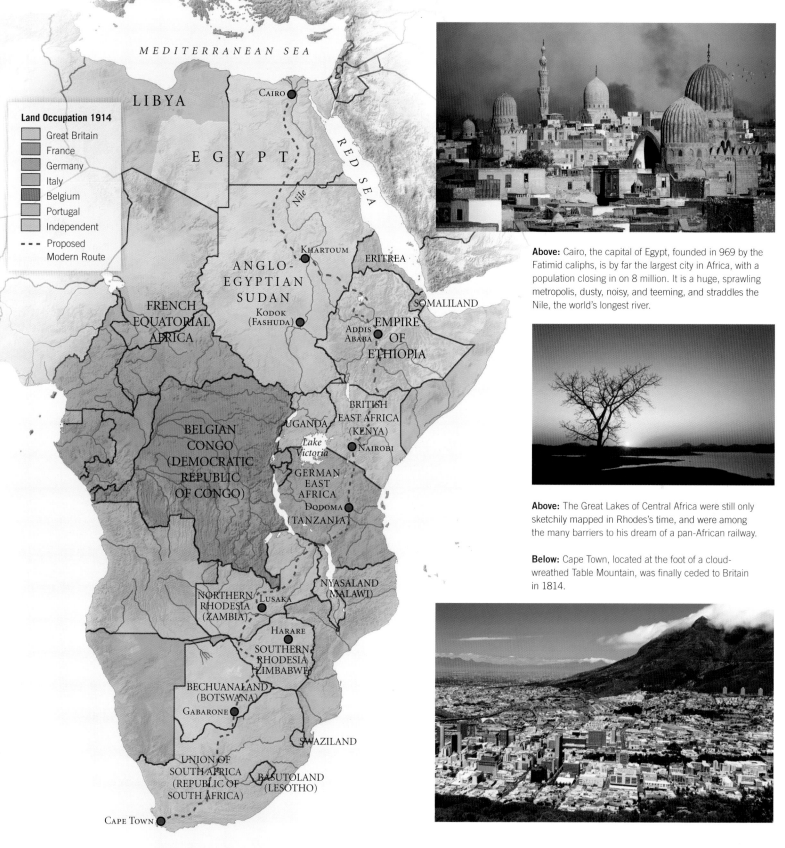

MEDITERRANEAN SEA

LIBYA

EGYPT

RED SEA

Nile

Land Occupation 1914
- Great Britain
- France
- Germany
- Italy
- Belgium
- Portugal
- Independent
- - - - Proposed Modern Route

CAIRO

KHARTOUM

ANGLO-EGYPTIAN SUDAN

ERITREA

SOMALILAND

FRENCH EQUATORIAL AFRICA

KODOK (FASHUDA)

ADDIS ABABA

EMPIRE OF ETHIOPIA

BELGIAN CONGO (DEMOCRATIC REPUBLIC OF CONGO)

UGANDA

Lake Victoria

BRITISH EAST AFRICA (KENYA)

NAIROBI

GERMAN EAST AFRICA

DODOMA (TANZANIA)

NYASALAND (MALAWI)

NORTHERN RHODESIA (ZAMBIA)

LUSAKA

HARARE

SOUTHERN RHODESIA (ZIMBABWE)

BECHUANALAND (BOTSWANA)

GABARONE

SWAZILAND

UNION OF SOUTH AFRICA (REPUBLIC OF SOUTH AFRICA)

BASUTOLAND (LESOTHO)

CAPE TOWN

Above: Cairo, the capital of Egypt, founded in 969 by the Fatimid caliphs, is by far the largest city in Africa, with a population closing in on 8 million. It is a huge, sprawling metropolis, dusty, noisy, and teeming, and straddles the Nile, the world's longest river.

Above: The Great Lakes of Central Africa were still only sketchily mapped in Rhodes's time, and were among the many barriers to his dream of a pan-African railway.

Below: Cape Town, located at the foot of a cloud-wreathed Table Mountain, was finally ceded to Britain in 1814.

THE SILK ROADS
Across the Roof of Asia

In two distinct periods, the Silk Roads, a name coined in 1877 by a German geographer, Ferdinand von Richtofen, provided the only direct overland routes between Europe and China. The first was from approximately 200 BC to AD 200, the second in the 13th and 14th centuries. In both cases, it was impelled by trade between vast empires—Roman, Parthian, Kushan, and Han China; then a re-emergent Europe and Mongol China—whose reach imposed order across the otherwise lawless and hostile deserts of Central Asia. However daunting a journey that could take over a year, in both periods exceptionally profitable contacts—cultural as much as purely commercial—developed.

Above: In the first period of the Silk Roads, it has been estimated that perhaps as much as 90% of China's exports were in the form of silk, destined to satisfy a captive Roman market and carried in caravans straggling over the reaches of Central Asia.

The trade route

In the 1st century AD, the writer Pliny complained that Roman demands for Chinese silk, the secret of whose production was unknown in the West, was unsustainably expensive and risked bankrupting the empire. Yet luxury goods from the West were also in demand in the East. A chance find in 1938 of a warehouse in Begram, Afghanistan, contained a number of lavish Roman works of art destined for markets in the East. Similarly, horses from Ferghana in Central Asia were highly prized by China's Han emperors, who believed the animals were of divine origin. In fact, a huge variety of goods were traded in both directions: carpets, gold, rubies, lapis lazuli, lacquer, jade, muslin, cotton, glass, porcelain, and slaves, as well as more common everyday items. A variety of strategically placed oasis towns grew rich on the trade, but the hazards of the journey, whether from bandits, extremes of temperatures, droughts, or hostile terrain were constant, and the bodies of men and animals littered the routes.

FIND OUT MORE

Life Along the Silk Road
Susan Whitfield

Silk Road: Monks, Warriors, and Merchants on the Silk Road
Luce Bulnois

The Silk Road: 2,000 Years in the Heart of Asia
Frances Wood

The Shadow of the Silk Road
Colin Thubron

Left: The level of trade between East and West during the period of the Mongol Peace was substantially greater than in the first period of the Silk Road over a thousand years before. Yet the peace under Mongol rule lasted barely 100 years before Central Asia once more fell victim to the depredations of bandits and nomads.

Left: Peking (also known as Beijing) marked the end of the Eastern trade route across Asia. Access to China allowed Western merchants to trade a wide range of goods—most notably Chinese silk in the time of the Roman Empire. However, the trading worked both ways, with many goods also being transported from the West to the East.

The road to conversion

The Mongol Peace of the 13th and 14th centuries allowed a remarkable re-opening of the Silk Roads. The Mongols were anxious to revive trade, but for some in the West, there was a further motive: to find converts to Christianity. The accounts they left provide the earliest detailed picture of the Silk Roads. In 1246, a Franciscan, John of Piano Carpini, with a Mongol escort, journeyed almost to the original Mongol capital Karakorum. An even more detailed account came from William of Rubruck, sent by Louis IX of France, who entered Karakorum on Palm Sunday in 1254.

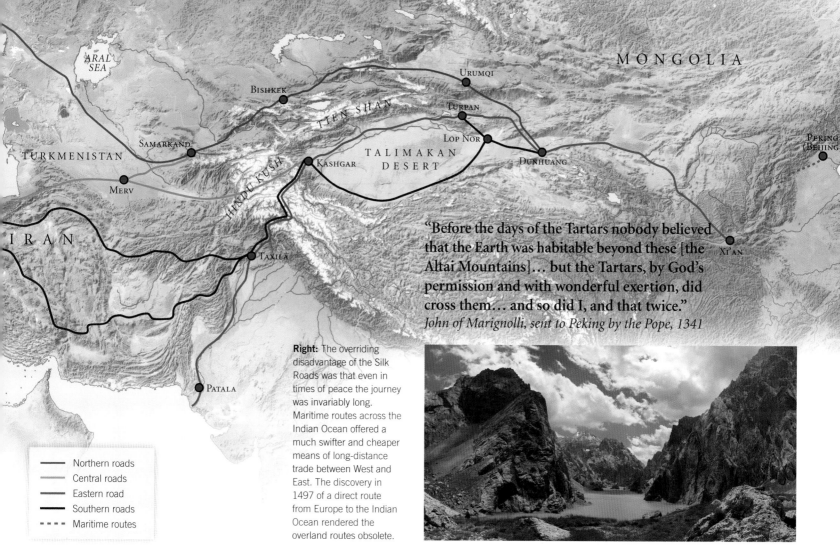

"Before the days of the Tartars nobody believed that the Earth was habitable beyond these [the Altai Mountains]… but the Tartars, by God's permission and with wonderful exertion, did cross them… and so did I, and that twice."
John of Marignolli, sent to Peking by the Pope, 1341

Right: The overriding disadvantage of the Silk Roads was that even in times of peace the journey was invariably long. Maritime routes across the Indian Ocean offered a much swifter and cheaper means of long-distance trade between West and East. The discovery in 1497 of a direct route from Europe to the Indian Ocean rendered the overland routes obsolete.

Map labels: ARAL SEA, MONGOLIA, BISHKEK, URUMQI, TIEN SHAN, TURPAN, SAMARKAND, LOP NOR, TALIMAKAN DESERT, TURKMENISTAN, KASHGAR, DUNHUANG, PEKING (BEIJING), MERV, HINDU KUSH, IRAN, TAXILA, XI'AN, PATALA

Legend:
— Northern roads
— Central roads
— Eastern road
— Southern roads
- - - Maritime routes

Rail travel has long captured the imagination of those seeking adventures in distant lands. For centuries, ocean-going ships were the only practical alternative to horseback for travel of any substantial distance, but shipping could rarely enter far into continental interiors. The invention of the railway in the 19th century transformed all this, and for 150 years reigned supreme.

RIDING THE IRON HORSE
Memorable railway rides

Until the middle of the 20th century the railways that had been built across most continents were the safest and most efficient way to travel for any long-distance passenger. Providing accommodation and berths from the most luxurious to the most basic, they really made their money from freight and short distance, commuter passengers. But in fact, it was the railroad that opened up many remote continental interiors to settlement and economic growth: it was the great railroad builders of North America who made possible the delivery of the mass migrants in the late

19th century to the prairies and plains of the Midwest and beyond.

In South America they provided a reliable means of transport to the most remote places before the age of the paved road, while in Africa and Australia—where the modern highway still remains a scarcity— railroads were essential to colonialists. In India and China the iron highway replaced the existing road networks in a way that transformed people's lives.

More recently, however, with the proliferation of the automobile and road transport, rail as a means of travel has been in decline across the globe. Over the last 40 years many of the classic lines—the Trans-Siberian Railway, the Canadian Pacific, and the Venice-Simplon for example—have been inventively marketed as luxurious and more convenient alternatives to flying.

Yet as automotive commuters become increasingly stuck in tailbacks and gridlock as they travel from suburb to city, and the "carbon footprint" becomes part of our individual responsibility, there is a chance that this great institution may yet survive. Perhaps ironically, it is the short-distance commuter and not the long-haul traveler who will keep the tracks alive.

THE TRANS-SIBERIAN RAILWAY
Moscow to Vladivostok

The Trans-Siberian Railway, or Great Siberian Way as it was known in Imperial Russia, is the longest continuous railway in the world. It runs 5,805 miles (9,342 km) from Moscow to Vladivostok on Russia's Pacific coast, the equivalent of almost one-third of the way around the globe, and spans 10 time zones. The journey itself on the fastest trains—though even these call at almost 100 stations—takes six days and four hours. Over 90,000 men labored to build it at the peak of construction in the late 1890s. They shifted, mostly by hand, 100 million cubic meters of earth (3.5 billion cubic feet), laid one million tons of rails, 12 million sleepers, and built 60 miles (95 km)of bridges and tunnels.

Left: Whatever the imperial and other splendors of Moscow, it remained among Europe's least accessible cities well into the 19th century, the result of transport methods little changed since the time of Catherine the Great in the 18th century. It was abundantly obvious that Russia had to modernize and, above all, to industrialize if it was not to be left fatally behind its competitors.

Left: The man who made the Trans-Siberian Railway possible was Sergei Witte, the chief architect of Russia's belated industrialization. He was the country's director of Railway Affairs between 1889–91, and as Finance Minister between 1892–1902, he was also responsible for financing it.

Across the northern steppes

The surge of Russian expansion across Siberia in the 17th century may have greatly boosted the country's economic potential, but the sheer scale of these vast territories made access a perennial problem. The almost complete absence of roads left rivers the only reliable means of transport and this was only possible when they were not frozen, meaning no more than eight months a year. As most of the rivers ran north to the Arctic Ocean they also did little to solve the difficulties of west–east travel, so journey times of well over a year were common. But if the development of railways in the 19th century suggested an obvious solution, the immense scale of the enterprise was exceptionally daunting. The terrain presented problems of its own, not least permafrost that turned into sodden wastes in the brief summer. Nonetheless, in 1886 Alexander III authorized that detailed planning be started and in May 1891, after a mammoth three-year survey, he ceremoniously laid the first foundation stone.

From Moscow's Yaroslavsky station

Station	Distance (Miles / km)	Time
Nizhny Novgorod	288 / 465	6 hrs
Perm	873 / 1,405	20hrs
Yekaterinburg	1,111 / 1,788	1d 2hrs
Omsk	1,672 / 2,691	1d 14hrs
Novosibirsk	2,064 / 3,322	1d 22hrs
Krasoyarsk	2,540 / 4,088	2d 11hrs
Irkutsk	3,220 / 5,182	3d 4hrs
Ulan Ude	3,505 / 5,641	3d 12hrs
Chita	3,853 / 6,201	3d 22hrs
Khabarovsk	5,308 / 8,542	5d 15hrs
Vladivostok	5,805 / 9,342	6d 4hrs

Left: The six-day ride on the Trans-Siberian Railway remains one of the world's great train journeys and an exceptional opportunity to experience the vastness of Russia and its natural splendors. The train rumbles across the country's seemingly limitless steppes on its epic crossing. Time for the traveler takes on a new dimension, the world passing by both remote and near at hand.

Cutting corners and costs

The eventual cost of the Trans-Siberian Railway was 1.455 bn roubles, a sum exceeded by the Russian treasury only by that it spent on the First World War, this despite the enforced employment of political prisoners in its construction (by 1900 there were over 1 million such exiles in Siberia). Materials and construction were also skimped wherever possible, and it was seriously proposed for example, that most of the river bridges eventually constructed should not be built at all and ferries used in their place. A possibly inevitable consequence of the cost-cutting was that when it was completed in 1905, the line was plagued by breakdowns and delays, and to ease the strain on the flimsy rails themselves, trains could travel at no more than 13 mph (21 km/h). It subsequently proved necessary to rebuild many stretches, a process completed in 1916.

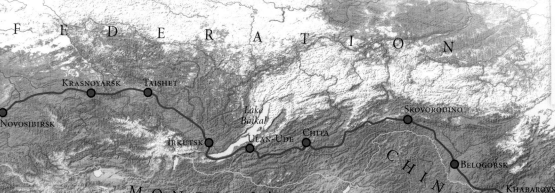

Below: The Russo-Japanese War of 1904–5 provided an enormous stimulus to complete the Trans-Siberian Railway so as to be able to transport men and supplies to Vladivostock and the Sea of Japan. However, it wasn't enough to prevent a humilating Russian defeat at the hands of an emerging Japan.

Above: Lake Baikal in southern Siberia is the world's largest and deepest freshwater lake and was a significant barrier for the Trans-Siberian Railway. In the winter of 1903–4 it was decided to lay a temporary line across the frozen lake, but the first train across broke through the ice and disappeared into the depths.

FIND OUT MORE

Trans-Siberian Handbook Bryn Thomas

To Russia With Love: A Traveler's Account of the Trans-Siberian Railway Sandy Weeks

The Road to Power: the Trans-Siberian Railway and the Colonization of Asian Russia Steven G. Marks

THE ORIENT EXPRESS
The romance of the railway

No train more precisely encapsulates the lure of pre-war travel at its most seductively glamorous than the Orient Express, a by-word for sophistication, luxury, and, on occasion, intrigue. It began life in 1883 as a service between Paris and Istanbul, and was deliberately intended to offer the latest in comfort. Numerous changes to its route followed, and today (at least officially), it is no more than the name of a daily train service between Strasbourg and Vienna. But since 1982 the entirely separate, privately owned Venice-Simplon Orient Express has also operated services between London and Venice that use lavishly restored pre-war carriages to recreate the appeal of the golden age of train travel.

Right: The Orient Express is one of the most immediately resonant names in the world of travel, instantly conjuring to mind the kind of elegance and style wholly missing from travel in today's remorselessly utilitarian age. However, a number of variations of trains designated "Orient Express" have existed, including the Arlberg Orient Express that ran all the way from London to Athens or Bucharest between 1930 and 1962.

East across Europe

The Orient Express was the brainchild of a Belgian, Georges Nagelmackers, who in 1876 founded the Compagnie Internationale des Wagons-Lits. His trains were the first to carry sleeping cars and restaurants, and the original Orient Express was the first to cross international borders as it traveled from Paris across Europe. From 1889 a direct service to Istanbul was inaugurated. In 1919, the Simplon Orient Express was introduced, in effect the Orient Express of popular imagination. It ran from Paris, via the 12-mile (19-km) Simplon tunnel under the Alps, to Milan, and Venice, before continuing to Istanbul. The same year, the Arlberg Orient Express was also launched, running from London to Budapest, from where it continued to Athens or Bucharest. Both ceased running during World War Two, and post 1945 their decline was gradual, but consistent. In 1977 the Simplon OE service to Istanbul was withdrawn. By 2001 it had been reduced to a Paris to Vienna service, and since 2007 no more than Strasbourg to Vienna.

FIND OUT MORE

Gavin Stamp's Orient Express (DVD)

The Orient Express: The History of the Orient Express Service from 1883 to 1950
Anthony Burton

Murder on the Orient Express Agatha Christie

Stamboul Train
Graham Greene

ISTHMUS OF KRA
Bangkok to Johor Bahru

A journey down the Isthmus of Kra, a ribbon of land only 40 miles (64 km) wide at its narrowest point, takes you from the glittering golden temples of Thailand down to gleaming high-rise Singapore. Beautiful beaches and incredible limestone scenery give way to the dense rainforests and towering mountains of the Malay Peninsula. See paddy fields with water buffalo, rubber plantations, luxuriant jungle, and stilt houses. And what better way to travel than on the Eastern & Oriental Express, the world-renowned luxury train that prides itself on its elegant compartments, delicious cuisine, and superb service.

Express way down

Leaving Bangkok, the first stop is the World War II "death railway," immortalized in the 1957 film *Bridge on the River Kwai*. Further south, Surat Thani station is the gateway to the impressive scenery and pristine beaches around Phuket. Once across the Malaysian border, catch the ferry to Penang's old colonial capital, Georgetown, with its mix of

British and Asian buildings, and sip a Singapore sling at the classic Eastern & Oriental Hotel. Negara National Park protects what could be the world's oldest tropical forest, but you are soon back in the modern world in hi-tech Kuala Lumpur, whose Petronas Twin Towers claimed the world's tallest building title from 1998 to 2004. Finally, on day three, the train crosses the Straits of Johor to Singapore, where you can conclude this glamorous trip by checking in at Raffles Hotel.

Above: The incredible limestone stacks around Phuket appear to defy gravity. Koh Tapoo (or Nail rock) is nicknamed James Bond Island, as it featured in the movie *The Man with the Golden Gun*. Local longtail boats and junks take tourists around the karsts, through mangrove forests, into caves and past floating villages built on rafts.

> "To travel by train is to see nature and human beings... in fact, to see life."
> *Agatha Christie*

Left: The city of Singapore was founded by Sir Stamford Raffles, whose 1822 city plan created separate ethnic areas for its inhabitants—Chinatown and Little India, in addition to traditional Malay houses and European-style villas. Now postmodern skyscrapers dominate the skyline, particularly around the commercial center of Raffles Square.

NEW ZEALAND
North Island to South Island

The spectacular backdrop to *The Lord of the Rings* films, New Zealand is a lush country with more sheep than people, and a sunny if rainy climate, in spite of its Maori name, Aotearoa, meaning "The land of the long white cloud." The most important cities, including the capital Wellington, are on North Island, a world apart from its volcanic center. South Island is the place for dramatic mountain scenery and for putting your body through its paces with jet-skiing, bungee jumping, or many other extreme sports. New Zealand's rail network is somewhat limited, but is nevertheless a good way to see highlights across both islands.

Above: The bubbling geothermal mud pools of Rotorua, such as the Champagne Pool in Wai-o-Tapu Thermal Wonderland, are an ethereal sight. The Lady Knox Geyser erupts as regularly as clockwork each morning, while evenings are ideal for retreating to the banks of Lake Rotorua to witness a traditional *haka* (Maori dance), but be ready for action!

South from Auckland

After flying in to the country's greatest city, Auckland, take the train across North Island to Wellington, detouring to see the geysers and bubbling mud pools of Rotorua, which will take your breath away in more ways than one! The glow-worm caves of Waitomo are truly enchanting, while Wellington is known as the "Windy City" for good reason. It is a short ferry ride to Picton on the South Island, where you can pick up the train to Kaikoura to see migrating sperm whales, before continuing to Christchurch, where punts glide down the river between old colleges. From here you can take the dramatic TranzAlpine Express across to Greymouth, with buses then taking you further south.

Above: Waitomo is world-famous for its glow-worms, (*Arachnocampa Luminosa*), which cast an eerie light over the grotto, entered via boat. Opera stars have performed in the huge subterranean cavern, while another highlight is Tomo, a deep limestone shaft.

Left: New Zealand is not known for the extent of its train network—which is somewhat slender—but for the awesome beauty of the routes. None is more famous than the TranzAlpine Express.

Above: Just offshore from Kaikoura there is a deep ocean trench that is the perfect territory for migrating sperm whales. The largest toothed animals in the world, the whales make regular hour-long dives down to 7,200 ft (2,200 m) to feed, and it is believed they have epic battles with giant squids. Herman Melville's *Moby Dick* was a sperm whale.

> "There's a real purity in New Zealand that's not an easy thing to find in our world anymore... There is a sense of isolation and also being protected."
> *Elijah Wood, Actor*

Above: Christchurch is reputedly more English than England. It is New Zealand's answer to Cambridge, though in actual fact took its name from Christ Church, Oxford. Punts glide down the shallow river between old colleges and willow trees.

AUCKLAND

Bay of Plenty

HAMILTON

Waitomo Caves

ROTORUA

NORTH ISLAND

GISBORNE

Lake Taupo
Mt. Tongariro

Mt. Taranaki

Mt. Ruapehu

Hawke's Bay

NAPIER
HASTINGS

Pukerua Bay

PICTON

WELLINGTON

Cook Strait

NELSON

TASMAN SEA

KAIKOURA

GREYMOUTH

SOUTH PACIFIC OCEAN

Franz Joseph Glacier
Aoraki/Mt. Cook

SOUTHERN ALPS

CHRISTCHURCH

SOUTH ISLAND

Milford Sound

QUEENSTOWN

Fjordland National Park

DUNEDIN

INVERCARGILL

HALF MOON BAY

STEWART ISLAND

▲▲ Peak

Peter Jackson

The world-famous director was born in Pukerua, New Zealand, in 1961. His breakthrough in the film industry came with *Heavenly Creatures* (1994), soon after which he decided to focus on his dream of turning Tolkien's epic fantasy into reality. Dogged initially with problems over the film rights, he eventually recorded all three parts of *The Lord of the Rings* simultaneously, using 150 locations in the rugged landscapes of New Zealand.

The films were released over three years (2001-03), instantly joining the ranks of the most popular films of all time and earning many awards, including 17 Oscars. Since then he has also worked on a remake of *King Kong*, the film that had inspired his passion for movies as a child.

FIND OUT MORE

Insight Pocket Guide: New Zealand
Craig Dowling

The Bone People Keri Hulme

Once Were Warriors Alan Duff

The Whale Rider Witi Ihimaera

www.tranzscenic.co.nz

COPPER CANYON
Through North America's deepest gully

Mexico's "El Chepe" railroad descends from Chihuahua to the Pacific seaboard through the dramatic Copper Canyon, a mile-deep scar in the volcanic rock of the Sierra Madre Occidental. The railroad was conceived as a fast route across Central America before the construction of the Panama Canal, but the complicated engineering—with 86 tunnels and 37 bridges—took almost a century to complete, finally opening in 1961. The train twists along the canyon, which is considerably deeper than the Grand Canyon in the USA, offering glimpses of the precipitous side canyons, pine forests, plummeting waterfalls, and peaceful lakes.

Left: The triple-domed church of Satevó Mission stands at the bottom of Copper Canyon, just 4 miles south of Batopilas, a silver mining town founded by Spanish conquistadores in 1632. The mission is thought to be 400 years old and its past is shrouded in mystery, due in part to its records being destroyed in fire. It has a fine but rickety bell tower with several old bells still in use.

> "The Copper Canyon is what the Grand Canyon would like to be when it grows up."
> *Anon*

Riding the canyon

The 13-hour journey is best started in Chihuahua, home of revolutionaries Pancho Villa and Father Miguel Hidalgo. The train passes through Cuauhtémoc, the largest Mennonite settlement in Latin America, before reaching the logging town of Creel, which is worth a stopover for the glorious day trek to the 850 foot (250 m) single-drop Basaseachic Falls. From Creel the train begins its descent into the canyon, stopping at El Divisadero where passengers get a fantastic view into the depths. Further south is the former silver-mining town of Batopilas, over a mile down, with the "lost cathedral" of Satevó nearby. The ride ends in Los Mochis on the coast.

Right: Barranca del Cobre, or the Copper Canyon, consists of six canyons in the vast state of Chihuahua in Northern Mexico. It covers 20,000 square miles (51,800 km²), with some points deeper than the Grand Canyon, and overall larger, though each individual canyon is smaller. The train ride is regarded as the most scenic on the continent.

IN THE ANDES
Ecuador's Devil's Nose railway

One of the greatest-ever railway engineering feats, the descent of Nariz del Diablo—or "The Devil's Nose"—masters a 5.56% (1:18) gradient down the mountain's 3,280 foot (1,000 m) near-vertical rock face, using a series of switchbacks (zigzag cuttings that allow the train to move forwards and backwards). The railway, constructed in 1899-1908, originally linked Ecuador's capital, Quito, to Guayaquil, but now only the section from Riobamba to Sibambe is operational. Have no fear though—this is by far the best stretch, with stunning views of smoking volcanoes and deep rocky gorges. The single carriage train, known as the *autoferro*, until recently allowed passengers to sit on the roof to admire the stunning scenery, dangling their feet out over the vertiginous drop.

Above: At 20,564 ft (6268 m), Chimborazo is Ecuador's highest peak, and its summit is the furthest point from the Earth's center. The upper slopes of this dormant volcano have large glaciers that provide water for the surrounding district.

Via volcanoes and switchbacks

The journey south from Quito crosses the equator and heads down the majestic "Avenue of the Volcanoes," named by explorer Alexander von Humboldt. None are more famous than 19,370 ft (5,897 m) Cotopaxi, the second highest active volcano in the world. Several of the small towns and villages along the way have colorful indigenous markets, selling local textiles. Riobamba, at the foot of Chimborazo, Ecuador's tallest mountain, was the first city founded by the Spaniards. The train heads from here to Alausí and then makes the hair-raising zigzag descent to Sibambe. Disembarking here, the journey can continue to the Temple of the Sun and other Inca ruins at Ingapirca and then on to the red roofs and cobblestone streets of colonial Cuenca.

Above: Used in many countries, switchbacks are a way of allowing a train to ascend or descend a large drop in a short distance, but nowhere is more dramatic than the Devil's Nose.

Left: Fifteen miles south of the Equator, Quito is the world's second highest capital (after La Paz in Bolivia), reaching nearly 9,842 ft (3,000 m) above sea level. Its outstanding colonial old town has made it a popular starting point for trips to the rest of the country and to the Galápagos Islands.

"The most difficult train in the world."
Anon

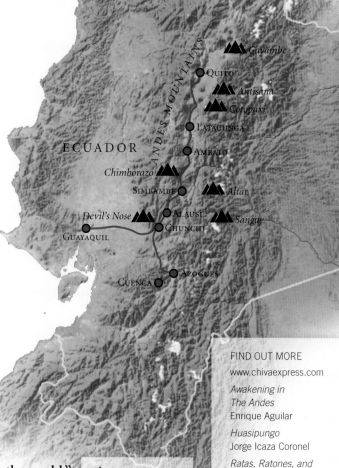

ECUADOR

ANDES MOUNTAINS

Cayambe
Quito
Antisana
Cotopaxi
Latacunga
Ambato
Chimborazo
Simbambe
Altar
Devil's Nose
Alausí
Sangay
Chunchi
Guayaquil
Cuenca
Azogues

▲▲ Peak

FIND OUT MORE
www.chivaexpress.com
Awakening in The Andes
Enrique Aguilar
Huasipungo
Jorge Icaza Coronel
Ratas, Ratones, and Rateros (Movie)

The Spring Festival
Across the roof of the world

On July 3, 2006, the inaugural train arrived in Lhasa, completing a 48-hour, 2,485 mile (4,000 km) journey across the "roof of the world" from Beijing. American writer Paul Theroux had claimed that the Kunlun mountains were "a guarantee that a railway will never get to Lhasa," but the Chinese have pulled off a remarkable feat of engineering. The track crosses permanently frozen areas, which require a high-tech cooling system to keep the frozen track-bed stable, and it reaches 16,640 ft (5,072 m) at the Tanggula pass—making it the world's highest railway. At this altitude, the carriages also have to be oxygenated to avoid altitude sickness. However, controversy has surrounded the project, and debate still rages as to whether the railway is a successful step in China's "Great Leap West" campaign to provide much-needed development to this impoverished corner of the country, or signals a "second invasion" of Tibet.

Above: In June, 1989, Tiananmen Square hit the world's headlines as tanks rumbled into the massive heart of Beijing and fired indiscriminately on unarmed protesters. The "Gate of Heavenly Peace" covers over 100 acres, making it the largest city square in the world. It is adorned with huge emblems of Chairman Mao, and thronged by those wishing to see his mausoleum.

Left: The Qingzang Railway into Lhasa has been described as "the realization of a 100-year-old Chinese dream." For much of the route, the train is watched by surprised yaks, antelope, and donkeys, but this formerly remote region is now being opened up thanks to a $4 billion investment. The Chinese government sees this as vital to improve commerce and extend their new-found wealth to Tibet.

FIND OUT MORE

My Land, My People
Dalai Lama

Wild Swans
Jung Chang

The Hotel on the Roof of the World: Five years in Tibet
Alec Le Sueur

Dragon in the Land of Snows
Tsering Shakya

A Traveller in China
Christina Dodwell

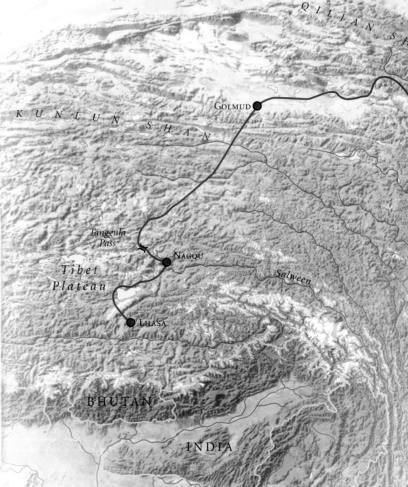

Beijing to Lhasa

Beijing's heart has an incongruous mix of the imperial splendor of the Forbidden Palace and the massive emblems of the cult of Mao in Tiananmen Square. The train heads for the former capital Xian, with its huge, thick city walls, and the bizarre Terracotta Warriors, a life-size army of 8,000 figures buried to protect Emperor Qin in the afterlife. Xining's history as a transit point on the Silk Road is borne out by its Buddhist Ta'er Monastery, Dongguan Mosque, and Taoist Beishan Temple. From Lanzhou, with its salt lakes, the railway heads across the grassy highlands of the remote Tibetan plateau, turning south at the garrison town of Golmud. The views are breathtaking (literally) as the train crosses the snow-capped mountains, dotted with herdsmen tending their yaks.

Finally the train reaches Lhasa, the "place of the gods," capital of Tibet, and spiritual center of Tibetan Buddhism. The Jokhang is the most sacred temple, while the Potala and Norbulingka palaces were the traditional winter and summer homes of the Dalai Lama.

> "A journey of a thousand miles begins with a single step."
> *Lao-tzu (604-531BC), The Way of Lao-tzu*

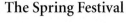

BEIJING

SHIJIAZHUANG
North China Platte

Huang He

XINING

LANCHOU

Huang He

XI'AN

Above: The iconic 1000-room Potala Palace was constructed by the fifth Dalai Lama, in 1645. It was named after Mount Potala, and was the abode of Avalokitesvara, a widely revered *bodhisattva* known for his compassion. After the 14th Dalai Lama fled into exile, the Chinese converted it into a museum and it is now an UNESCO World Heritage Site.

The Spring Festival

The Spring Festival celebrates the lunar new year, generally in late January or early February. It is traditionally a time for people to return home to their families, and signals the start of spring. Homes are decorated with red scrolls or papercuts incorporating the Fu character for "happiness," and *jaozi* dumplings or *niangao* rice cakes are eaten to bring good fortune in the coming year. Evil spirits are driven away with firecrackers, and dragon and lion dances celebrate the triumph of good over evil. It is not completely over until the Lantern Festival on the 15th day.

In Tibet the new year is celebrated with the Losar Festival, where customs include making offerings to family shrine deities, and the performance of traditional *zhega* and Tibetan Opera.

Left: Beijing's Summer Palace, set around the stunning Kunming Lake, was created by Emperor Qianlong in 1750, reproducing gardens from palaces around the country. In 1998, UNESCO described it as an "outstanding expression of the creative art of Chinese landscape garden design, incorporating the works of humankind and nature in a harmonious whole".

39

THE CANADIAN PACIFIC RAILROAD
Vancouver to Montreal

The coast-to-coast rail journey across Canada joins two of the country's most popular and liveable cities—Vancouver and Montreal. The trains traverse the magnificent Rockies, using the legendary spiral tunnels to achieve the steepest part of the climb. They then head across the wide-open prairies of middle Canada to reach the shores of the Great Lakes, and follow the St Lawrence Seaway into the heart of French-speaking Canada. The scenic wonders of Banff National Park and Niagara Falls are the highlights, but other stops can introduce Canada's First Nations Communities, its Mounties, or its treasure trove of dinosaur remains. For a longer journey you could add in a diversion from Winnipeg into the wild expanses of the northern tundra in search of the October polar bear migration around Churchill, or continue from Montreal to the real Atlantic shoreline at Halifax.

Above: Vancouver is widely regarded as one of the most liveable cities in the world: a clean, well-planned city with plenty of culture and good museums. It is set to host the Winter Olympics in 2010 (along with Whistler). It is also considering a joint bid with the nearby US city of Seattle for the 2028 summer Olympics.

Across the Rockies

Vancouver, settled in 1862 after the discovery of coal, is the starting point for the two-day Rocky Mountaineer train ride. The train heads through Fraser Canyon, past the rushing waters of Hell's Gate, and deep into the breathtaking scenery of the Rockies. Spend several days enjoying the shimmering turquoise waters of Lake Louise in Banff, Canada's first national park in 1885, and exploring the icefields of Jasper, before catching the train to Calgary, a modern city with a Wild West feel. If you're there in July catch the world-famous Calgary Stampede of bucking broncos, calf roping, and steer wrestling. On the long trek across the prairies, stop at Moose Jaw to get an insight into the gangster world of Al Capone, who used its tunnels as a hideout in the 1920s. Close to cosmopolitan Toronto are the thundering Niagara Falls, "honeymoon capital of the world," where you can experience a Maid of the Mist boat ride through the spray. Finally you reach the fascinating French-English mix of Montreal, with its colorful basilica of Notre Dame and outstanding Museum of Fine Arts. It's a city that can be enjoyed even in the depths of winter—simply venture into its Underground City, a climate-controlled world below street level.

Left: The thunder of the Niagara Falls can be heard from miles away, the frothing water crashing over a 170 ft (52 m) high cliff some 2,624 ft (800 m) wide. The boat, *Maid of the Mist*, takes visitors up close to the base of the falls.

Right: The rows of steep mountain ranges that run down through British Columbia provided a major challenge to the engineers of the Canadian Pacific Railway, but today they create a magnificent backdrop for the route. The railway also passes through land once inhabited by the Blackfoot First Nation, whose chief, Crowfoot, was given a life's pass on the railway in return for the tribe's co-operation.

Canadian Pacific Railway

When British Columbia insisted on having a national railway as a condition of joining the Confederation of Canada in 1871, plans for the world's longest railway line were laid and it was eventually completed in 1885 using government cash and land grants. An engineering triumph of the time, this "act of insane recklessness"—according to the opposition leader Alexander Mackezie—connected the two coasts of Canada, over 2,000 miles (3,220 km) apart, and became the main means of traversing the country's vast area. The toughest section was around Kicking Horse Pass, where a 4.5% gradient was required—way above the recommended limits for railways, even today. As a result, safety switches were installed, and spiral tunnels constructed, which opened in 1909.

> **"If we can't export the scenery, we'll import the tourists."**
> *William van Horne, first president of the Canadian Pacific Railroad*

MANITOBA

Lake Winnipeg

PORTAGE LA PRAIRIE
WINNIPEG
KENORA
Crow Lake
Lake Nipigon
THUNDER BAY
Lake Superior

ONTARIO

AMERICA

Lake Michigan

Lake Huron

SUDBURY

QUEBEC

MONTRÉAL

GUELPH
Lake Ontario
NIAGARA FALLS

Lake Erie

ATLANTIC OCEAN

Above: Montreal is the fifth-largest French-speaking city in the world. Explorer Jacques Cartier landed at the foot of "Mont Réal" in 1535 and claimed the St. Lawrence river valley in the name of France.

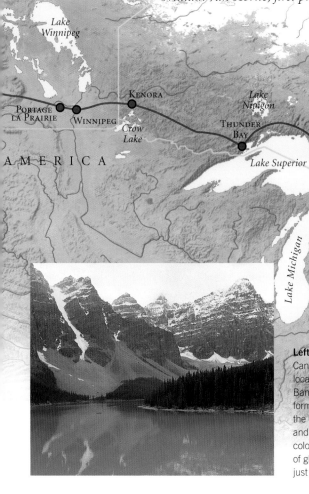

Left: Lake Louise, one of Canada's most photogenic locations, is a highlight of Banff National Park. It was formed 10,000 years ago at the end of the last ice age, and its serene turquoise color is due to the deposits of glacial silt suspended just beneath the surface.

FIND OUT MORE

www.rockymountaineer.com

www.cprheritage.com

The National Dream: The Great Railway, 1871-1881 Pierre Berton

Men of the Last Frontier Grey Owl

Cat's Eye Margaret Atwood

THE PALACE ON WHEELS
Around the old Empire

Travel in royal style through historic Rajasthan, the land of the Maharajahs, known for romance and chivalry. The luxury Palace on Wheels rail tour conjures up all the classic images of India—jungle-clad hills sprinkled with village life, temples teeming with colorfully-clad people, bustling cities graced with grand forts, and beautiful palaces—and if you're lucky a glimpse of a regal tiger in the wild. But the best of all has to wait until the end—the lavish splendor of the Mughal Empire, which culminated in the most sublime monument to love, the Taj Mahal.

A round route from Delhi

From the megacity of Delhi you head to the pink city of Jaipur, home to the attractive Palace of the Winds and an ancient observatory. The golden walled city of Jaisalmer rises shimmering out of the desert, with fine *havelis* (mansions) towering over charming narrow streets populated by ambling holy cows. Next is the blue city of Jodhpur, with its fabulous fort. By now it is time to go in search of the elusive tiger in Ranthambore National Park. The gaunt walls of Chittorgarh fort recall the great battles of the Rajput era, while Udaipur and its lakes showcase the delicate beauty of its palaces. Then it's on to Agra and the incomparable magnificence of the Taj Mahal.

Right: Climb onto an elephant's back for the dramatic ascent to the sandstone Amber Fort, just outside Jaipur. The palace is paved with white marble, and boasts a grand hall of thousands of intricately set mirrors, allowing it to be lit entirely by a single candle. It was built around 1600 by Raja Man Singh. Looming above is Jaigarh Fort, home to the world's largest cannon on wheels.

Left: The endangered Bengal Tiger roams the great national parks of India and neighboring countries. The best chance to see tigers in the wild is at Ranthambore National Park.

Below: The Taj Mahal, situated by the Yamuna River in Agra, is the crowning glory of the Mughal legacy of exquisite mausoleums in the region.

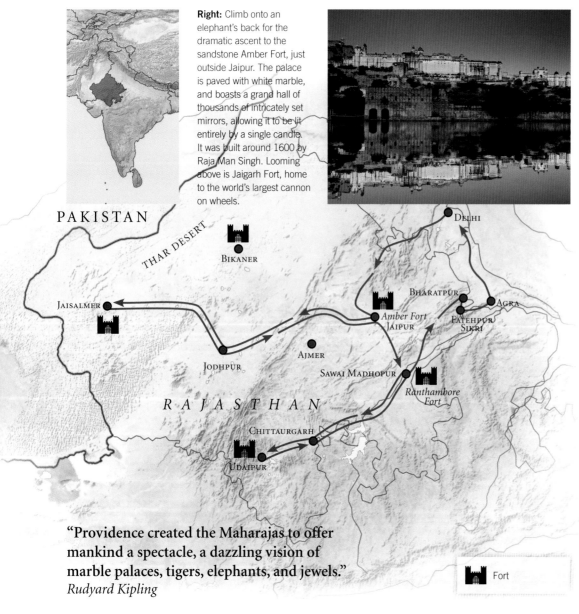

PAKISTAN

THAR DESERT

BIKANER

JAISALMER

JODHPUR

AJMER

SAWAI MADHOPUR

Ranthambore Fort

R A J A S T H A N

CHITTAURGARH

UDAIPUR

DELHI

BHARATPUR

Amber Fort
JAIPUR

FATEHPUR SIKRI

AGRA

Fort

"Providence created the Maharajas to offer mankind a spectacle, a dazzling vision of marble palaces, tigers, elephants, and jewels."
Rudyard Kipling

THE BLUE TRAIN
Pretoria to Cape Town

The Blue Train chuffs through grasslands, desert, mountains, and wine valleys on its two-day, 994 mile (1,600 km) route from the administrative capital Pretoria to vibrant Cape Town. It is a great introduction to the many faces of South Africa—a country made wealthy by diamond mining, made weary by apartheid, and made wonderful by nature. The Blue Train's sleek azure engine and spacious carriage suites—the epitome of Edwardian luxury—are the whimsy of steam train enthusiast Rohan Vos. His Rovos Rail trains also run up to the Victoria Falls or to the Mozambique border via Kruger National Park, and once a month, a 25-day trip reaches Dar Es Salaam—as far north as Cecil Rhodes' grand dream of a Cape to Cairo railway ever reached.

South to the Cape

Pretoria, with its British-era government buildings, is a good place to join the train, which then speeds on to the diamond capital, Kimberley, where Cecil Rhodes made his fortune. The Big Hole is supposedly the largest pit dug by manual labor in the world—almost 31 million tons (28 million tonnes) of rock was removed in order to recover three tonnes of diamonds. Carrying on across the semi-desert Karoo you make a brief visit to Matjiesfontein, a microcosm of Victorian England—complete with London double-decker bus—before arriving at Cape Town, one of the most liveable cities in the world. Here you can end the way you began, taking in those apartheid reminders, including Robben Island, the notorious prison where Nelson Mandela spent 18 years.

Above: Travel in the style of kings on board the Blue Train. The opulent suites have goose-down duvets and marble-tiled bathrooms. Enjoy fine dining with meals cooked by top chefs and world-class South African wines.

Below: At 3,562 ft (1,086 m) high and almost 2 miles (3 km) across, Table Mountain looms over Cape Town. Flanked by Lion's Head and Devil's Peak, it's most easily accessed via cable car, with magnificent views over the city.

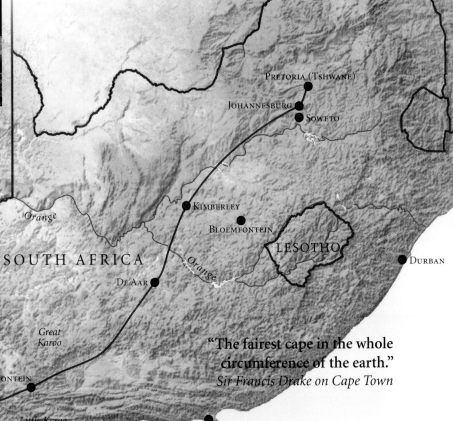

"The fairest cape in the whole circumference of the earth."
Sir Francis Drake on Cape Town

43

If a journey is to be fully savored, and every nuance teased out, then take it easy—the slower the pace, the greater the pleasure. It's that simple. A landscape glimpsed from a highway leaves a blur of random impressions, but covered on foot, the same landscape reveals itself as a whole. The beauty is invariably in the detail.

TRACKS AND TRAILS
On foot or on horseback

Traveling slowly was a point that William Cobbett fully understood. Traipsing round Britain in the 1820s to gather the material for his compelling portrait of rural Britain, *Rural Rides*, he wrote "You must go either on foot or on horse-back." A hundred years earlier, Daniel Defoe had much the same experience, with the result, the book *A Tour Through the Whole Island of Great Britain*, precisely reflecting the measured pace of his progress.

These are both experiences that can—at least partly—be recreated by journeying along some of Great Britain's national paths. The South West Coastal Path takes in the whole of the south west tip of the country, starting from Minehead and leading counterclockwise around the most westerly and southerly points on the mainland before ending at Poole Harbor. Meanwhile, in northern England the Pennine Way provides walkers with opportunities to contemplate landscapes infused with history as they travel along the "backbone of Britain".

Robert Louis Stevenson's travels with his donkey in France's Cevennes mountains inject an idiosyncratic Gallic flavor to the same message: slow is always best, and it's a point easily exported.

Those with a taste for Latin American flair can imagine themselves *gauchos* in the rich grasslands of the pampas, exploring ancient Jesuit churches and working ranches. Alternatively, a trek into the Andes will lead to the ruins of the lost Inca city of Machu Picchu, a treasure hidden for almost 400 years.

The pioneering spirit that drove America's westward expansion can be relived by following Daniel Boone's heroic crossing of the Cumberland Gap in the 18th century, the first breaching by white settlers of the previously impenetrable barrier of the Appalachians.

THE INCA TRAIL
To the lost city of Machu Picchu

The Incas of pre-conquest Peru had an efficient network of trails for communicating across their vast empire. Messengers would run 6 mile (10 km) sections in relays—and reputedly fish could be brought over 150 miles (250 km) from the coast in less than a day. The restored 25 mile (40 km) path known as the Inca Trail heads through spectacular Andean scenery, past fine Inca remains, to the ultimate lost city—Machu Picchu. It is a mysterious site—perhaps a royal city with walls once clad in gold and silver, or maybe just a minor village—but whatever the truth it was deserted within a century of construction in the 1400s, and lost to the jungle. Only the local Amerindians knew of its existence and told tales of the once-great city on the Urubamba River.

Hitting the trail

Spend time in Cusco to acclimatize to the altitude, which at upwards of 9,500 ft (3,000 m) causes shortness of breath, before taking the train for a magnificent ride through the Urubamba Valley, and disembarking at km 88, 25 miles (40 km) short of Machu Picchu. The first short stretch of the trail goes up to Wayllabamba, which is a possible first night's stop, while the second day has a tough ascent to Warmiwanusqa (Dead Woman's Pass) at almost 14,000 ft (4,200 m). The third day passes the ruins of Runkurakay and Sayacmarca, before going through an Inca tunnel in the mountains. You will also see the ritual baths of Phuyupatamarca before camping at the beautiful terraced ruins of Wiñay Wayna, with baths and ceremonial buildings. Finally on the fourth day an early start brings you to Intipunko (the Sun Gate) and there before you is Machu Picchu, perched on a ridge between towering peaks, with the river meandering far below.

Hiram Bingham

Hiram Bingham (1875-1956) grew up in Hawaii before completing his education in mainland USA, and becoming a lecturer in South American history. In 1908 on his way home from a conference in Chile, he stopped off in Peru to visit Choquequirao. He was

so thrilled that he returned three years later with the Yale Peruvian Expedition. Local guides led him to Machu Picchu on July 24, 1911—the first European ever to go there, as it was never found by the invading Spanish conquistadors of the 16th century. In later life he became governor of Connecticut and a US senator. He married Alfreda Mitchell, the grand-daughter of the founder of Tiffany & Co, the jewelry company.

Left: The magnificent Urubamba River winds between precipitous jungle-clad peaks and opens out into the Sacred Valley nearer to the former Inca capital of Cusco. Nearby sites include the bustling market at Pisac, and the imposing Inca fortress of Ollantaytambo.

Below: Machu Picchu consists of 140 buildings with perfect mortarless stone walls. It was erected by people who did not know of the wheel, but used astronomy to align their temples with sunrise on the solstices.

Left: Much of Peru in the Andes or in the southern *altiplano* (high plain) is over 9,500 ft (3,000 m) above sea level. This causes shortness of breath, so all visitors to the region must take time to acclimatize before any exertion such as hiking the Inca Trail.

Ruins

Below: One of the highlights of the Inca Trail, Wiñay Wayna is a perfect set of village ruins overlooking the Urubamba River. Its name means "eternal youth" and it consists of a series of terraced houses connected by a steep staircase. There is also an agricultural area, and a system of fountains, which could perhaps have been baths.

Mandor

Aguas Calientes

Aguas Calientes

Urubamba

Machu Picchu

Intipunku

Aobamba

Urubamba

Wiñay Wayna

Phuyupatamarca

Above: Dead Woman's Pass (or Warmiwanusqa) is the highest point on the Inca Trail, at 13,780 ft (4,200 m). It got its name because the mountains are supposed to resemble a dead woman, though a little imagination is required. A maximum of 500 trekkers are permitted to start the trail each day. The Short Inca Trail, an 8.7 mile (14 km) route along the last leg of the trip, is an alternative.

Chaqulcocha

Runkurakay

Sayacmarca

Pacamayo

Warmiwanusqa Pass

Llulluchapampa

To Cusco

Tres Piedras

Wayllabamba

"Then up the ladder of the earth I climbed through the barbed jungle's thickets until I reached you, Machu Picchu."
Pablo Neruda

WITH STEVENSON IN THE CEVENNES
Travels with a donkey

In 1878 Robert Louis Stevenson embarked on a long trek through the Cevennes in the south of France, accompanied by a donkey, resulting in the publication of *Travels with a Donkey in the Cevennes* (1879). Stevenson had bought his donkey from one Father Adam and named her Modestine: "At length she passed into my service for the consideration of sixty-five francs and a glass of brandy. The sack had already cost eighty francs and two glasses of beer, so that Modestine, as I instantly baptized her, was upon all accounts the cheaper article. Indeed, that was as it should be; for she was only an appurtenance of my mattress, or self-acting bedstead on four castors." Modestine proved a lazy, but amusing traveling companion, and the pair set out on September 22 from Le Monastier in the north of the region.

Across the Cevennes

Journeying south through Langogne, Cheylard, Luc, La Bastide, Chasserades, Bleymard, Pont de Montvert, Florac, St. Germain de Calberte, and St. Jean du Gard, Stephenson's descriptions of his encounters, the countryside, and events are unforgettable; the self-made bedding and constant alterations to Modestine's load; the dreaded "Beast of the Gévaudan;" the innkeeper of Bouchet St. Nicolas; the monks of Our Lady of the Snows; the country of the Camisards, and the suffering poor of La Vernède. Finally, having traveled 120 miles (193 km) through a sparsely populated countryside, the unlikely pair arrived at Alais on October 3.

Into the wilderness of this world

"The journey which this little book is to describe was very agreeable and fortunate for me... we are all travelers in what John Bunyan calls the wilderness of this world—all, too, travelers with a donkey; and the best that we find in our travels is an honest friend. He is a fortunate voyager who finds many. We travel, indeed, to find them. They are the end and the reward of life...."
Stevenson's foreword to Travels with a Donkey in the Cevennes

Above: The Cevennes was known for its community of Huguenots (French Protestants), who were largely protected from reprisals by Catholics due to the region's mountainous terrain.

Above: Stevenson began his journey at Le Monastier, "a pleasant highland valley notable for the making of lace, for drunkenness...for unparalleled political discussion."

AROUND BRITAIN WITH DANIEL DEFOE
A celebration of the the British Isles

Best known as the author of *Robinson Crusoe*, Daniel Defoe, born in London around 1660, was the personification of the "brilliant scoundrel" of late Stuart and early Georgian Britain. His career was astonishingly varied and included a series of doomed business ventures, as well as a spell in prison. He can be considered among the founding fathers of the English novel, as well as one of the first journalists as he was the author of an extraordinary array of pamphlets and journals on a bewildering number of subjects. Between 1724 and 1727, he also produced an extraordinarily vivid account of Britain—in effect one of the first travel books—*A Tour Through the Whole Island of Great Britain*.

Above: Scotland was united with England only 20 years before Defoe's journey and was still economically backward, barbarous, and wild. Defoe was anxious to see it fulfill its economic potential, which he believed it could most obviously do if people were better informed about its state.

Record of a nation

Defoe's purpose was unashamedly to celebrate not just the variety of Britain but its rapidly increasing prosperity and new political, Protestant, parliamentary stability. If there was a clear political motive at work, as important was the technique, all but revolutionary at the time, of first-hand reporting he brought to bear. Defoe was incorrigibly curious, as interested in oyster fishing as in high politics, as moved by landscapes as by local history, as intrigued  by royal dockyards as by improving agricultural techniques. The result is a richly detailed record of pre-industrial Britain, a multifaceted portrait of an increasingly confident if still overwhelmingly agrictural nation. It is an exceptional testament not just to his unflagging industriousness but to a rare gift for reportage.

FIND OUT MORE

A Tour Through the Whole Island of Great Britain
Daniel Defoe
ed. Patricia Rodgers

Daniel Defoe
John J Richetti

The Strange Life and Surprising Adventures of Daniel Defoe
Richard West

"As the work itself is a description of the most flourishing and opulent country in the world, so there is a flowing variety of materials; all the particulars are fruitful of instructing and diverting objects."
Daniel Defoe, Preface to the First Volume, 1724

Below: Although fascinated by politics and local history, Defoe was also intrigued by the working world of fisherman and farmers in pre-industrial Britain.

Right: In an age when the overwhelming majority of the population of Britain were unlikely to travel more than a few miles from the place of their birth, knowledge as a whole of the state of the newly unified kingdom of Great Britain was patchy at best. It was Defoe's enduring achievement to help reinforce a sense of an emerging national identity.

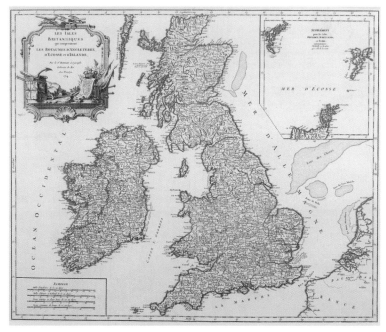

THROUGH THE CUMBERLAND GAP
Blazing a trail across the Appalachians

In the mid 18th century the Appalachian Mountains formed a substantial barrier to westward migration for pioneers from the Thirteen Colonies. This wild and lawless frontier was a traditional hunting ground of the American Indians, but in 1769 American pioneer Daniel Boone headed through the one dip in the formidable Cumberland Mountain ridge and found the great bluegrass meadow of Kentucky, with bountiful buffalo, deer, and turkeys. Six years later he took 35 axemen to blaze the Wilderness Road through the Cumberland Gap, setting up a colony at Boonesborough, and opening up the middle of America. Today, small farms—renowned for their horse-breeding—are set amid rolling hills of bluegrass and crops of corn and tobacco. The corn is used to make Kentucky's famous bourbon whiskey, and the region has many distilleries.

Above: The English explorer Thomas Walker named Cumberland River after Prince William Augustus, Duke of Cumberland, shortly after the Battle of Culloden (1746).

Daniel Boone

Daniel Boone (1734-1820) was a hunter and woodman from Pennsylvania. He first ventured into Kentucky in 1767, and crossed the Cumberland Gap two years later. He blazed the Wilderness Road through the Gap in 1775, founding Boonesborough (southeast of Lexington), and by the end of the century, 200,000 pioneers had followed.

In 1776 Indians took his daughter and two other girls, and Boone's rescue of them is fictionally portrayed in the novel and film *The Last of the Mohicans*. Boone himself was also later captured, but befriended Chief Blackfish who "adopted" him as a son. In later life Boone headed out into the new frontierlands of Missouri, claiming Kentucky was "too crowded." The countless tales of Boone's adventures have turned him into a legend larger than life.

Left: The American folk song "Cumberland Gap," first sung by the 18th-century westward-trekking pioneers, crossed the Atlantic when Lonnie Donegan made a hit with his skiffle version in 1957. It remained No.1 in the UK charts for five weeks—the first folk song ever to top the listings.

FIND OUT MORE

The Last of the Mohicans
James Fenimore Cooper

A Walk in the Woods
Bill Bryson
(Appalachian Trail)

Daniel Boone
(Movie)

www.nps.gov/cuga

ALEXANDRIA

Kentucky

Licking

LOUISVILLE

LAWRENCEBURG   LEXINGTON

BOONESBOROUGH

LORETO

Logans Fort

MT. VERNON

KENTUCKY

Cumberland

MIDDLESBORO

Cumberland Gap   Fort Patrick Hen

TENNESSEE   Holston   Fort Wat.

Fort

Above / above right: Skyland Road winds up to Pinnacle Overlook at 2,440 feet (743 m). From here you can experience spectacular views that change with the seasons, looking out over the Gap into Kentucky, Virginia, and Tennessee. The 21-mile (34 km) Ridge Trail leads on to Gibson's Gap, Butcher's Gap, and Chadwell Gap. Near here is Hensley Settlement, inhabited from 1904 to 1951. The blacksmith's, springhouse, and schoolhouse have all been restored. The Ridge Trail continues through Bailes Meadows to the White Rocks Overlook at the eastern edge of the park, where limestone caves conceal stalagmites and flowstone cascades, as well as colonies of bats.

Along the pioneer trail

Starting at Roanoke, the end of the Great Wagon Road from Philadelphia, head for Bristol along the first leg of Daniel Boone's pioneer trail into Kentucky. A notoriously difficult part of the route crosses the Clinch and Powell mountains, before passing through the Devil's Racepath gap and following the foothills of the Cumberland Mountain ridge, whose white sandstone cliffs would have loomed over the pioneers.

The old wagon trail through the Cumberland Gap is being restored in the National Historic Park, where you can explore Gap Cave and climb to Pinnacle Overlook for breathtaking views over the Gap and the small, sparkling lakes set among wooded mountain peaks. North across Bluegrass Country is the Daniel Boone National Forest with a 65 ft (20 m) tall, 79 ft (24 m) span natural bridge, beside the Red River Gorge. George Washington's 18th century whiskey distillery at his home in Mount Vernon has been restored, as has Fort Boonesborough, at the end of the original Wilderness Road.

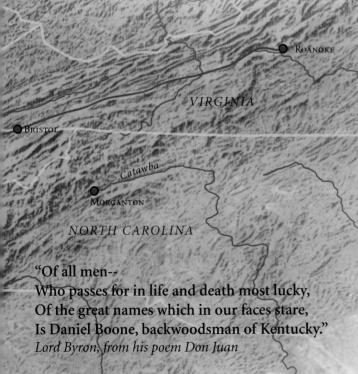

ROANOKE

VIRGINIA

BRISTOL

Catawba

MORGANTON

NORTH CAROLINA

"Of all men--
Who passes for in life and death most lucky,
Of the great names which in our faces stare,
Is Daniel Boone, backwoodsman of Kentucky."
Lord Byron, from his poem Don Juan

Above: A trail up a crack in the side of the arch beside the Red River Gorge is known as *Fat Man's Misery*. Daniel Boone is believed to have slept in one of the rock shelters in the park.

RIDING THE PAMPAS
The grasslands of South America

Argentina is the land of the *gaucho*, the cowboys that roam the wide-open grasslands of the pampas, from the foothills of the Andes across a northern swathe of the country into Uruguay. Stay at the colonial estancias near Cordobá, Argentina's former capital, and ride out on a *criollo*, the unique Argentine breed of horse, to round up the cattle and learn to lasso. Afterwards enjoy a traditional *asado*—beef barbecue—and some fine Argentinean wine beside the pool. The more sporty can try their hand at polo, or enjoy mountain biking and paragliding, while those seeking culture can visit the 17th century Jesuit churches and *estancias*, reminders of the age when missionaries brought European learning and skills to the region, before their expulsion by the Spanish king in 1767.

The flavor of Latin America

After the long flight to Buenos Aires, take a couple of days to enjoy its colorful tin houses, its 19th century European-style parks and gardens, and the hottest tango in the world. Then it's time for the short flight to the second city, Cordobá, some 435 miles (700 km) northwest in the foothills of the Sierra Chicas, nestled between the grasslands and the saltpans of the pampas. The old colonial heart, dating from 1573, centers on the Manzana Jesuitica complex of church, residence, and university. The work of the Jesuits was funded by its own ranches-cum-monasteries, the oldest of which is Caroya (1616). Jesús Maria, with its beautiful double-arched cloister, houses the National Jesuit Museum, while the town is famous for its Gaucho Festival of folklore and horse-breaking each January. Santa Catalina's church is one of the best examples of "colonial Baroque" in Argentina. Traveling back towards Cordobá via the other *estancias*, you'll pass the crumbling Eden hotel in German La Falda, and Cosquín, which comes alive in January during its Folklore Festival.

Left: Buenos Aires, literally "fair winds," is a cosmopolitan mix of peoples and architecture. European immigrants have built villas reminiscent of Paris or Barcelona, while other *barrios* abound with traditional painted tin houses. Tango developed from the dancing of the rough, sweaty gauchos with Buenos Aires' ladies of the night. It was not until the 1920s that this passionate dance became accepted by the upper class.

Above: The Jesuits founded their first rural settlement—of church, cloister-residence, mill, and farmland—at Caroya in 1616. Since then it has been a college, arms factory, hostel, and now national monument.

Right: At Alta Gracia Estancia the Jesuits built a *tajamar* to form a reservoir. "Che" Guevara grew up in the town, and Spanish composer Manuel de Falla died here.

Martín Fierro

The impoverished gaucho hero of José Hernández's epic poem has become the Don Quixote of Argentine literature. The ballad's earthy language conjures up the harsh life of gauchos in the late 19th century as modernization attempted to destroy their very existence. Beginning with Fierro's rural life, it follows his conscription into the army to fight Indians on the frontier. He deserts only to find his home and family gone, and is outlawed for taking part in (and provoking) knifefights. He takes shelter with the Indians but soon becomes their captive. His return to "civilization" brings him back to face the consequences of his violent life.

Below: Gauchos use lassos to catch cattle and boleadoras (three leather-covered stone or wooden balls attached to a rope) to disable them. Living a rugged life, on a diet of beef, bread, and *mate* (Latin American tea), the gaucho's main possession is usually his horse.

FIND OUT MORE

On the Pampas
Maria C. Brusca

Tschiffely's Ride
Aimé Tschiffely

Imagining Argentina
Lawrence Thornton

Martín Fierro
José Hernández

Assassination Tango
(Movie)

www.ridingholidays.
com/argentina-
cordoba.htm

"My joy is to live as free as the bird in the sky."
Martín Fierro by José Hernández

Dos Lunas

Capilla del Monte

Santa Catalina

Jesús María

Jesús María

Caroya

Caroya

La Cumbre

La Candelaria

La Falda

Los Potreros

Río Ceballos

Unquillo

Cosquín

Villa Allende

La Calera

Córdoba

Manzana Jesuítica

Primero

Villa Carlos Paz

Alta Gracia

Alta Gracia

Segundo

Estancia

Ranch

WILLIAM COBBETT
Rural Rides

Cobbett, born in Surrey in 1763, was one of the most paradoxical, provoking, and compelling figures of his age. He was chiefly a political journalist, founding his own newspaper (the *Political Register*) and producing an unofficial record of parliament, *Parliamentary Debates*, as well as authoring numerous pamphlets. He was awkward, difficult, suspicious, and riddled with prejudices—he abominated the drinking of tea and the eating of potatoes, for example. However, he was a relentless opponent of political corruption and a fierce champion of political reform, convinced that the accelerating impact of industrialization was overwhelmingly disastrous, enriching town dwellers at the direct expense of the rural poor.

Above: Cobbett's *Rural Rides* consisted of a series of journeys made on horseback throughout the Southeast and Midland regions of England.

A picture of England

Cobbett wrote what were subsequently published in 1830 as his *Rural Rides*; a series of what he called "letters" in the Political Register between 1821 and 1830. They are without question the most complete picture of rural England in the early years of the Industrial Revolution, a vast "rolling panorama" of landscapes and peoples, dashed off with a typically bravura mix of "eloquence and invective." They form a magnificently idiosyncratic whole, a vivid and deeply personal series of impressions, musings, denunciations, and first-hand descriptions. Throughout, there is an abiding sense of his absolute love of the English countryside—and his equally heartfelt hatred of cities, London in particular—and of the lives of those, above all the poor, who had shaped it and been shaped by it.

FIND OUT MORE
Rural Rides
William Cobbet
ed. Ian Dyck, 2001

William Cobbet
G.K. Chesterton

The Life and Adventures of William Cobbet
Richard Ingrams

"My object was, not to see inns and turnpike-roads, but to see the country: to see the farmers at home, and to see the labourers in the fields; and to do this you must go either on foot or on horseback."
William Cobbett, Rural Rides, September 25, 1822

Below: The Great British landscape—and the people who lived and worked the land—were the catalyst for Cobbett's *Rural Rides,* which were undertaken in response to agricultural proposals made by Parliament in 1821.

Below: Cobbett visited Dover in 1823, making a series of caustic remarks about the Napoleonic fortifications on the Western Heights. "The question that every man of sense asks is: What reason had you to suppose that the French would ever come to this hill to attack it... This is, perhaps, the only set of fortifications in the world ever famed for mere hiding. There is no appearance of any intention to annoy an enemy. It is a parcel of holes made in a hill, to hide Englishmen from Frenchmen."

THE PENNINE WAY
The backbone of England

Britain's best-known path extends from Edale in Derbyshire to Kirk Yetholm in the Scottish borders. Inspired by the Appalachian Trail in the 1930s, journalist Tom Stephenson campaigned to make the Pennine Way an official trail, eventually succeeding when the final section was opened in 1965. While the trail is a challenge, this 267 mile (429 km) trek is not renowned for its toughness, with its highest point, Cross Fell, a mere 2,930 ft (893 m). It does, however, pass through some of the finest scenery in England, from Derbyshire's Peak District, the Yorkshire Dales, and the moors of Northumberland.

Above: Malham Cove is one of Britain's most striking natural wonders, a 236 ft (72 m) high amphitheatre-shaped cliff, with a limestone pavement above it. Once a tremendous waterfall thundered over the edge, but the water now seeps through the limestone, emerging as a peaceful stream below.

Edale to Kirk Yetholm

Don your walking boots, wrap up against the English weather, and settle in to a pint of beer at the Old Nag's Head in Edale, before heading north for dramatic Kinder Scout. Past Haworth, the Way enters the glorious Dales and reaches Malham Cove, with its limestone pavement, and the rocky Gordale Scar. The path then climbs Pen-y-Ghent, part of the Three Peaks Challenge, and one of the area's most striking summits. After crossing the Coast-to-Coast Walk at Keld, it's time for a beer at England's highest pub—the Tan Hill Inn. Across Teesdale, with its plummeting waterfalls—High Force and Cauldron Snout—the Way follows Hadrian's Wall past excellent Roman forts at Housesteads and Vindolanda. From here it is not far to Kirk Yetholm, and the chance for a final pint before returning to the daily grind.

> "A long green trail from the Peak to the Cheviots. Just a faint line on the Ordnance Maps which the feet of grateful pilgrims would, with the passing years, engrave on the face of the land."
> *Tom Stephenson*

FIND OUT MORE

Pennine Way Companion
Alfred Wainwright

The Pennine Way
Tom Stephenson

One Man and his Bog
Barry Pilton

www.nationaltrail.co.uk/PennineWay

Above: Rising to 2,085 ft (636 m), Kinder Scout is the Peak District's highest mountain. It is part of a large gritstone plateau, with the summit itself also known as the Dark Peak. It is known for its rocky outcrops, the dramatic waterfall known as Kinder Downfall, and pretty streams such as Jaggers Clough. The crossing of this peatland area by the Pennine Way is causing some worries due to erosion. Over 10,000 people walk the entire Pennine Way each year, and as many as 200,000 walk shorter stretches, putting immense pressure on fragile ecosystems.

Above: The Dent Head Viaduct, in the heart of the beautiful Yorkshire Dales, is part of the famed Settle to Carlisle railway. The route has been threatened with closure several times, but has been maintained as one of the most scenic rail journeys in England.

THE SOUTH WEST COAST PATH
Around the western tip of England

Since 1978, the South West Coast Path has been one of Britain's 15 officially designated National Trails, and at 630 miles (1,014 km) long it is the longest footpath in the country. Other than 18 short river-mouth ferry crossings it is continuous, following the coasts of Somerset, Devon, Cornwall, and Dorset. Its two end points are Minehead and Poole, and between these two towns are two UNESCO World Heritage Sites (the Jurassic Coast in south Devon and Dorset, and the Cornwall and West Devon Mining Landscape), as well as a number of National Parks and Heritage Coasts.

Minehead to Poole

By convention, the South West Coast Path is normally described counterclockwise, from Minehead to Poole, but there is no limit to the ways it can be walked. The overwhelming majority of walkers do small stretches at a time, dipping in and out  as mood and circumstance allow. More hardy types may want to tackle longer and more demanding lengths, spending a week or more walking them. To walk the Path in one go, covering anywhere from 10 to 16 miles (16–26 km) a day, is generally estimated to take eight weeks. Whether tempted by a stroll, or determined to tackle the whole route, information is available on suggested routes, graded from easy to hard, short to long, and the facilities en route, and detailed information is easily found on aspects of the Path such as landscapes, geology, and history.

> "With all its ups and downs and ins and outs, the route is … a monstrous roller-coaster … through history and heritage, scenic splendor and the wonders of the natural world."
> *Paddy Dillon, The South West Coast Path*

Left: The rocky, windswept splendor of Lands End. The nearest land due west is Newfoundland in Canada, almost 2,000 miles (3,220 km) away. Just over a mile out to sea is the Longships lighthouse, built in 1873 and standing on a sea-lashed outcrop.

Right: Tin has been mined in Cornwall since the Bronze Age, 4,000 years ago and the country is dotted with tin mines. The industry reached its zenith in the 19th century, but has been a tale of steady decline ever since. The last working mine was closed in 1998.

FIND OUT MORE
South West Coast Path Eric Wallis
The South West Coast Path Paddy Dillon
www.southwestcoastpath.com (Official website)
www.swcp.org.uk
(South West Coast Path Association)

Harbors stud the South West Coast Path. The harbor at Minehead (**above**) boasts a pier built in 1616, while Poole Harbor (**left**) is claimed to be the second-largest natural harbor in the world after Sydney, Australia. Today, it is one of the most important yachting centers in Britain.

Below: Durdle Door is a dramatic limestone arch jutting 400 feet into the sea. It is a celebrated local beauty spot.

Points of interest

The South West Coast Path takes in an immense variety of landscapes and other places of interest. Among the sites and scenery are the highest cliffs in mainland Britain (Great Hangman, Somerset), the most westerly and most southerly points of mainland England (Land's End and Lizard Point, Cornwall), the smallest parish church in England (Culborne Church, Somerset), and the longest village street (Combe Martin, Devon). This is to say nothing of two officially recognized nudist beaches at Budleigh Salterton, Devon, and Studland Bay, Dorset. This means the path provides a permanently changing series of views, alternately commanding and domestic, with the only constant being the sea. It is not always easy going, however—to walk the whole path means negotiating 26,719 steps, crossing 302 bridges, and straddling 921 stiles.

The vast sweep of history manifests itself in myriad ways, with those making journeys doing so for reasons every bit as various. War, trade, curiosity, culture, religion, or just a determination for a new and better life are just some of the motives that drive the constant human impulse to travel to new lands.

IN THE STEPS OF HISTORY
The routes of adventure

Two medieval travelers, one an Italian and a Christian, the other a North African Muslim, undertook two extraordinary journeys across what was then in effect almost the entire known world. The first was Marco Polo in the 13th century, the second Ibn Battuta in the 14th. Both not only visited China, but left accounts of their travels that provide invaluable first-hand insights into medieval Eurasia and, in the case of Ibn Battuta, Africa.

The Greek, Pausanias, provides a similar example. His *Description of Greece*, written in the 2nd century AD, is an exceptionally detailed description of the cultural achievements of the ancient Greek world.

Military genius made possible the journeys of two towering figures of the Ancient World: Alexander the Great, whose whirlwind of conquest hugely extended the boundaries of the Greek world; and Hannibal, whose daring came close to toppling the might of an emerging Rome in the 3rd century BC.

Almost 1,300 years later, the First Crusade saw different kinds of armies on the move, all making their way across Europe to the Holy Land, determined to wrest control of the Christian holy places from Muslim rule.

More recent conflicts have given rise to other journeys in this chapter: Mussolini's "march" on Rome and Mao Zedong's infinitely more grueling "Long March." Though espousing diametrically opposed political positions—Mussolini a fascist, and Zedong a communist—both successfully extracted the maximum propaganda from their travels.

The great westward expansion of 19th century America provided further reasons for hundreds of thousands of settlers to seek new lives, even fortunes, in the frontier territories, whether riding the wagon trails or rushing to the goldfields.

ALEXANDER THE GREAT
Conquest of the east

In 334 AD, at the age of 21, Alexander, king of Macedonia, began a blaze of conquest across the ancient world that in barely 10 years took him to Afghanistan and India, the limits of the then-known world for the Greeks. He began with certain advantages. By 337, his father, the brutal Philip II, was effectively ruler of all Thrace and most of Greece. But the speed with which Alexander extended Macedonian rule was dizzying: the whole of Asia Minor fell to him, Egypt was annexed, and Achaemenid Persia, the most serious military threat to the Greek world for over 150 years, was obliterated.

✗ Battlesites
— Main Routes of Alexander
- - - Return sea route of partial force
▭ Extent of Alexander's Empire
▬ States allied to Alexander

Against the odds

One of the most remarkable aspects of Alexander the Great's conquests was that they were made in the face of numerically much stronger forces. In his two crushing victories over the Persians—at Issus in 333 and Gaugamela in 331—he fielded forces

of 30,000 and 40,000 against Persian troops 100,000 and 200,000 strong respectively. Though he progressively expanded his army, recruiting troops in the lands he conquered, Macedonian soldiers remained at its heart. They were exceptionally loyal to Alexander personally and in turn he treated them with great tact, lavishing them with honors and plunder, and regularly sending veterans back to Greece. Alexander led his troops with the kind of reckless courage that saw him regularly wounded, most seriously in India where he came close to death after being shot in the lung by an arrow. But his generalship was no less a product of precise planning. At its height, his army was over 50,000 strong and required 120 tons of supplies a day, yet it was still capable of traveling almost 20 miles (32 km) at a stretch.

Left: Babylon, one of the major power centers in the Middle East, fell to Alexander in 331 BC and it was in this ancient center of former Persian power that Alexander died, on June 10, 323 BC at the age of 33. It was long thought he had either been poisoned or had died of malaria, but recent research indicates he died of typhoid.

Left: The Battle of Issus, fought in November 333 in southern Anatolia, was one of the most significant in Alexander's shattering conquest of Achaemenid Persia. The Persian forces were lead by Darius III, the Persian emperor, in person, who was desperate to avenge Alexander's victory over his forces the previous year at Granicus. Here it is shown in a painting from 1602 that is currently housed in the Louvre, Paris.

The quest for knowledge and power

Alexander's motive in continuing eastwards into Central Asia and then, in 327, to India following the destruction of Achaemenid Persia has long been the subject of dispute. Was it because he wanted to make himself ruler of the whole world? Had he come to believe, as was claimed on his behalf, that he was divine? Certainly, Greek knowledge of India was speculative at best: that it could be no larger than Persia and that, beyond it, was only the Great Outer Sea, a vast ocean encircling the globe. The reality proved disturbingly different, an alien and seemingly endless arid land apparently leading only to further unknown great rivers and kingdoms. Convincing his armies to continue became increasingly difficult and at the Hyphasis river, in September, 326 BC, Alexander reluctantly agreed to return. The journey took a year, his army following the course of the Indus south to the Arabian Sea, where half his forces then embarked on ships. The remainder continued overland across the Makran desert, suffering appalling losses due to heat and thirst.

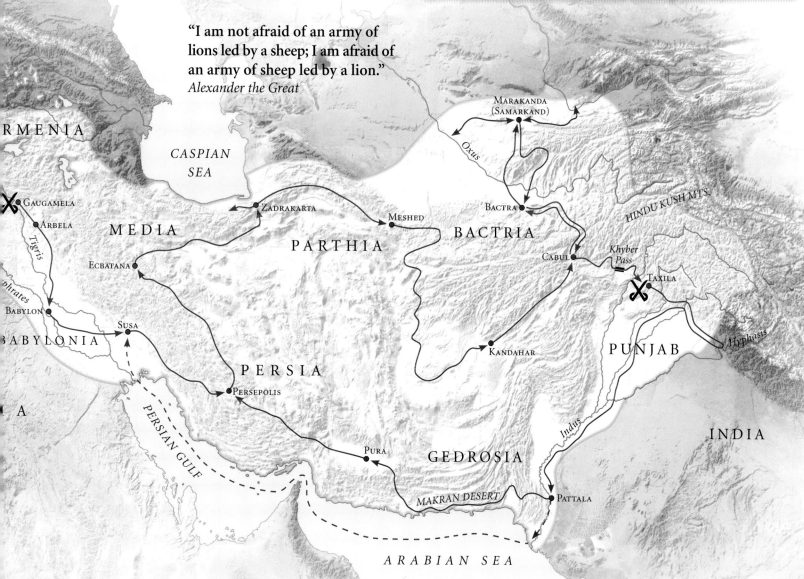

"I am not afraid of an army of lions led by a sheep; I am afraid of an army of sheep led by a lion."
Alexander the Great

MARCO POLO
Venice to the Orient

The re-establishment of the Silk Road was made possible in the early 13th century by Mongol conquests of Eurasia. If, initially, this sparked an uncertain renewal of trade between East and West, it also provoked a lasting curiosity in Europe about the Orient, the fabled Cathay—China—above all. In 1260, two Venetian merchants, the Polo brothers, Niccolò and Maffeo, reached China. In 1271, they returned there, accompanied by Niccolo's 17-year-old son, Marco. His account of their epic journey and of their 17-year stay in China—the "Description of the World"—colored and inspired European perceptions of the Orient for generations, decisively reinforcing the Western belief of the East as a land of exotic, limitless riches.

> "If you put together all the Christians in the world, with their Emperors and their Kings, the whole of these Christians—aye, and throw in the Saracens to boot—they would not have such power or be able to do so much as this Kublai, who is Lord of all the Tartars in the world."
> *Marco Polo*

Chinese wonders

Marco Polo provided an astoundingly vivid narrative of the three-and-a-half-year, 5,600-mile (9,010 km) journey he, his father, and his uncle made to reach China. If no reliably authenticated version exists today, his story, inflated or not, remains a compelling tale of fortitude and exploration. Above all, however occasionally overwrought, it also provides a remarkable first-hand account of Mongol China in the 13th century. Having reached Kublai Khan's capital, Shang-tu, in

1275, Polo noted that the palace was "painted within with pictures and images of beasts and birds... a wonder to see." He rapidly became a "court favorite," charged with a variety of diplomatic missions and his astonishment at the sophistications of China is evident. His commentary covered paper money, the use of coal for fuel—"a kind of black stone... which maintains the fire better than wood"—and official mail that traveled at the amazing rate of 250 miles (400 km) a day. He also produced the first Western account of Japan—*Cipangu*—and its "measureless quantities" of gold.

Above: Venice had emerged as a leading power in the eastern Mediterranean in the 12th century, controlling much of the trade between Europe, the Middle East and the Orient. The interests of the Italian city-state were naturally inclined to the East.

FIND OUT MORE

The Travels of Marco Polo
ed. Henry Yule

Marco Polo, Venetian Adventurer
Henry H. Hart

Marco Polo and the Discovery of the World
John Larner

Above: In addition to being one of the oldest continuously inhabited cities in the world, Samarkand was one of the major cities of the Silk Roads and a key staging post between Europe and the Orient. When Marco Polo passed close by it, the city was among the most populous in central Asia.

Il Milione

Marco Polo, his father, and his uncle, returned from China by sea, leaving in 1292. In its way, it was no less epic a journey than their original overland trek to the East: a two-year voyage from Ch'uan-chou in southern China via Indo-China, Malaya, and India, to Hormuz in the Persian Gulf, followed by a hardly less arduous overland haul to Trebizond on the Black Sea and a final sea leg, via Constantinople, to Venice, where they arrived in 1295. Polo's account of his travels, popularly known as *Il Milione*—The Million—was written by him in prison, reputedly dictated to a fellow prisoner after he had been captured by the Genoese in 1298 following a war between Genoa and Venice, whose forces Polo had joined. Its impact was immediate. Though often dismissed as "fantastic and unreliable," it nonetheless provided a lasting stimulus to further European efforts to tap the apparent riches of the East. Released from prison in 1299, Polo died in Venice at the age of 70, rich and established, in 1324.

Below: Shang-tu in northern China was the summer capital of Kublai Khan. Polo described the palace there as "built of marble and many other ornamental stones." It stood in 16 miles (25 km) of park land "diversified with springs and sprawling lawns." Leaving the city at the end of August each year, the Khan is said to have traveled with "an entourage of 10,000 snow-white mares."

MONGOLIA

GOBI DESERT

PEKING (BEIJING)

YARKAND

KASHGAR

TAKLIMAKAN DESERT

HINDU KUSH

TIBET

LANCHOW (LANZHOU)

YELLOW SEA

HIMALAYA

CHINA

HANGCHOW (HANGZHOU)

AMOY (XIAMEN)

BROACH

INDIA

BAY OF BENGAL

PAGAN (BAGAN)

SOUTH CHINA SEA

CALICUT

COCHIN

INDIAN OCEAN

IBN BATTUTA
Across the Muslim World

Ibn Battuta, born in Tangier in 1304 and trained as a lawyer, was not just the greatest traveler of his age, but among the most remarkable of any. In 1325, on a pilgrimage to Mecca, he formed the desire to travel "through the Earth," and by his death (in either 1368 or 1369), he was widely claimed to be the most traveled man in the world. In a series of exceptional undertakings, he visited the Middle East, reached Kilwa in East Africa, traversed the lands of the Golden Horde and Central Asia, crossed into India, and continued by sea to China. He later traveled across the Sahara to Mali in West Africa.

"So I braced my resolution to quit all my dear ones, female and male, and forsook my home as birds forsake their nests."
Ibn Batutta, My Travels

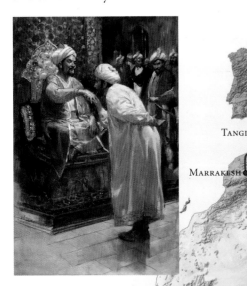

Above: When Ibn Battuta reached Delhi in 1341, the Muslim Delhi Sultanate, ruled by the erratic but brilliant Sultan Muhammed Ibn Tughluq, was at the peak of its power. Ibn Battuta spent seven years in India, before being sent as an ambassador to China.

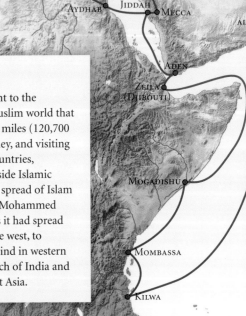

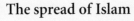

Left: Ibn Battuta's crossing of the Sahara took him to the court of the Mansa Musa, whose rule was a by-word for opulence and ritual. Battuta's descriptions of these desert travels are among the most complete of the trans-Saharan camel routes. "There is no visible road—nothing but sand blown by the wind."

The spread of Islam

It is an extraordinary testament to the immensity of the medieval Muslim world that despite covering about 75,000 miles (120,700 km) on his near 30-year journey, and visiting what today are 44 different countries, Ibn Battuta rarely strayed outside Islamic territory. So explosive was the spread of Islam after its foundation in 622 by Mohammed that within less than 100 years it had spread from its Arab heartlands in the west, to southern France, and east to Sind in western India. By 1200 it included much of India and by 1290 had reached southeast Asia.

Ibn Battuta's *Rihla*

Geographical knowledge in the Islamic world, both academic and practical, was exceptionally sophisticated, and substantially in advance of anything Europe could boast at the time. The Haj, the ritual pilgrimage to Mecca that all Muslims were expected to make at least once, was an important part of this culture, and had long made the idea of substantial journeys common among Muslims. Ibn Battuta's own visit to Mecca in 1325 was the first of three he made to it, and although arduous it would prove no more than the prelude to a life almost entirely given to wanderings. His motives in undertaking these vast journeys remain uncertain, and the only source is his own account, the *Rihla* or, simply, "My Travels." Yet his reports have since been accepted by scholars as being almost entirely authentic, even if elements may owe more to storytelling than first-hand reporting.

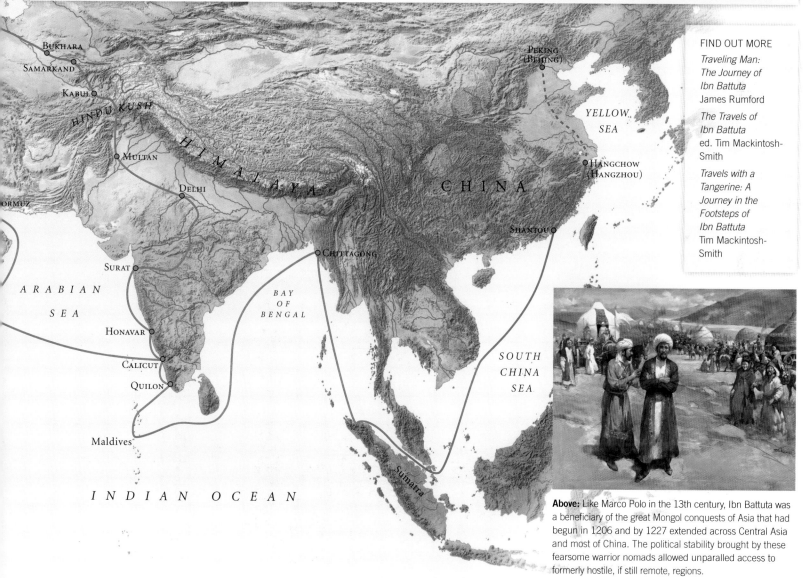

FIND OUT MORE

Traveling Man: The Journey of Ibn Battuta
James Rumford

The Travels of Ibn Battuta
ed. Tim Mackintosh-Smith

Travels with a Tangerine: A Journey in the Footsteps of Ibn Battuta
Tim Mackintosh-Smith

Above: Like Marco Polo in the 13th century, Ibn Battuta was a beneficiary of the great Mongol conquests of Asia that had begun in 1206 and by 1227 extended across Central Asia and most of China. The political stability brought by these fearsome warrior nomads allowed unparalled access to formerly hostile, if still remote, regions.

PAUSANIAS
Classical Greece Revealed

Much of what is known about ancient Greece comes from a Greek writer of the 2nd century AD. His name was Pausanias and it seems likely that he came from Asia Minor. He was unusually well traveled, having visited much of the Middle East, Egypt, southern Italy, and Rome, but it was for his travels on the Greek mainland that he is remembered. He recorded them in a 10-volume work, the *Periegesis*, or, simply, "Description of Greece." Though exceptionally comprehensive, with many digressions on landscapes and natural phenomena, his chief interest was the buildings, statues, monuments, history, and mythology. In short, the cultural glories of ancient Greece.

"There is but one entry to the Acropolis. It affords no other, being precipitous throughout and having a strong wall. The gateway has a roof of white marble, and down to the present day it is unrivalled for the beauty and size of its stones."
Pausanias, Periegesis, Book 1

It is a curiosity that Pausanias's Description of Greece remained almost entirely unknown until little more than 100 years ago. 19th century scholars, where they were aware of it all, nearly uniformly dismissed it as of little or no value. The ruined temples (**above**), many no less imposing than the commanding Acropolis in Athens (**above left**), were precisely logged by the busy Greek, as was a host of statuary (**left**).

To Rome with Hannibal
Across the Alps

Hannibal (c.247 – c.183 BC) became the Carthaginian commander fighting the Romans on the Iberian Peninsula in 221 BC following the death of his father, Hamilcar Barca, and his brother-in-law, Hasdrubal. In 218, Rome started the Second Punic War, hoping to force Hannibal back to Carthage. Instead, he headed northeast from Spain and took the war to northern Italy. Subjugating Gallic tribes on the way—and supported by them in the Po valley—Hannibal proved immensely skilful at fighting in hostile terrain. This culminated in his legendary crossing of the Alps in September, 219.

"How much more serious was the defeat of Cannae, than those which preceded it can be seen by the behavior of Rome's allies; before that fateful day their loyalty remained unshaken, now it began to waver for the simple reason that they despaired of Roman Power."
Polybius

Into Italy

In northern Italy, Hannibal won battles at Ticinus and Trebia against the Roman general Scipio. He crossed the Apennines, but at the River Arno lost much of his force, including his elephants. Unwilling to concede, Hannibal fought onwards, destroying the Roman Army of Gaius Glaminius at Lake Trasimene in 217 and ravaging Campania and Apulia. The following year saw the Carthaginian commander secure a massive tactical victory at Cannae, in one of the bloodiest battles in history. Despite inferior numbers, Hannibal's army clashed with the troops of the consuls Varro and Paullus, annihilating up to 70,000 Romans. Parts of Italy now supported Hannibal's cause, but he was prevented from making a full assault on Rome by dwindling forces, a lack of reinforcements from Carthage, inadequate siege weapons, and a reluctance by Italian city-states to fully embrace his cause. As a result, Rome could effect a war of attrition, reducing Hannibal's power to little more than minor operations.

Battlesites

218 Hannibal crosses the Alps

ALPS

GAUL

Rhone

TURIN
Ticinus 218
Po
Trebia 218

ARRETIUM
L. Trasimene 217

NARBO

Ebro

CORSICA

ROME
Tiber

CANNAE

CAPUA

ADRIATIC SEA

SPAIN

SARDINIA

TARENTUM

Saguntum 219 SAGENTUM

CROTON

CARTAGENA

MEDITERRANEAN SEA

SICILY
SYRACUSE

CARTHAGE
Zama
(Hannibal returns to Carthage but is defeated by Scipio Africanus)

Right: With 40,000 infantry, 10,000 cavalry and 40 elephants, Hannibal crossed the Alps in September 219 BC in the face of a harsh climate, ambushes, and skirmishes with native tribes.

FOLLOWING THE FIRST CRUSADE
Reclaiming the Holy Land

The First Crusade sparked an intermittent and frequently savage conflict between the Christian West and the Muslim East that continued for centuries. It was launched in 1096 in response to an urgent plea the previous year by Pope Urban II to protect the Orthodox Christians of the beleaguered Byzantine Empire, and to recover Palestine—the Holy Land—from Muslim rule. Yet though driven by piety, as often as not the Crusade was riddled by internal rivalries, political imperatives, and the desire for territorial conquest. In scenes that lurched between the absurd and the brutal, a series of armies struggled across Europe and fought their way across the Middle East.

It took almost a year for Jerusalem (**above**) to fall, and besiegers and besieged alike suffered appallingly from thirst and hunger. When on July 15, 1099 the city was eventually stormed, an orgy of bloodletting followed. Almost the entire population—Muslim, Jewish, and Christian alike—was killed as the Crusaders surged through it (**right**).

The People's Crusade

Urban's impassioned call for a crusade at Clermont, France, in November 1095 was a reply to a no-less-impassioned request for military aid by the Byzantine emperor, Alexius I Comnenus, against the Seljuk Muslims, who had driven the Byzantines out of Asia Minor. The response was immediate and overwhelming. In addition to nobles and knights—chiefly from France and the Rhineland—an improbable collection of peasants, town dwellers, servants, itinerants, and monks, as well as women and children, flocked to "take the Cross," setting off in two distinct waves. In April, defying the pope who had called for these Christian armies to leave on August 15 (the Feast of the Assumption), the People's Crusade, led by a charismatic French monk named Peter the Hermit, began its epic journey. It traveled overland from Cologne to the Danube, and on into Hungary and Serbia, leaving a trail of devastation in its wake. When on August 1 Constantinople was reached, Emperor Comnenus instantly had this vast disorganized rabble shipped over the Bosporus to Asia Minor. Here a series of brutal skirmishes were fought until, on October 21, the Seljuks annihilated the People's Crusade.

Left: The Crusaders established a series of Christian states: Edessa, Tripoli, Antioch, and Jerusalem, tenuously sustained by the building of massive fortresses, of which Krak des Chavliers is the most spectacular example. Its fall in 1291 ended the brief period of Crusader rule.

"Let those who have been fighting against their brothers and relatives now fight in a proper way against the barbarians. Let those who have been serving as mercenaries for small pay now obtain the eternal reward."
Urban II, Council of Clermont, 1095

Right: In 1096, the Council of Clermont marked a key moment in the evolution of an increasingly self-aware and self-confident Christendom. These were medieval Europe's emerging independent states, often in conflict, but united by a common Christian faith and all owing alligiance to their spiritual leader, the pope. Shared hostility towards a more technically advanced Muslim world would remain a central feature of its identity for centuries.

The Prince's Crusade

In stark contrast to the growing chaos and eventual destruction of the People's Crusade, the Barons' or Princes' Crusade was an infinitely better led and more effective military force. Though never more than 10,000 strong (and in the end reduced to little more than 1,500), this was never a unified band, but four main groups that took a number of different overland routes to Constantinople, which was reached between October 1096 and May 1097. Here it was joined by the remnants of the People's Crusade and despite considerable tensions between the Crusaders and Alexius I—who demanded they swear an oath of loyalty to him before agreeing to equip and provision them—they enjoyed remarkable success. They were helped in large measure by internal divisions among the Muslims, who were rarely able to field unified forces, and ultimately, after lengthy sieges, they took Nicaea in 1097, Antioch in 1098, and Jerusalem in 1099.

FIND OUT MORE
*The First Crusade:
A New History*
Thomas Asbridge

*The First Crusade:
Conquest of the
Holy Land*
David Nicolle and
Christa Hook

*A History of the
Crusades, Vol. 1*
Steven Runciman

*NORTH
SEA*

NGLAND

HOLY
ROMAN
EMPIRE

POLAND

RATISBON

VIENNA

KINGDOM
OF
FRANCE

LYONS

VIENNE

HUNGARY

BLACK SEA

CORSICA

ROME

BARI

DURAZZO

OCHRIDA
(OHRID)

EASTERN EMPIRE

CONSTANTINOPLE
(ISTANBUL)

BRINDISI

NICAEA

SARDINIA

CAESAREA

M E D I T E R R A N E A N

S E A

TARSUS

ANTIOCH

S E L J U K
EMPIRE

CRETE

CYPRUS

TRIPOLI

DAMASCUS

JAFFA

JERUSALEM

THE MARCH ON ROME
Mussolini's takeover of Italy

Mass strikes, a governmental crisis, and the threat of civil war in Italy were all the motivations needed by Benito Mussolini, leader of the Fascist Party, to announce to a Fascist conference in Naples on October 24, 1922 that he would march on Rome and seize power. He shrewdly retired to Milan, but not before instructing his ruthless paramilitary troops—his Blackshirts—to occupy strategic points around the country as he laid the groundwork for a possible *coup d'état*.

On October 26, the liberal Prime Minister, Luigi Facta, was warned that Mussolini was trying to unseat him, but he didn't believe the claims, thinking he could share power with Mussolini. However, to meet the threat posed by the Blackshirts gathering outside Rome he announced a military state of siege. King Victor Emmanuel III refused to sign the order, fearing that a weakened Facta could not prevent the outbreak of civil war, and believing that Mussolini wasn't a threat as big business, the military, and the liberal right-wing establishment supported him.

Left: The "March on Rome" was pure propaganda. Mussolini massively exaggerated the numbers of Blackshirts in Rome at the time, although following his inauguration, on October 31 his followers marched in an ostentatious parade.

Left: It is claimed that almost 40,000 of Mussolini's Blackshirts entered Rome between October 27 and October 29, 1922, on the instruction of the leader of the Fascist Party. They encountered little resistance, and King Victor Emmanuel II telephoned Mussolini on October 29 to invite him to Rome to form a new government.

THE KLONDIKE GOLD RUSH
"Gold! Gold! In the Klondike!"

After George Carmack found a large nugget of gold in Bonanza Creek in 1896, over 100,000 prospectors made a frenzied rush for Canada's new goldfields in the fierce Yukon terrain. Less than half made it—only to find all claims already staked. Settlements sprang up along the way to supply the prospectors, and Dawson City at the confluence of the Yukon and Klondike rivers swelled to 40,000 to become the largest city north of San Francisco. However, when new gold was discovered in Alaska in 1899 many miners upped and left. The Klondike rush had generated $50 million, but few managed to make or keep their fortunes. It was a wild and lawless time, kept in check by Canada's Mounties.

Left: The 33 mile (53 km) Chilkoot Trail from Dyea, Alaska, to Bennett, British Columbia, was originally used by the Tlingit Indians. Once the Gold Rush began, Canadian Mounties checked that each arriving prospector was carrying the specified "ton of gear" required to sustain them for a year.

Above: Gold is still mined in Dawson City, with its colorful wooden houses, although it is tourism that now brings in more income. Diamond Tooth Gertie's is a gambling hall with can-can girls, while there are also interpretative displays about Jack London, and chances to pan for gold yourself.

FIND OUT MORE

The Son of the Wolf
Jack London

Songs of a Sourdough
Robert Service

The Volcano of Gold
Jules Verne

The Gold Rush
(Movie)

To the goldfields

Prospectors had three choices: an overland route from Edmonton, a river voyage up the Yukon River from western Alaska, or the most popular option—up from Seattle or Vancouver by ship to tiny Skagway, over the arduous Chilkoot or White Pass trails, and then down the Yukon. Skagway's narrow gauge railway was originally a mining construction, but now runs just for tourists. You can still trek the Chilkoot trail, crossing the twice-yearly caribou migration route, or take the Klondike Highway. The rapids on the Yukon gave name to Whitehorse, with its 3-storey "log skyscrapers." Just off route is the fantastic ice-age environment of Kluane National Park. From Lake Laberge the Highway diverges from the Yukon until Dawson City, the "Paris of the North."

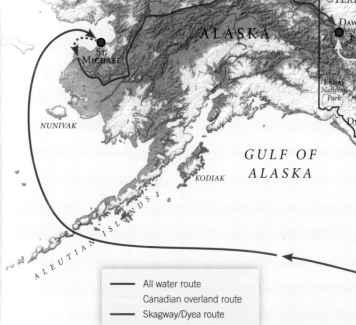

— All water route
Canadian overland route
— Skagway/Dyea route

Westward Ho!
The Trails West

Since independence in 1789, a permanent drive to the apparently virgin lands to the west had powered American expansion. By 1840, America's effective western frontier had been pushed to the Mississippi. Over the following 30 years, with their numbers steadily increasing, a stream of new settlers—farmers, prospectors, businessmen, drifters, and dreamers—followed the uncertain trails beyond the great river, crossing the seemingly limitless Great Plains to the Rockies and the Pacific beyond. Until the completion of the first transcontinental railroad in 1869 this meant a six-month trek in ox-drawn wagons, with disease, hunger, and thirst as much a threat as the increasingly hostile native population and the elements. Thousands struggled through, with perhaps 10% perishing in the attempt.

Oregon and California Trails

Although a series of trails were developed, the two principal routes—as arduous as they were long—were the Oregon Trail and, branching south from it, the California Trail. The former led northwest to what are now the states of Oregon and Washington, the latter southwest to the heart of California. Like almost all the wagon trails, they began in Missouri. The 2,000 mile (3,220 km) trek westward almost invariably proved more gruelling than even the most pessimistic might have imagined, as they experienced a painfully slow, apparently endless plod to the west.

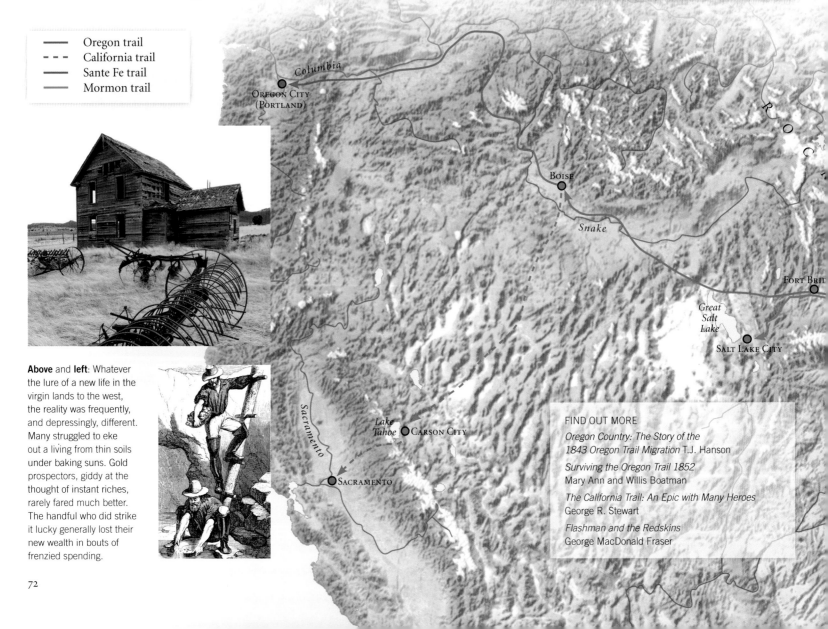

- ——— Oregon trail
- - - - California trail
- ——— Sante Fe trail
- ——— Mormon trail

Above and **left**: Whatever the lure of a new life in the virgin lands to the west, the reality was frequently, and depressingly, different. Many struggled to eke out a living from thin soils under baking suns. Gold prospectors, giddy at the thought of instant riches, rarely fared much better. The handful who did strike it lucky generally lost their new wealth in bouts of frenzied spending.

FIND OUT MORE

Oregon Country: The Story of the 1843 Oregon Trail Migration T.J. Hanson

Surviving the Oregon Trail 1852 Mary Ann and Willis Boatman

The California Trail: An Epic with Many Heroes George R. Stewart

Flashman and the Redskins George MacDonald Fraser

Recommended food allowances for the Oregon Trail (per adult):

Flour 150 lbs (68 kg)
Corn meal 20 lbs (9 kg)
Bacon 50 lbs (23 kg)
Beans 15 lbs (7 kg)
Rice 5 lbs (2.25 kg)
Sugar 40 lbs (18 kg)
Dried fruit 15 lbs (7 kg)
Salt 5 lbs (2.25 kg)
Coffee 10 lbs (4.5 kg)
Tea 2 lbs (0.9 kg)

Diets were supplemented by bison, which were killed in huge numbers.

The price of heading west

Riding the wagon trails was expensive. The cost for an average family was around $1,000, while the wagon itself cost a further $400. The wagon trains were generally several hundred strong, led by a wagon master elected by the settlers, who was helped by a scout—many of which were Indians. In addition, as many as 2,000 cattle and 10,000 sheep were frequently included, creating huge clouds of dust. The wagons were used to carry food, whatever household goods settlers had brought along—though many were frequently abandoned if the pace slowed too much—the very young, and the very old. Those with horses rode, but most just walked, so an average of 10 miles (16 km) a day was as much as could be expected, with the settlers invariably leaving in the spring to reach and cross the Rockies before the snows set in. Of the many risks, the greatest was disease—cholera above all—and the victims were hastily buried, or simply abandoned to their inevitable fate so as not to slow the wagons.

"Our manifest destiny is to overspread the continent allotted by Providence for the free development of our yearly multiplying millions."
John L. O'Sullivan, 1845

Right: The Rocky Mountains presented a formidable barrier to the trekkers and the Donner Party precisely highlighted their perils. Leaving in May 1846, they reached the mountains dangerously late and were forced to construct a makeshift camp. In mid-December, 15 set out for help. Only seven survived, but the remaining members of the party were progressively rescued. Of the 87 who set out, 39 died.

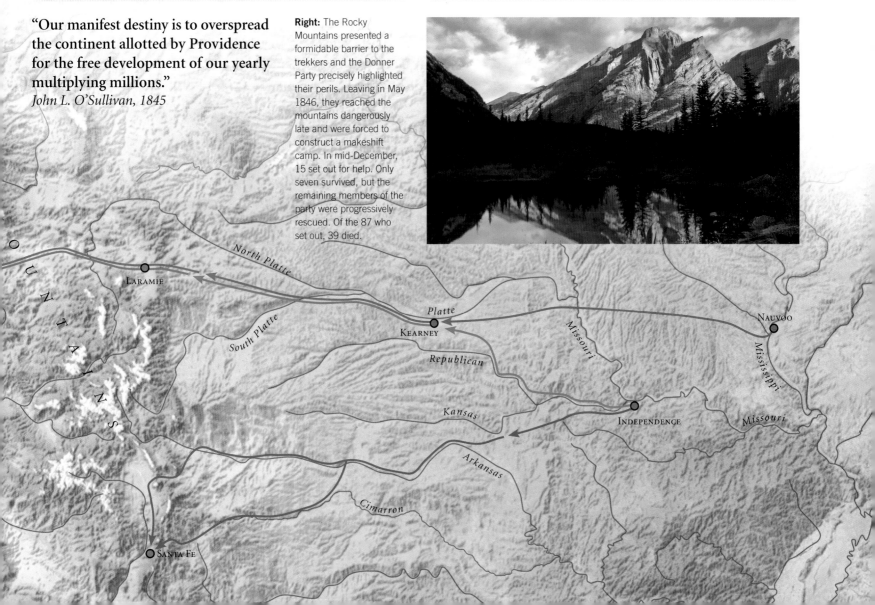

THE LONG MARCH
The Great March of the Red Army

The Long March was decisive in preserving the beleaguered forces of the fledging Chinese communist party during the bitter civil war that racked China in the 1920s and '30s. It involved a forced march by the tattered remnants of the Red Army north and west from their stronghold in Jiangxi province in south China to Shaanxi in the north. It took one year and five days and, officially at least, covered 8,000 miles (12,875 km). Despite horrendous losses—86,000 troops set off, but only 8,000 arrived—it not only kept intact the Chinese communists as a fighting force, but saw the emergence of a new leader of the communists: Mao Zedong.

Left: The hazards of the Long March may have been real enough—the crossing of the Xiang river, for example—but in 2003, two Britons, Ed Jocelyn and Andrew McEwan, traced the route. They concluded that the communists had covered 3,700 miles (5,955 km), not the 8,000 miles (12,975 km) asserted in the offical record.

Though heralded in communist propaganda as proof of the inevitable triumph of communism over the degenerate Nationalists of Chiang Kai-shek (**left**), the Long March remains controversial. Much of the official record is hard to prove. Similarly, the role of Mao (**above**) is murky. It has been claimed that far from struggling on foot with his troops he was carried in a litter.

When Shaanxi (**above and right**) was eventually reached, Mao had emerged as the undisputed leader of the Chinese communist party, his superiority engineered in a series of bitter power struggles. His dominance would never subsequently waver and his absolute rule as leader of the country from 1949 to his death in 1976 was reinforced by a grotesque personality cult.

The struggle for power

Since the fall of the Manchu dynasty in 1911, China was wracked by turmoil as rival groups competed for power. Chaos and brutality followed, but by the late 1920s the Nationalist Kuomintang, under Chiang Kai-shek, had achieved a clear ascendancy. His own position established, Chiang Kai-shek set out to eliminate his only remaining rivals, the communists. From 1930 onwards, the communists had been forced out of the cities into the mountainous and remote south of the country. But, by September 1933, they had been encircled by the much larger Kuomintang forces. With their numbers and territory shrinking, the First Red Army began a daring break-out on October 16, 1934. Their initial aim was to link with the Second Red Army, believed to be in Hubei to the northwest, though it was already retreating westward. The Long March had begun.

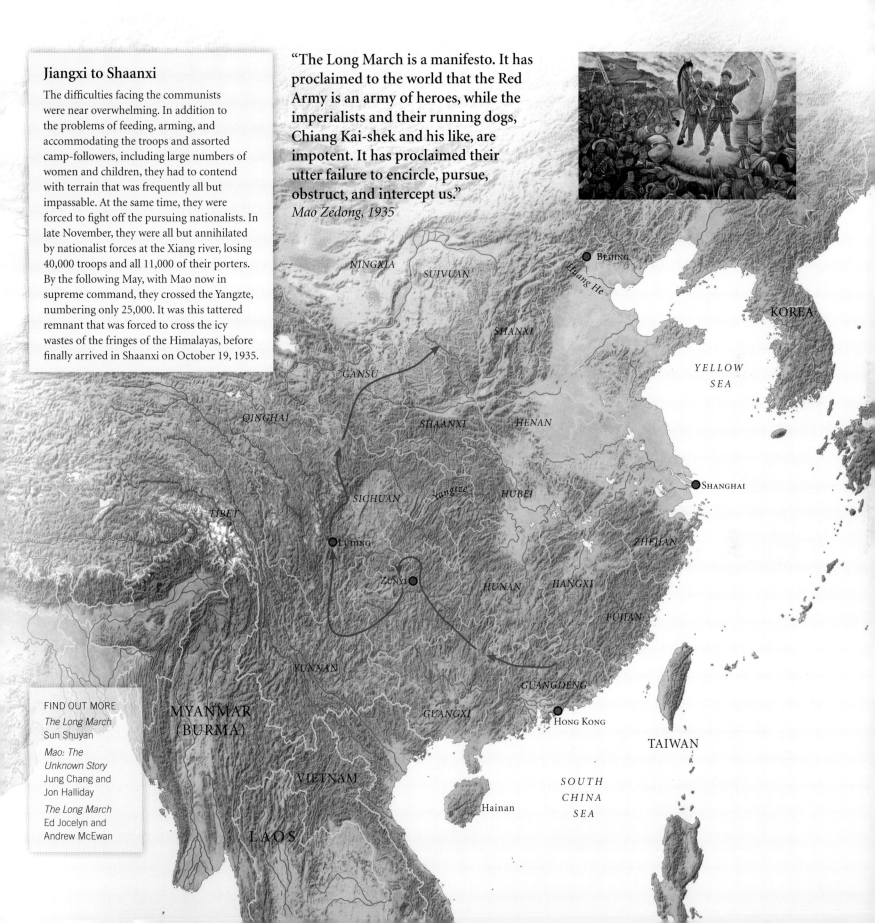

Jiangxi to Shaanxi

The difficulties facing the communists were near overwhelming. In addition to the problems of feeding, arming, and accommodating the troops and assorted camp-followers, including large numbers of women and children, they had to contend with terrain that was frequently all but impassable. At the same time, they were forced to fight off the pursuing nationalists. In late November, they were all but annihilated by nationalist forces at the Xiang river, losing 40,000 troops and all 11,000 of their porters. By the following May, with Mao now in supreme command, they crossed the Yangzte, numbering only 25,000. It was this tattered remnant that was forced to cross the icy wastes of the fringes of the Himalayas, before finally arrived in Shaanxi on October 19, 1935.

"The Long March is a manifesto. It has proclaimed to the world that the Red Army is an army of heroes, while the imperialists and their running dogs, Chiang Kai-shek and his like, are impotent. It has proclaimed their utter failure to encircle, pursue, obstruct, and intercept us."
Mao Zedong, 1935

FIND OUT MORE
The Long March
Sun Shuyan

Mao: The Unknown Story
Jung Chang and Jon Halliday

The Long March
Ed Jocelyn and Andrew McEwan

NINGXIA

SUIYUAN

Beijing

Huang He

KOREA

SHANXI

YELLOW
SEA

GANSU

QINGHAI

SHAANXI

HENAN

Yangtze

HUBEI

Shanghai

SICHUAN

ZHEJIAN

TIBET

Luding

Zunyi

HUNAN

JIANGXI

FUJIAN

MYANMAR
(BURMA)

YUNNAN

GUANGDENG

GUANGXI

Hong Kong

TAIWAN

VIETNAM

Hainan

SOUTH
CHINA
SEA

LAOS

The ten overland journeys of exploration covered in this chapter highlight a central feature of almost all such ventures from almost all periods: they demanded not just great daring but reserves of fortitude, moral courage, and determination on a scale that can stun the imagination. This was a world in which suffering was commonplace.

EXPLORER
Tortuous trips for the intrepid traveler

Writing of his two journeys across the Empty Quarter of Arabia in 1946–7 and 1948–9, the English explorer, Wilfred Thesiger, said "…we endured almost incessant hunger and, worse still, thirst." It is a complaint that precisely echoes the experiences of most of the remarkable figures covered in this chapter. Like almost all the explorers of the great arid wasteland that is the interior of Australia, both Edward Eyre, who traversed the Nullarbor Plain in 1840–1, and John Stuart, who in 1862 crossed Australia from north to south, suffered agonies of thirst, the search for water dominating almost every moment of their appalling treks.

Lack of water may not have plagued the 19th century explorers of Africa, but torments of another kind awaited. Tropical disease and hostile natives proved a fatal combination for Mungo Park as he sought to trace the river Niger in 1805, and every member of his expedition died. Henry Stanley, who crossed Africa in 1876–7, lost 114 of his native guides, porters and soldiers. John Speke, discoverer of the source of the Nile in 1862, suffered astonishing privations during his ventures, which seem in the end to have unhinged him—in 1864 he died by his own hand.

The Spanish conquests of Aztec Mexico and Inca Peru by, respectively, Hernán Cortés in 1519–21 and Francisco Pizarro in 1532 illustrate another central truth of European exploration: that the confrontation of Europeans and native peoples, especially in the New World, almost invariably led to conflict and subjugation, with European arms—backed by a brutal readiness to use them—overwhelming entire nations. Even the expedition to the shores of the Pacific by Lewis and Clark helped pave the way for the effective elimination of America's native peoples.

Francisco Pizarro
To the Heart of the Inca Empire

The burst of Spanish exploration and conquest in the New World, so decisively reinforced by Cortés' subjection of Mexico in 1521, was continued on an even more spectacular scale with the takeover of the Peruvian Inca empire by Francisco Pizarro a little over 10 years later. In little more than a year, a force of 188 Spaniards defeated a highly organized state of five million. Success depended on a combination of superior military means—steel, guns, and armor against the Incas' weapons of sharpened stones and padded cotton armor—and religious zeal. Fuelled by Pizarro, a man of unscrupulous and driving ambition, the Incas' defeat was as inevitable as it was astonishing.

With Atahuallpa dead and Cajamarca secured, Pizarro marched south to Cuzco, the Inca capital in the Andes (**left**), following the Inca highway over a variety of dramatic mountain landscapes (**below**). He entered the city on November 15, 1533. Though efforts to oust the Spaniards continued, Peru effectively capitulated. Pizarro's army was augmented by 27 horses, an animal unknown to the Incas, who believed them a form of terrifying, four-legged human.

The end of an empire

Despite its sophistication, Inca Peru was a state that had existed for less than 100 years, so it was vulnerable to determined incursion. Its network of paved roads—over 9,000 miles (14,485 km) in all—made travel through the country swift, greatly facilitating Pizarro's advance. At the same time, the country had been in the grip of civil war since 1525, leaving it weak and divided, while a series of diseases imported by the Europeans were

cutting a deadly swathe through all classes. Nonetheless, the prospect of the nation succumbing to a force as apparently insignificant as Pizarro's seemed remote, even when he reached Cajamarca in mid-November, 1532. He confronted Atahuallpa and promptly arrested the Inca, calculating that such a hierarchical society would be unable to function without its ruler. He was right. Pizarro demanded a vast ransom for Atahuallpa's release—a room of the palace to be filled nine-feet deep with gold and silver. When it was paid, Pizarro responded by having Atahuallpa murdered.

The Spaniards' desire for gold knew no limitls, but for the Incas, this lust was inexplicable: they prized gold for its decorative qualities alone and, baffled, assumed the *conquistadores* wanted it as food. The Spaniards' greed led to near permanent tension among the invaders, chiefly between the followers of Pizarro and his one-time collaborator, Diego de Almagro. In 1541, Pizarro was murdered in Lima (**above**), the capital of Spanish Peru, by supporters of Almagro.

Isthmus of Panama

PANAMA

QUITO

TUMBES

SECHORA
DESERT

CAJAMARCA

*PACIFIC
OCEAN*

LIMA

CUZCO

Above: However relentless Pizarro's drive for conquest, Inca Peru did not yield all its secrets. The city of Machu Picchu, high in the Andes, remained entirely unknown to the Spanish conquerors during the three centuries of Spanish rule. It was discovered by the wider world only in 1911. Its precisely engineered dry-stone walls reveal an impressively advanced technological accomplishment.

"When I set out to write … about the conquest and discovery that our Spaniards made here in Peru, I could not but reflect that I was dealing with the greatest matters one could possibly write about in all of creation."
*Pedro Cieza de León,
Chronicles of Peru, 1553*

The march on Cajamarca

The initial key to Pizarro's success was Spain's exploration of the Pacific after its discovery by Balboa, the first European "to gaze upon the Pacific," and who, in 1513, had crossed the Isthmus of Panama. Pizarro had accompanied Balboa and it was natural that so restless a man should take the lead in subsequent Spanish attempts on the Pacific coast of South America. The goal was "a province called Birú," first reported in 1522.

Between 1524 and 1527, Pizarro led two expeditions into Peru, enduring extraordinary hardship, but confirming the region's abundant riches. In January 1531, now with royal sanction, he set off for a third time. It took almost two years of reconnaissance—and some hesitation—before, in September, 1532, Pizarro pushed inland from his base at Tangaiaia on the Pacific to confront Atahuallpa, the "divine Inca" himself, at Cajamarca in the Peruvian highlands.

LEWIS AND CLARK
The search for the South Sea

Thomas Jefferson, president of the United States from 1801–9, was acutely aware of the vast lands to the west of his fledgling republic. He was no less acutely aware that the destiny of America was likely to be shaped by them. These immense regions of untold wealth were not just potentially desirable in themselves, but held the promise of a new route to the South Sea and the riches of the Orient. Yet reliable information about them was non-existent so, in 1804, he commissioned an expedition to probe them. The Discovery Corp was to be led by two army officers, Meriwether Lewis and William Clark, and their two-and-a-half year journey transformed knowledge of the West.

A teacherous journey

Considering they were venturing into the unknown, the party came out of its epic two-year and four-month, 8,000 mile (12,875 km) journey remarkably unscathed. Only one man was lost, Sgt. Charles Floyd, who on August 20, 1804, died from appendicitis.

Their most arduous days were the first crossing of the Rockies—the Bitterroot Mountains—in September 1804, described as "the most terrible mountains I ever beheld." The situation was not helped by perilously low food levels and the first snows falling.

West from the Mississippi

Lewis and Clark's 33-strong party began their journey on May 14, 1804, from Camp Dubois on the Mississippi river, then almost as far west as official knowledge of the frontier extended. They necessarily traveled by river, spending more than a year on the Missouri.

Not only was this faster and more reliable than traveling overland, but it helped with one of the prime goals of their mission, which was to verify whether a navigable river route to the Pacific existed. Geography was only one goal, however, as they were also charged with making detailed records of animal and plant life, and reporting on the native Indian inhabitants. They traveled in three boats—a 55 foot (16.75 m) keelboat and two flat-bottomed canoes or *pirogues*—spending their first winter amid the freezing temperatures of North Dakota at a hastily constructed camp, Fort Mandan. As conditions and terrain dictated, they were occasionally forced to travel on horseback, or in dugout canoes that they built themselves.

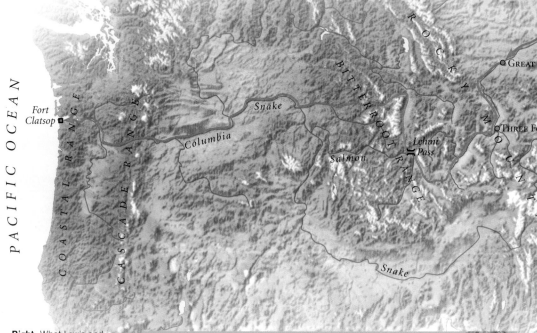

Right: What Lewis and Clark called the Bitterroot Mountains provided an alarming shock to the party as the vast flatlands of central America—the Great Plains—were expected to continue all the way to the Pacific. Instead, they were abruptly ended by the Rockies, at first sight an apparently insurmountable barrier to the route west.

Left: The harshness of much of the North America landscape was forcefully brought home to Lewis and Clark by their first winter in the Badlands of North Dakota, a rugged, unforgiving landscape, parched in summer, frozen in winter, that even today remains among the most sparsely populated in the United States.

Above: Hopes that the Missouri would provide a practical route to the Pacific were dashed in June 1805 when the expedition reached the Great Falls— five falls spread over 20 miles (32 km). It took over a month to bypass them, with the party's boats and provisions carried by hand.

Right: A Blackfoot Indian, photographed much later in the century, perhaps contemplating his peoples' fate at the hands of the white man.

FIND OUT MORE

Lewis and Clark through Indian Eyes
Alvin Josephy

The Journals of Lewis and Clark
ed. Anthony Brandt

The Essential Lewis and Clark
Landon Y. Jones

"Great joy in camp we are in viuew of the Ocian, this great Pacific Octean which we been so long anxious to See. and the roreing or noise made by the waves brakeing on the rockey Shores (as I suppose) may be heard disti[n]ctly."
William Clark, November 7 1805

Missouri

Yellowstone

Great Plains

Fort Mandan

BADLANDS

PIERRE

Fort Pierre

Missouri

COUNCIL BLUFFS

Mississippi

Camp Dubois

SAINT LOUIS

Missouri

HERNÁN CORTÉS
Into Aztec Mexico

The Spanish conquest of Mexico in 1521 remains among the most audacious in history. A force of less than 600 men, led by Hernán Cortés, part visionary, part wide-eyed fanatic, took on and defeated an entire nation. Over the summer of 1519, Cortés led his tiny army deep into the heart of Aztec Mexico, brutally overcoming all opposition, the defeated Mexicans then flocking to join him. In the face of this growing force, the Aztecs could offer no resistance. The Spanish conquest was never straightforward though, with divisions among the Spanish in the New World, and a belated Aztec uprising coming close to derailing it. But in the end it was as emphatic as it was daring.

FIND OUT MORE
Conquistadors
Michael Wood

History of the Indies of New Spain
Diego Durán,
ed. Doris Heyden

Conquest: Cortés, Montezuma, and the Fall of Old Mexico
Hugh Thomas

Above: The imposing Piramide de los Nichos in Veracruz underlines the exceptionally sophisticated nature of central American society. Completed in the 7th century, it stands 82 feet (25 m) high with each of the four sides 115 feet (35 m) long.

Above: This panel dating from 1521 shows *The Taking of Tenochtitlan by Cortés*. Like Pizarro who followed, Cortés managed to overwhelm an entire nation with an initially small force, in this case only 600 men.

A ruthless leader

The measure of Cortés's leadership—calculating, ruthless, and unbending—was provided by his decision to scuttle all but one of his 11 ships after he had landed at what is now Veracruz, to persuade the men he left behind not to "betray" him by sailing away.

Having recruited several thousand Tlaxcalans to his army, he massacred what he claimed were 3,000 of the inhabitants of Cholula (other reports speak of 30,000 dead).

His brutal intent only too clear, the Aztec emperor, Montezuma II, had little option but to allow Cortés to enter Tenochtitlán, the capital, unopposed. Less than 10 days later, Cortés summarily arrested Montezuma.

The following year the Aztecs rose and the Spaniards were forced to flee. It took a further year for Cortés to retake the city, but when he re-entered it on August 13, 1521, he had conquered a territory larger than Spain itself.

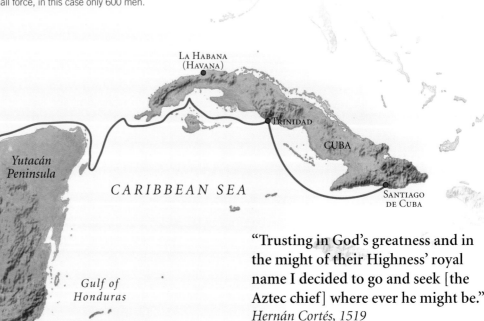

GULF OF MEXICO

LA HABANA (HAVANA)

TRINIDAD

CUBA

Gulf of Campeche

Yutacán Peninsula

CARIBBEAN SEA

SANTIAGO DE CUBA

TENOCHTITLÁN (MEXICO CITY) TLAXCALA

VERACRUZ

Popocatépetl

Peak

Gulf of Honduras

"Trusting in God's greatness and in the might of their Highness' royal name I decided to go and seek [the Aztec chief] where ever he might be."
Hernán Cortés, 1519

PACIFIC OCEAN

MUNGO PARK
West Africa

For late 18th century Europeans the mystery of the river Niger in West Africa was one of the most tantalizing in geography; where did it go? This was partly a matter of academic speculation, but more particularly of greed. The fabled gold mines of West Africa exercised an astonishing hold on Western imaginations and the Niger appeared the obvious means of transporting these presumed millions. Mungo Park, a Scottish doctor, first explored the river in 1795, traveling overland from the Gambia and discovering to his amazement that it flowed east. He returned in 1805, determined to navigate it to its end, but despite lavish funding the expedition was a disaster. Park was never seen again.

Right: It was only in 1830 that Richard Lander demonstrated that the Niger flowed south and west to the Gulf of Guinea. Before then, it was variously believed simply to dry up somewhere in the Sahara, to join with the Nile or, as Park believed, to link with the Congo. However slowly, the gaps on the map were being filled.

A failed expedition

The British government funded Park's second expedition, sending him off with a party of 40 soldiers. Accompanied by various porters and guides, again traveling from the Gambia, they took four months to reach the Niger, by

which point all but 11 of the Europeans were dead—victims of dysentery or fever. A further six died before Park, the four remaining soldiers, a guide, and three slaves set off down the Niger in a converted 40-foot (12 m) canoe. Their fate was not discovered until the mid-1820s, when three British explorers, Hugh Clapperton and the Lander brothers, Richard and John, were broadly able to confirm the report of a native guide—the expedition's sole survivor. According to him, Park and his companions sailed almost 1,000 miles (1,609 km) before their boat ran aground and the Europeans—Park among them—were either killed by locals or drowned.

FIND OUT MORE

Travels in the Interior Districts of Africa
Mungo Park. introduction by Kate Ferguson Marsters

Barrow's Boys
Fergus Fleming

Two Rivers: Travels in West Africa on the Trail of Mungo Park
Peter Hudson

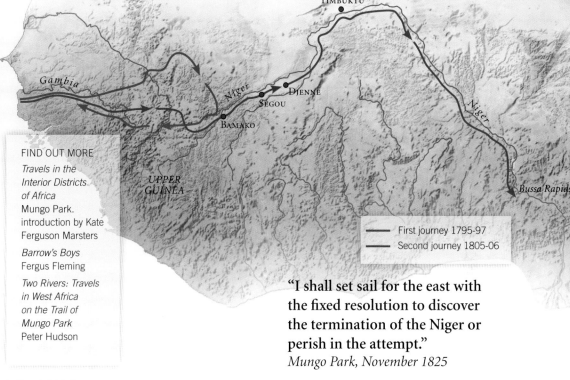

First journey 1795-97
Second journey 1805-06

TIMBUKTU
Gambia
Niger
DJENNE
SEGOU
BAMAKO
UPPER GUINEA
Niger
Bussa Rapids

> "I shall set sail for the east with the fixed resolution to discover the termination of the Niger or perish in the attempt."
> *Mungo Park, November 1825*

Left and right: As Europeans painfully penetrated West Africa, it proved an increasing disappointment. Far from yielding limitless wealth, it was gradually revealed as impoverished and disease-ridden, while its peoples were uncooperative and hostile. Even the Niger itself, studded with shallows and rapids, was essentially useless for long-distance trade.

John Speke
The source of the Nile

No geographical question exerted a greater hold on the imagination of Victorian Britain than the source of the Nile. It went beyond mere controversy; it excited and inflamed passions, sparking furious claims and wild speculations. In part, this was a simple question of wanting to fill the vast blank that was the map of equatorial Africa. More particularly, the Nile occupied a near mythic place in European imaginations as the river that had given birth to Ancient Egypt. Predictably, when a British army officer, John Speke, identified Lake Victoria as its source in July 1862, few believed him. It was only in April 1875 that Henry Stanley was able to show that Speke had been right.

Left: The placid waters of Lake Victoria belie the extraordinary controversy generated by a "mere" geographic problem. It wasn't just the educated public who were swept up in the drama. Burton and Speke themselves developed a cordial loathing of one another. Their strained relations assumed a tragic twist in September 1859 when Speke, hunting in Somerset, shot himself.

Above and below: For much of its length, the Nile itself may be easily navigated. But reaching it overland from the East African coast presented huge problems, especially after 1860, when the spread of sleeping sickness made animal transport impossible, so all overland travel had to be on foot. In addition, European explorers were wholly dependent on unwieldy trains of native porters.

"The Nile is settled"

Speke (**left**) had first journeyed to East Africa with Richard Burton (**below**), legendary explorer of Arabia, in 1857–8, when the pair discovered Lake Tanganika (though Speke, having temporarily lost his sight, never saw it). In August 1858, with Burton incapacitated and left in camp, Speke ventured northwards and discovered the southern shores of Lake Victoria, which he instantly took for the headwaters of the Nile. Backed by the Royal Geographical Society, he returned in 1860 with another British officer, James Grant, and traveled along the north shore of Lake Victoria.

On July 28, 1862, he reached what he called the Ripon Falls, an outflow of water from the lake and the true source of the Nile. As he put it in his first triumphant telegram to England: "The Nile is settled."

Hostile conditions

The difficulties confronting the mid-19th century European explorers of Africa were legion. In the first place, travel was possible only along the more or less well-established Arab slave-trade routes from the coast. Yet these depended on the permanently unstable relations between the slave traders and the tribal leaders of the interior. Good relations with both was crucial, yet offending neither called for a permanently taxing and, on occasion, impossible balancing act in which negotiations could drag on for months. Once under way, the hazards only multiplied. Not only were the distances daunting, but disease was a persistent and frequently debilitating hazard. Every European explorer was regularly laid low by tropical illnesses of varying degrees of unpleasantness.

—— Speke and Burton (1857-58)
—— Speke (1858)
—— Speke and Grant (1860-62)

Below: The complex geography of East Africa always hindered the discovery of the source of the Nile. It was made more difficult by the lingering influence of Classical geographers. Livingstone was convinced of the existence of the Fountains of the Nile, described by the 5th-century BC Greek geographer Herodotus.

Above: After Speke had reached the Ripon Falls in July 1862, he failed to clear up a further mystery. From Lake Victoria, the Nile flows through two further lakes: Kyoga and Albert. Speke tracked the river through the former, but not the latter. Only in 1864 was it confirmed that the Nile flowed through and out of Lake Albert.

FIND OUT MORE
The Sad Story of Burton, Speke, and the Nile
W.B. Carnochan

Burton and Speke
William Harrison

Speke and the Discovery of the Source of the Nile
Alexander Maitland

White Nile

Albert Nile

Victoria Nile

Lake Albert

Lake Kyoga

BUGANDA

KAMPALA

Ripon Falls

Lake Edward

Lake Kivu

Lake Victoria

Lake Tanganyika

UJIJO

TABORA

PEMBA I.

ZANZIBAR

ZANZIBAR

BAGAMAYO

MAFIA I.

"Here at last I stood on the brinks of the Nile … a magnificent stream 600 to 700 yards wide, dotted with islets and rocks."
John Speke, The Discovery of the Source of the Nile, 1864

ALFRED RUSSEL WALLACE
In Indonesia

If less well known than Charles Darwin, his near contemporary, Alfred Russel Wallace, born in Wales in 1823, was just as important in formulating the theory of natural selection, conceiving the idea entirely independently of Darwin. Like Darwin, whose first tentative steps in the working-up of his theory came during his five-year voyage around the world on HMS Beagle, Wallace also traveled extensively. Indeed, he was perhaps the single most important scientific traveler of the 19th century. Between 1848 and 1852 he was in the Amazon, then, more famously still, he visited the Malay Archipelago between 1854 and 1862 and it was here, in 1858, while recovering from malaria, that he conceived his theory of natural selection.

Natural selection

During his eight years in Indonesia, Wallace visited every major island at least once, making 60 or 70 separate journeys and covering around 14,000 miles (22,500 km). No less remarkable, when he returned to England (bringing with him two live birds of paradise) he also had with him "310 mammals, 100 reptiles, 8,050 birds, 7,500 shells, 13,100 butterflies, 83,200 beetles, and 13,400 other insects," some 125,600 specimens in all, over one thousand of which were new to science. Astonishingly, he was essentially self-taught. He had received little formal education, having been forced to leave school aged 13 when his father, an improvident lawyer, fell on hard times. When Wallace discovered natural history in his early 20s, its "staggering diversity" sparked in him a profound and enduring love of the natural world that verged on the mystical.

Right: Despite his advocacy of natural selection, Wallace always believed a divine purpose lay behind it. He was a fierce opponent of what came to be called Social Darwinism—the belief that privilege reflected virtue and could be used to defend social divisions, and by the end of his life he had become a staunch socialist.

In Darwin's shadow

A key component in Wallace's development of the theory of natural selection was his realization that the animals of the western and eastern halves of Indonesia are of two different types. Those to the west are essentially Asian in character, while those to the east are Australian. The natural conclusion was that the western islands must have once formed part of a continuous Asian landmass, while the eastern islands formed part of an Australasian landmass. The distinction is all the more striking because the division (known ever since as the Wallace Line) separates the islands of Bali and Lombok, which at their closest are only 20 miles apart. Wallace discovered the distinction extended to many birds as well, giving clear evidence of their natural reluctance to fly across even relatively narrow stretches of water.

Above and right: Bali, lushly tropical and vividly colored, was to prove a particular source of inspiration to Wallace. Its teeming varieties of animals and plants was a veritable paradise for the natural historian and precisely like Darwin, Wallace took inexhaustible delight in the wonders of tropical lands never before subjected to scientific investigation.

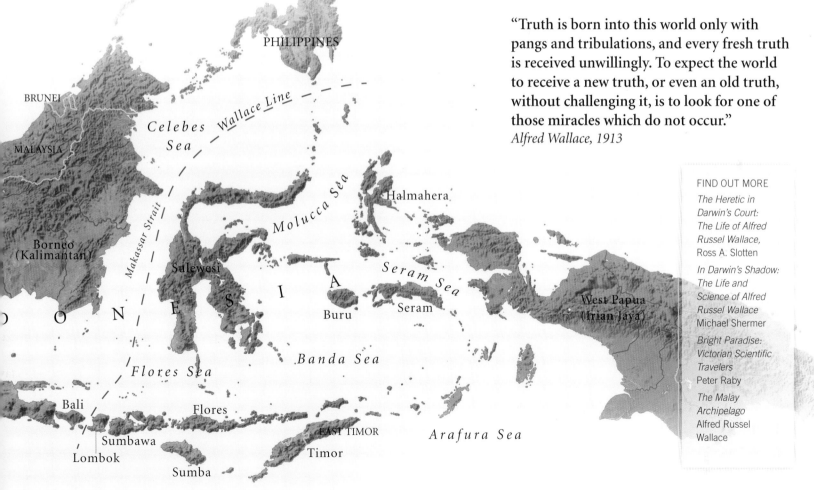

> "Truth is born into this world only with pangs and tribulations, and every fresh truth is received unwillingly. To expect the world to receive a new truth, or even an old truth, without challenging it, is to look for one of those miracles which do not occur."
> *Alfred Wallace, 1913*

FIND OUT MORE

The Heretic in Darwin's Court: The Life of Alfred Russel Wallace, Ross A. Slotten

In Darwin's Shadow: The Life and Science of Alfred Russel Wallace Michael Shermer

Bright Paradise: Victorian Scientific Travelers Peter Raby

The Malay Archipelago Alfred Russel Wallace

EDWARD JOHN EYRE
Across the Nullarbor Plain

The early exploration of Australia, beginning in the late 18th century with tentative journeys inland from the first settlements of the southeast, had revealed a pastoral idyll. It was assumed the interior would prove similarly inviting. Yet a series of 19th century journeys, epics of suffering, showed that not only did the major river systems confidently predicted not exist, but the country was little more than a vast, hostile waste of scrubland, desert, and soaring temperatures that was not only largely uninhabited, but largely uninhabitable. Among these intrepid early pioneers was Edward Eyre. Already an experienced traveler in Australia, in 1840–1 he crossed the daunting wastes of the Nullarbor Plain; 1,200 miles (1,930 km) of relentless heat and waterless scrubland.

FIND OUT MORE

Explorers of Australia
Geoffrey Badger

In Search of Edward John Eyre
Geoffrey Dutton

Edward John Eyre: The Hero as Murderer
Geoffrey Dutton

Waterless Horizons: The Extraordinary Life of Edward John Eyre
Malcolm Uren and Robert Stephens

Journal of Expeditions into Central Australia
Edward Eyre

Along the coast

Eyre's goal was purely practical: to determine if a viable stock route existed between Adelaide and the west of the country. By the time he left on November 3, 1840 he had already established that no viable route existed to the north, so he determined to travel along the coast of the Great Australian Bight. By January 7, after his party of nine Europeans, two Aborigines, 13 horses, and 40 sheep had endured a desperate struggle over intractable sand dunes, they reached the waterholes of Yeer Kumban Kauwe. Here, Eyre recognized the party was too large to continue safely so they turned back, reaching their original depot, Fowler's Bay, on February 23. Two days later, Eyre, John Baxter, and three Aborigines set off again, retracing their steps westward. It proved a journey of suffering and misery, dominated by ever-more frantic searches for water.

Right: Eyre's later career was controversial. After serving as an administrator in New Zealand he was made governor of Jamaica where he was responsible for the suppression of the Morant Bay rebellion of 1865. More than 2,000 Jamaicans rose in violent protest against economic conditions, of which 439 were killed and a further 354 executed. The furor in Britain effectively ended Eyre's career.

———— Nullarbor Route

– – – – Eastern Explorations

• • • • • • Albany-Freemantle Journey

FREEMANTLE

Cape Leeuwin

ALBANY

Rossiter Bay (Lucky Bay)

Point Malcolm

GRE

NULLARB

GR
VICTOR

Eyre had considerable respect for the Aborigines (**left**). This was not merely because so many of them spontaneously helped him, above all showing him where to find water in profoundly hostile regions, but because he recognized that the coming of Europeans could only mean their effective eradication. "It is lamentable," he wrote, "to think that the progress and prosperity of one race should lead to the downfall and decay of another."

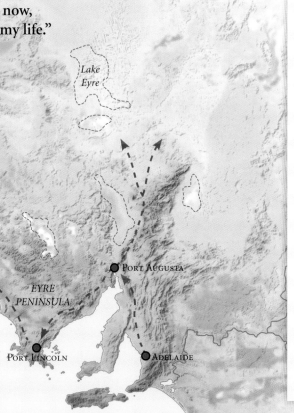

> "In the wildest and most inhospitable wastes of Australia... I was left with a single native, and who for aught I knew might be in league with the other two, who were perhaps even now, lurking about with the view to taking my life."
>
> *Edward Eyre on the death of John Baxter*

Lake Eyre

SERT

LAIN

Yeer Kumban Kauwe Waterholes

Head of Bight

Fowlers Bay

JSTRALIAN BIGHT

EYRE PENINSULA

● PORT AUGUSTA

● PORT LINCOLN

● ADELAIDE

On to King George's Sound

The nadir was reached on April 29. By this point a grim despair had settled over the party as they were reduced to gathering dew with a sponge, and eating wallabies and roasted eucalyptus roots (and, once, eagle stew). Two of the Aborigines had already run away, returning shamed faced and starving five days later, only to murder Baxter and make off with most of the remaining stores. The limestone cliffs over which they were traveling were so hard that Eyre and the remaining Aborigine, Wylie, were unable to dig even the shallowest of graves, so Baxter's body was left wrapped in a cloth. By mid-May, Eyre and Wylie were succumbing to "creeping apathy and torpor," their only consolation the knowledge of a further well at Lucky Bay. In the event, it wasn't a well they found there, but a French whaler. It was deliverance. For 12 days they fed, drank, and rested before, with extraordinary resolution, they set off to complete the last 300 miles (480 km). Ironically, their greatest threat now was not a shortage of water but a surfeit, as bitterly cold rains drenched and froze them. Journey's end, King George's Sound (today Albany), was reached on July 6.

John McDouall Stuart
From Adelaide to Darwin

Despite the gradual discovery that the huge heart of Australia, far from being a fertile, well-watered extension of the more temperate coastal regions, was a waterless wasteland, worn flat by eons of erosion, efforts to penetrate it still continued. No figure was more important in these painful discoveries than John Stuart, a Scot, who between 1858 and 1862 led six major expeditions north into the center of the continent and finally across the whole of Australia to the Indian Ocean. His motive was partly practical—to find a route for a telegraph line linking north and south—and partly geographical, based on a characteristically Victorian determination to fill in the still substantial blanks on the map of Australia.

Across the heart of Australia

Stuart's introduction to the unforgiving realities of inland travel in Australia came in 1844–5 in an expedition northwards from Adelaide led by Charles Sturt in search of a presumed great inland sea. They found only wasteland. Starvation and agonies of thirst were its hallmarks from the start; scurvy its inevitable climax. Stuart was so wracked by the experience that it took him a year to recover.

Nonetheless, between May 1858 and January 1861, on five separate journeys, Stuart pioneered a viable route northward from Adelaide, gradually pushing past Alice Springs, over the MacDonnell Ranges to Tennant Creek, and eventually to Newcastle Waters in the Northern Territory. His practical purpose of finding a route along which a telegraph line could be laid led to increasing government support and to the departure on October 25, 1861, of his sixth and final expedition, the South Australian Great Northern Exploring Expedition. On July 24 1862, after a nine-month, 2,000 mile (3,220 km) crossing of Australia, Stuart and his party finally reached the Indian Ocean.

Tennant Creek (**above**) was little more than a parched water hole, and even for the Aborigines (**left**), Australia provided a meager existence. This was underlined by Stuart's physical decline. For the last 600 miles (965 km) of the return to Adelaide he had to be dragged, partly blind, on a stretcher. He died four years later, at 50, his health ruined.

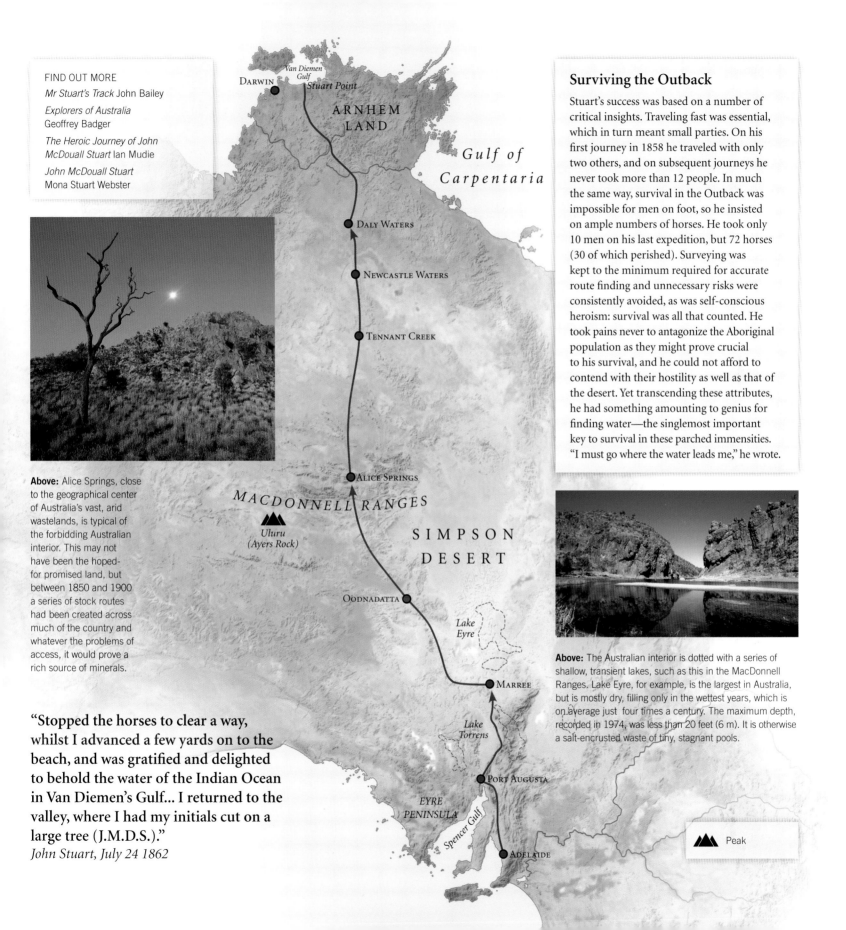

FIND OUT MORE

Mr Stuart's Track John Bailey

Explorers of Australia
Geoffrey Badger

*The Heroic Journey of John
McDouall Stuart* Ian Mudie

John McDouall Stuart
Mona Stuart Webster

DARWIN
*Van Diemen
Gulf*
Stuart Point

ARNHEM
LAND

*Gulf of
Carpentaria*

DALY WATERS

NEWCASTLE WATERS

TENNANT CREEK

Above: Alice Springs, close to the geographical center of Australia's vast, arid wastelands, is typical of the forbidding Australian interior. This may not have been the hoped-for promised land, but between 1850 and 1900 a series of stock routes had been created across much of the country and whatever the problems of access, it would prove a rich source of minerals.

ALICE SPRINGS

MACDONNELL RANGES

*Uluru
(Ayers Rock)*

SIMPSON
DESERT

OODNADATTA

*Lake
Eyre*

*Lake
Torrens*

MARREE

"Stopped the horses to clear a way, whilst I advanced a few yards on to the beach, and was gratified and delighted to behold the water of the Indian Ocean in Van Diemen's Gulf... I returned to the valley, where I had my initials cut on a large tree (J.M.D.S.)."
John Stuart, July 24 1862

PORT AUGUSTA

*EYRE
PENINSULA*

Spencer Gulf

ADELAIDE

Surviving the Outback

Stuart's success was based on a number of critical insights. Traveling fast was essential, which in turn meant small parties. On his first journey in 1858 he traveled with only two others, and on subsequent journeys he never took more than 12 people. In much the same way, survival in the Outback was impossible for men on foot, so he insisted on ample numbers of horses. He took only 10 men on his last expedition, but 72 horses (30 of which perished). Surveying was kept to the minimum required for accurate route finding and unnecessary risks were consistently avoided, as was self-conscious heroism: survival was all that counted. He took pains never to antagonize the Aboriginal population as they might prove crucial to his survival, and he could not afford to contend with their hostility as well as that of the desert. Yet transcending these attributes, he had something amounting to genius for finding water—the singlemost important key to survival in these parched immensities. "I must go where the water leads me," he wrote.

Above: The Australian interior is dotted with a series of shallow, transient lakes, such as this in the MacDonnell Ranges. Lake Eyre, for example, is the largest in Australia, but is mostly dry, filling only in the wettest years, which is on average just four times a century. The maximum depth, recorded in 1974, was less than 20 feet (6 m). It is otherwise a salt-encrusted waste of tiny, stagnant pools.

Peak

HENRY MORTON STANLEY
Conquest of the Congo

Henry Morton Stanley burst to global prominence following his celebrated meeting with Dr Livingstone on the shores of Lake Tanganyika in October 1871. In 1874 he returned to Africa, traveling inland from Zanzibar. His goal was twofold: to confirm Lake Victoria as the source of the Nile, and to discover whether the great river Lualaba, discovered by Livingstone in 1871, was in fact the Congo. To do so, he proposed to navigate it from Central Africa to its mouth on the Atlantic. It was an astounding proposition, yet unlike earlier explorers who were compelled by the search for geographical knowledge and to import Christian civilization, Stanley's goal was unambiguously imperialistic.

Left: Stanley's trump card was a 40 foot (12 m), five-sectioned boat, the Lady Alice. It was central to his explorations of the lakes, as well as his descent of the Congo. Yet carrying it through the jungles of the Congo as well as round the river's many rapids proved nightmarish, reducing his porters to prostration.

7,000 miles along the Congo

Stanley was not only extraordinarily single-minded, but also exceptionally well financed. His huge caravan of porters and guides, 250 strong, were driven and cajoled by him across the continent, amounting almost to "a private army." Having successfully sailed around Lake Victoria—at one point shooting dead at least 33 natives as a "punishment"—and explored Lake Tanganyika, he set off down the Lualaba in November 1876. The river's importance was obvious; if it was indeed the Congo, then it would provide ready access to

and from what were rapidly emerging as the riches of central Africa. In Nyangwe, a tiny Swahili settlement, he recruited the local ruler, an Arab slave trader known as Tippu Tip, paying him $5,000 for 300 of his soldiers to accompany him downriver.

It proved a nine-month purgatory of suffering, starvation, and disease. The straggling caravan was repeatedly attacked by local war parties up to 2,000 men strong and there were also vast cataracts to be negotiated, the largest, the Livingstone Falls, consisting of 32 rock-strewn torrents. When Stanley finally reached the Atlantic on August 5, 1877, he had covered 7,088 miles (11,407 km) in exactly 999 days at a cost of 114 dead.

"If you Wasungu [white men] are desirous of throwing away your lives, it is no reason why we Arabs should... you look only for rivers and lakes and mountains, and you spend your lives for no reason..."
Tippu Tip to Stanley

The Stanley who descended the Congo was a driven man in every sense, forcing obstacles aside with enormous energy and an almost complete absence of tact.

FIND OUT MORE
Blood River: A Journey to Africa's Broken Heart
Tim Butcher

Stanley: The Impossible Life of Africa's Greatest Explorer
Tim Jeal

Imperial Footprints: Henry Morton Stanley's African Journeys
James L. Newman

WILFRED THESIGER
Across the Empty Quarter

The Empty Quarter of Arabia, the *Rub' al Khali*, is the world's largest sand desert, covering 250,000 square miles (647,497 km²) of pristine, arid wilderness in which immense sand dunes roll endlessly to the horizon. It is a profoundly hostile environment, barely capable of sustaining life, yet it was this bleak landscape that Wilfred Thesiger, a man who abominated the 20th century and all its works, twice crossed between 1946 and 1949. Its attraction for him was not simply its untouched emptiness; he was drawn at least as much by its inhabitants, the Bedu, a people for whom he developed an extraordinary admiration. As he put it: "The harder the life, the finer the man."

Escaping the modern world

Thesiger's two great sweeps across the Empty Quarter, both made with small Bedu parties, provided the kind of intense experiences he sought from similarly hostile and remote regions and among similarly "primitive" peoples all his life. Over the desert "lay a silence we have now driven from our world." Survival depended on finding a handful of wells containing water almost too bitter to drink, and while thirst was a permanent companion, hunger was "almost incessant." At night, temperatures plummeted below

freezing, and by day they soared, the temperature of the sand reaching 176°F (80°C). Distances were measured not in miles, but in "hours on camel-back." On his first journey, his companions had no choice but to abandon him for three days while they searched for food. Thesiger, starving, spent the time in a state bordering on delirium. On both journeys, he was acutely conscious that this was a world on the brink of extinction: that change, invariably for the worse, could not be held back, and that oil wealth would inevitably put an end to a way of life that had endured for centuries. In many ways, his two epic crossings were the 20th century's last ventures of pure exploration.

> "These travels in the Empty Quarter would for me have been a pointless penance but for the comradeship of my Bedu companions... they met every challenge, every hardship with the proud boast: 'We are Bedu.'"
> *Wifred Thesiger, The Life of My Choice, 1987*

Above: Thesiger revelled in emptiness and the kind of barbaric, threatening grandeur he found in the Empty Quarter. The greater the isolation, the greater the purity and value of the experience. 20th century civilization, in conventional terms, amounted in his view to a despoiling not just of the world, but of its peoples.

FIND OUT MORE

Wilfred Thesiger: The Life of the Great Explorer
Alexander Maitland

A Vanished World
Wilfred Thesiger

Arabian Sands
Wildred Thesiger

—— 1946-47
—— 1947-48

PERSIAN GULF

QATAR

UNITED ARAB EMIRATES

Strait of Hormuz

Gulf of Oman

MUSCAT

RED SEA

MEDINA

RIYADH

SAUDI ARABIA

Liwa Oasis

OMAN

JIDDAH

MECCA

Rub' al Khali (Empty Quarter)

MUGHSHIN

Dhofar

YEMEN

Hadramout

AL MUKALLA

ADEN

Gulf of Aden

INDIAN OCEAN

Literature and travel are natural companions. This is more than just a matter of travel writing *per se*. It is more a question of how the *genius loci*—the spirit of a place—is captured in fiction, coloring subsequent views so that it is almost always seen at least partly through the author's eyes.

OFF THE PAGE
Leisurely tours with your favorite authors

Three American authors embody this trend. The Mississippi, for example, is indelibly associated with Huckleberry Finn and Tom Sawyer. These are characters whose richly idiosyncratic river life are stamped on popular imaginations across the Western world by their creator, Mark Twain. In exactly the same way, John Steinbeck delivered vivid recreations of northern California in the 1920s and '30s—a time of simultaneous optimism and despair—while Ernest Hemingway developed an early and lasting fascination with Spain, writing about it with a passion that still inspires devotees in search of the peoples and places he captured.

Much less intense, if hardly less precise evocations of England's softer landscapes are offered by the early 18th century chronicler of the landed classes' human foibles, Jane Austen. Hers is a world of elegant parkland and genteel country seats that consistently delights. The same period's growing taste for wilder, more romantic landscapes is no less importantly represented by the Lakeland poets, Wordsworth, Coleridge, and Southey, who decisively helped inculcate a general taste for the "sublime" in nature.

Travel writing itself is represented in this chapter by two unusual, not to say eccentric journeys: around the Highlands and Islands of Scotland by Samuel Johnson and James Boswell in 1773; and, nearly 200 years later, across the Hindu Kush by Eric Newby, fashion retailer turned intrepidly incompetent adventurer. The Grand Tour, by contrast, offered high culture to the 18th century's aristocratic youths, resulting in travel becoming the pursuit of learning. Jules Verne's classic *Around the World in 80 Days* offered a very different, distinctively 19th century view of the world: a world that technology, with the steam ship and the train, was dramatically shrinking.

JULES VERNE
Around the World in 80 Days

The publication in 1873 of Jules Verne's novel, *Around the World in 80 Days*, almost precisely marks the birth of modern tourism. Where almost any journey, let alone one around the globe, had previously been arduous, slow, and perilous, steamships and railways had transformed travel, making it, at least for those with sufficient means, safe, comfortable—on occasion luxurious—and above all rapid. Almost at a stroke, the wider world was brought within range. But as the book's engagingly picaresque plot makes clear, even steam-powered Victorian travel was not always reliable. The hero, Phileas Fogg, completes his journey with just seconds to spare.

Fogg's planned itinerary		
London to Suez	train, steamer	7 days
Suez to Bombay	steamer	13 days
Bombay to Calcutta	train	3 days
Calcutta to Hong Kong	steamer	13 days
Hong Kong to Yokohama	steamer	6 days
Yokohama to San Francisco	steamer	22 days
San Francisco to New York	train	7 days
New York to London	steamer	9 days

A very British affair

Though Verne was French, the hero of his book is British, the redoubtable, intensely cultivated, and always correct Phileas Fogg, who embarks on his epic as a bet: to prove the world could be circled in no more than 80 days. For Verne, as for so many later 19th century Frenchmen, the Victorian gentleman and monied man of leisure was a figure of legend, admired for his sang froid as much as for his impeccable manners. Yet there is a further British theme running through the book: its empire, then approaching its height and to which the novel is almost a guided tour. For Verne, among the many virtues of Britain's vast empire was the civilising impact of technology. He saw the introduction of railways to India, for instance, as a natural corollary to the white man's duty to spread the self-evident virtues of European notions of justice, trade, and Christianity to heathen primitives, however colorful.

Above: *Around the World in 80 Days* gripped imaginations from the start. Its fame soared further with the release of a star-studded film in 1956. In 2004 a further film was made. Both saw Fogg ride in a balloon, a mode of transport that never featured in the book.

"An Englishman never jokes about anything as important as a bet. I hereby wager £20,000 with anyone who wishes that I will carry out the tour of the world in 80 days or less, i.e. in 1,920 hours or 115,200 minutes. Will you accept?"
Phileas Fogg

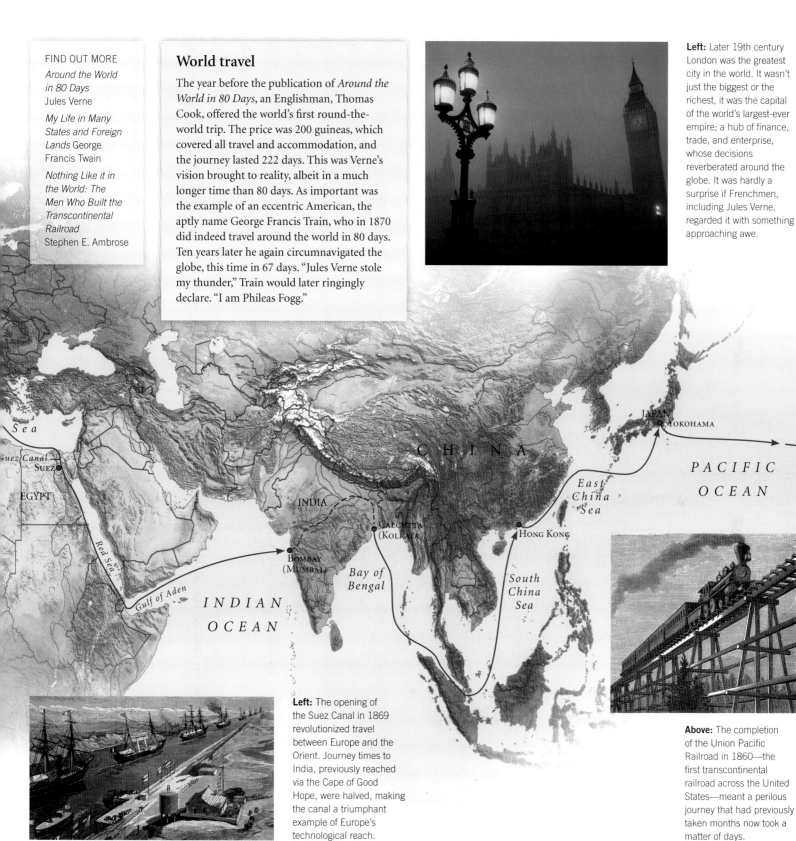

World travel

The year before the publication of *Around the World in 80 Days*, an Englishman, Thomas Cook, offered the world's first round-the-world trip. The price was 200 guineas, which covered all travel and accommodation, and the journey lasted 222 days. This was Verne's vision brought to reality, albeit in a much longer time than 80 days. As important was the example of an eccentric American, the aptly name George Francis Train, who in 1870 did indeed travel around the world in 80 days. Ten years later he again circumnavigated the globe, this time in 67 days. "Jules Verne stole my thunder," Train would later ringingly declare. "I am Phileas Fogg."

Left: Later 19th century London was the greatest city in the world. It wasn't just the biggest or the richest, it was the capital of the world's largest-ever empire; a hub of finance, trade, and enterprise, whose decisions reverberated around the globe. It was hardly a surprise if Frenchmen, including Jules Verne, regarded it with something approaching awe.

Left: The opening of the Suez Canal in 1869 revolutionized travel between Europe and the Orient. Journey times to India, previously reached via the Cape of Good Hope, were halved, making the canal a triumphant example of Europe's technological reach.

Above: The completion of the Union Pacific Railroad in 1860—the first transcontinental railroad across the United States—meant a perilous journey that had previously taken months now took a matter of days.

THE GRAND TOUR
A classic vacation

From the end of the 17th century to the last years of the 18th, the "Grand Tour" became an essential adjunct to the education of any young man of means in Britain, as well as many Germans, Scandanavians, and Americans. It involved an extended visit to continental Europe that could last anywhere from a few months to several years. The aim was to broaden the outlook of the youthful Grand Tourists, and expose them to the culture and highly polished courtly life of pre-revolutionary France and the glories of Classical and Renaissance Italy, with Rome its pre-eminent focus. It had a profound impact on the arts in Britain, decisively confirming the supremacy of Classicism.

Above: The lure of a licentious port city such as Marseilles could prove irresistible for the young Grand Tourist, who was easily subsumed by the delights of the flesh.

Below: By the mid-18th century, the Alps had been transformed from a dangerous barrier into a "sublime" landscape to be thrillingly admired for its own wild sake.

Right: Rome's hold on cultivated 18th-century imaginations never slackened. This was the city and the civilization that defined Europe. Without knowledge of it—and its language, painfully drummed into generations of unwilling schoolboys—no man of means could be thought educated. It was in direct emulation of this enduring model that 18th century English aristocrats sought to recreate its imagined pastoral idyll. The gardens of Stourhead (**above**) in Wiltshire are Rome reborn in a chilly climate.

The first tourists

There was no one route followed by those on the Grand Tour—in addition to France and Italy, many also visited Germany, Austria and the Low Countries, and by the end of the period Greece was also increasingly visited. However, there were certain well-established constants. From Calais, reached after Channel crossings from Dover, Paris was the first major

goal. Italy was then reached by sea—generally from Marseilles or Nice—or more commonly across the Alps, itself a perilous if spectacular undertaking. Venice, famed for the licentiousness of its Carnival, was the next target, after which Florence, Rome, and Naples beckoned. One consequence of this pan-Italian travel was an enormous art trade between Italy and Britain. Whole schools of Italian painting grew up to feed this appetite, while antiquities (forged or genuine) were also exported in vast numbers. When Lord Burlington returned to England in 1719 he had 878 pieces of luggage, while Charles Townley's collection of Roman antiquities formed one of the centerpieces of the British Museum's collections.

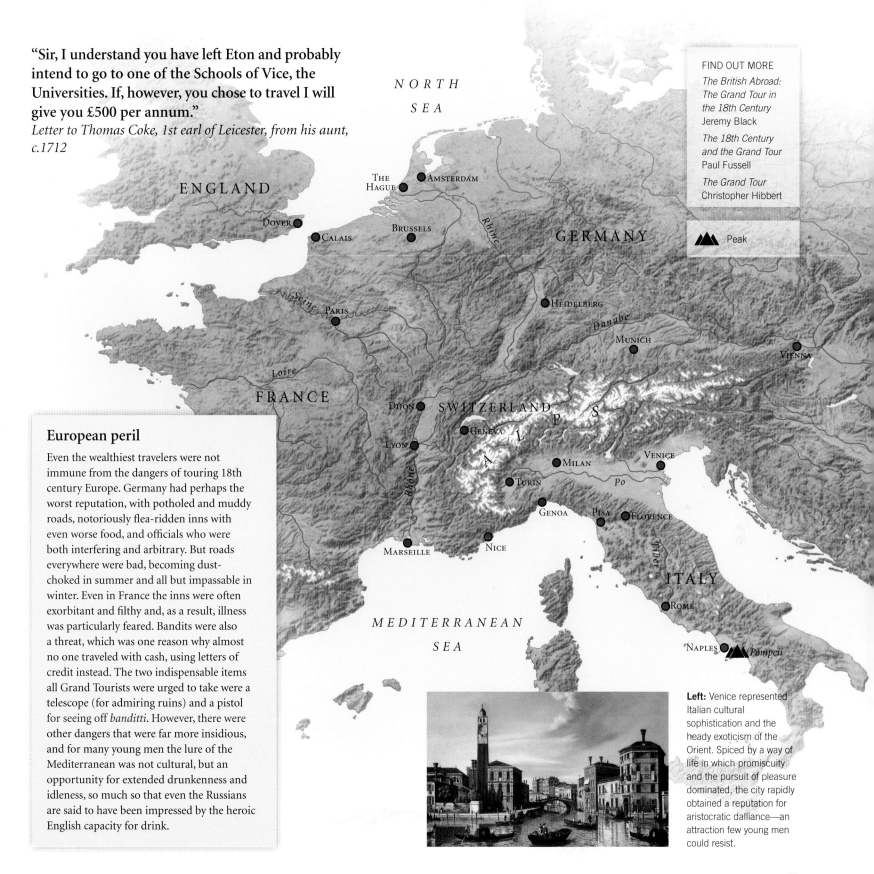

"Sir, I understand you have left Eton and probably intend to go to one of the Schools of Vice, the Universities. If, however, you chose to travel I will give you £500 per annum."

Letter to Thomas Coke, 1st earl of Leicester, from his aunt, c.1712

FIND OUT MORE

The British Abroad: The Grand Tour in the 18th Century
Jeremy Black

The 18th Century and the Grand Tour
Paul Fussell

The Grand Tour
Christopher Hibbert

▲▲ Peak

European peril

Even the wealthiest travelers were not immune from the dangers of touring 18th century Europe. Germany had perhaps the worst reputation, with potholed and muddy roads, notoriously flea-ridden inns with even worse food, and officials who were both interfering and arbitrary. But roads everywhere were bad, becoming dust-choked in summer and all but impassable in winter. Even in France the inns were often exorbitant and filthy and, as a result, illness was particularly feared. Bandits were also a threat, which was one reason why almost no one traveled with cash, using letters of credit instead. The two indispensable items all Grand Tourists were urged to take were a telescope (for admiring ruins) and a pistol for seeing off *banditti*. However, there were other dangers that were far more insidious, and for many young men the lure of the Mediterranean was not cultural, but an opportunity for extended drunkenness and idleness, so much so that even the Russians are said to have been impressed by the heroic English capacity for drink.

Left: Venice represented Italian cultural sophistication and the heady exoticism of the Orient. Spiced by a way of life in which promiscuity and the pursuit of pleasure dominated, the city rapidly obtained a reputation for aristocratic dalliance—an attraction few young men could resist.

WORDSWORTH, COLERIDGE, AND SOUTHEY
The Lake Poets

The "Lake Poets," or "Lake School" of poets, was a term first used in 1817 to collectively describe three English writers; William Wordsworth (1770-1850), Samuel Taylor Coleridge (1772–1834), and Robert Southey (1774–1843). There was actually no common "school" of thought linking their works, but what they did have in common was their location—the remotely beautiful Lake District in northern England.

Wordsworth was a native son of the Lake District, born in Cockermouth, Cumberland. In 1795, he moved to Dorset with his sister Dorothy, where he first met Coleridge and Southey. Wordsworth and Coleridge became firm friends before Wordsworth moved back to northern England in 1799, settling at Dove Cottage, Grasmere. The following year, Coleridge and his wife, Sarah Fricker, also headed to the Lakes, moving in to nearby Greta Hall, Keswick, where they were joined in 1802 by the Southey family (the poets' wives were sisters) and the "Lake Poets," as they later became known, were together.

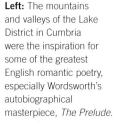

Left: The mountains and valleys of the Lake District in Cumbria were the inspiration for some of the greatest English romantic poetry, especially Wordsworth's autobiographical masterpiece, *The Prelude.*

Right: Samuel Coleridge Taylor battled against opium addiction for much of his life. When this started to affect his marriage to Sarah Fricker, Southey and his wife (Sarah's sister) moved in to Greta Hall.

The Lake District

The Lake District lies within the county of Cumbria, in the north west of England, and covers approximately 885 square miles (2,292 km²). It is one of few places in the country to have mountains, and the scenery is a stunning blend of peaks—including England's highest, Scafell Pike—and lakes, including 12 of the country's largest bodies of water, and the country's deepest, Wastwater.

With over 2,000 miles (3,500 km) of public rights of way, walkers can trek through some of the most spectacular scenery England has to offer.

Left: Southey was Coleridge's friend, brother-in-law, and foster father to his children, inspiring Southey's classic *The Story of the Three Bears.* He was poet laureate from 1813 until his death, when Wordsworth took the post.

Left: Dove Cottage, Grasmere, home of William Wordsworth and his sister Dorothy from 1799.

Below: If you don't fancy walking the Fells, you can take to the water on one of the great lakes, where dinghy sailing, waterskiing, and canoeing are all on offer against a stunning natural backdrop.

JANE AUSTEN'S ENGLAND
The romance of the countryside

Jane Austen (1775–1817) was born in the village of Steventon, Hampshire, where her father was rector. She was educated mostly at home, and enjoyed reading, dancing, and country walks—all reflected in her novels. Her father retired in 1801 and moved the family to Bath, but in this new town Austen proved quite unproductive. However, in 1809, with her father dead, Austen's brother George gave her and her mother a cottage in the village of Chawton, Hampshire. Their quiet life here proved to be Austen's most prolific period, as she revised earlier novels and wrote three more. She also completed *Persuasion*, which was posthumously published with a revision of *Northanger Abbey*. Austen fell ill in 1816, and was writing *Sanditon* when she was moved to Winchester for medical care in May 1817. She died on July 18 and was buried in Winchester Cathedral. Jane Austen's novels are an affectionate, yet satirical portrayal of the sensibilities, manners, and follies of society in southern England.

Principal Settings in Jane Austen's Novels

Jane Austen used both real and fictitious places as her locations.

Northanger Abbey (1798): Bath, Northanger Abbey, Somerset.

Sense and Sensibility (1811): Norland Park, Sussex; Barton Park and Delaford, Devonshire; London.

Pride and Prejudice (1813): Netherfield and Longbourn, Hertfordshire; Rosings, Kent; Derbyshire; descriptions of London and Brighton.

Mansfield Park (1814): Mansfield Park, Sotherton and Thornton Lacey, Northamptonshire; Portsmouth, Hampshire; descriptions of Bath and London.

Emma (1815): Hartfield in Highbury, Donwell Abbey and Randalls, Surrey.

Persuasion (1817): Kellynch Hall, Somerset; descriptions of Bath.

Stately home

SCOTLAND
GRETNA GREEN
NEWCASTLE UPON TYNE
ENGLAND
Chatsworth
BAKEWELL
MATLOCK
BIRMINGHAM
WARWICK
WALES
Blenheim Palace
HATFIELD
OXFORD
LONDON
BRISTOL
READING
WESTERHAM
BATH
STEVENTON
RAMSGATE
EPSOM
WINCHESTER
CHAWTON
SOUTHAMPTON
LYME REGIS
BOURNEMOUTH
BRIGHTON

Above: The rural landscape of Hampshire was the backdrop to one of Austen's most prolific periods of writing.

Left: Jane Austen's literary work continues to entertain new audiences, with television and movie adaptations of classic works such as *Pride and Prejudice*, *Emma*, and *Sense and Sensibility*.

Below: Jane Austen lived in this 17th-century house in Chawton, Hampshire, from 1809 until shortly before her death in 1817.

MARK TWAIN
From Hannibal to New Orleans

Whether you know it as "Big River," "Big Muddy," "Ole Man River," or "Moon River," the mighty Mississippi flows through our collective consciousness like no other. When combined with its major tributaries, the Missouri and the Jefferson, the Ohio and the Arkansas, this waterway extends for almost 4,000 miles (6,435 km), and the system drains almost the whole of the American Midwest between the Appalachian Mountains to the East, and the cordillera of the Rockies in the West—making it the second largest river basin in the world. Who best to guide us down the waterways of the lower Mississippi than former riverboat pilot, raconteur, and wit, Mark Twain?

Left: In Twain's time, as today, the waters of the Ohio, Missouri, and Mississippi were crowded with many craft, from skiffs to shallow cargo barges, often driven downstream by the current, and hauled back up by horses or propelled by long sweeps.

Below and Right: The French were among the first settlers in the Midwest, colonizing the mouth of the river at New Orleans in 1718. The French Quarter in New Orleans remains the heartland of blues and jazz, despite hurricane damage in 2005.

Hannibal to New Orleans

Starting our journey at the historic town of Hannibal, as Twain and Huckleberry Finn did (although Twain called it Petersburg) we drift downstream some 100 miles (160 km) to St. Louis. The "Gateway of the West," St. Louis was the assembly point for thousands of early settlers heading across the prairies and badlands, commemorated by its enormous arch. A further 200 miles (320 km) brings us to the confluence of the Mississippi with the Ohio, near Cairo (one of many settlements given Biblical names by the first Protestant settlers in the upper Midwest states). Entering the convoluted meanders below this will gradually bring us to Memphis, the home of rock 'n' roll, after which we enter the Deep South. One of the decisive battles of the Civil War was fought at Vicksburg, besieged on a bend in the river as we enter Blues country. New Orleans nestles in the enormous "bird's foot" delta at the mouth of the great river, and, although it lies inland, it remains susceptible to hurricanes and storm surge, as in the disaster of 2005.

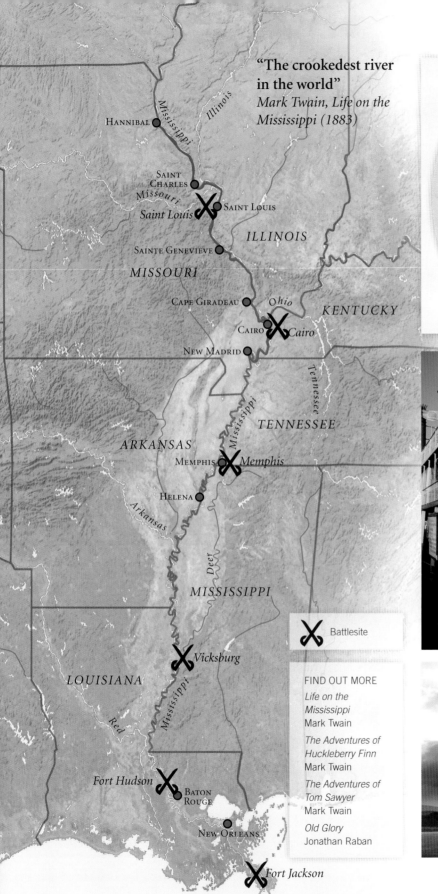

"The crookedest river in the world"
Mark Twain, Life on the Mississippi (1883)

Mark Twain

Mark Twain (1835-1910) was born Samuel Langhorne Clemens in Florida, Missouri, but his family soon moved to the river port town of Hannibal. He worked as a journalist, before becoming a steamboat pilot, which brought him into contact with a gallery of colorful characters who traveled and worked on the river. During the Civil War he began writing stories and articles for publication, earning a reputation as a keen and amusing observer of everyday life. By the 1870s he had moved to Harford, Connecticut, but returned to the Mississippi life for several of his major works.

X Battlesite

FIND OUT MORE

Life on the Mississippi
Mark Twain

The Adventures of Huckleberry Finn
Mark Twain

The Adventures of Tom Sawyer
Mark Twain

Old Glory
Jonathan Raban

Above: In the past, hundreds of flat-bottomed Mississippi steamboats plied the river between Hannibal and New Orleans, carrying cargo and passengers.

Left: During the American Civil War, the Mississippi was the site of many key battles, as Union forces fought to win control of the vital waterway from the Confederates.

VOLTAIRE, CASANOVA, AND MOZART
The Enlightenment experience

The Enlightenment—the intellectual revolution that spread across 18th century Europe—profoundly affected Western views of the world. Rational and humane, rejecting superstition, championing learning, and fiercely opposed to privilege, it decisively shaped the modern world. It was above all international, and while its leading figures were French and British, they found ready echoes as far afield as America and Russia. Voltaire was perhaps its embodiment, but Mozart and the controversial figure of Casanova also profited from this internationalism, traveling widely across Europe as representatives as much as beneficiaries of this new intellectual order.

Voltaire

Voltaire was among the most feted men in Europe, recognized as not just one of the leading thinkers of his age, but of any age. Yet since his early 20s, his was a life spent more or less permanently with one eye on the nearest  frontier over which to make an enforced dash to freedom. As an adult, he only twice lived for extended periods in France. In much the same way, he was effectively in exile, in England from 1726–9 and he found himself in a similar position, in Holland in 1736–9, and again in 1742–3, this time in Brussels. He also spent three years in Prussia, invited there in 1750 by Frederick the Great to spread the brilliant spotlight of his learning across an emerging, aspirant nation.

Above: Internationalism was a key feature of 18th century Europe. National borders in the modern sense were as much concepts as absolute limits. For those with the means—or the necessity—pan-European travel was relatively easily undertaken and a city such as Paris could be thought as much European as exclusively French.

> "All men are equal; it is not their birth but virtue itself that makes the difference."
> *Voltaire, Eriphile, 1732*

Both Brussels (**left**) and Venice (**right**) are prime examples of the permanently shifting borders of 18th century Europe. Brussels only emerged as capital of an independent Belgium as late as 1830, while 18th century Venice was variously an independent republic and part of an aggresively expansionist emerging Austrian Habsburg empire.

SWEDEN

STOCKHOLM

BALTIC SEA

PRUSSIA

BERLIN

WARSAW

HOLY ROMAN EMPIRE

POLAND

BRUSSELS

Prague

Bohemia

SALZBURG

GIREY

MUNICH

VIENNA

BUDAPEST

KINGDOM OF HUNGARY

SWITZ.

VENICE

VENICE

SAVOY

PARMA

TUSCANY

PAPAL STATES

OTTOMAN EMPIRE

NAPLES

KINGDOM OF THE TWO SICILIES

ERRANEAN SEA

ATHENS

FIND OUT MORE

History of My Life
Giacomo Casanova,
ed. Willard R. Trask

Voltaire: the Universal Man
Derek Parker

Mozart: A Cultural Biography
Robert Gutman

Casanova

It would seem hard to imagine any 18th century European traveled more widely or more often than the Venetian-born Casanova, a sometime priest, soldier, businessman, diplomat, magician, medicine-man, and

libertine. In 1743, at the age of only 18, he was forced to flee Venice, as he was again in 1749. Between 1755 and 1774, he endured a near 19-year exile from his native city after becoming the first man to escape the city's notorious I Piombi prison, where he was incarcerated on charges of witchcraft. In 1783, he was expelled again, this time ending up in Bohemia where he spent the last 14 years of his life. In between, he had visited—in many cases multiple time—Spain, France, England, Holland, Germany, Austria, Poland, and Russia.

Mozart

In June 1763, Leopold Mozart took his family on a three-year visit across Europe. From Salzburg, they traveled to Paris, arriving in November. The following April, they left for London, where they stayed until July 1765

when they left for the Low Countries. By May 1766, they were back in Paris, and by November, traveling via Switzerland, they had returned to Salzburg. The purpose had been to show off the child

Mozart, only seven when the family left, but a child musical prodigy of astonishing gifts; a "God-given miracle" in the words of his father, Leopold. Travel remained a constant theme of Mozart's life until his death in 1791, chiefly shuttling back and forth between Salzburg, Vienna, Munich, and Prague in a search for commissions.

Left: Modern Salzburg is a town consumed by Mozart, easily the Austrian city's most famous son. Memories of him are everywhere, with the city shamelessly cashing in on his legacy. Yet the composer's feelings towards his birthplace were ambivalent, a reaction to his frustration as the court composer to Salzburg's prince-archbishop of 1773–7.

Johnson and Boswell
Around the Western Isles of Scotland

Between August and November 1773, Samuel Johnson and his companion and biographer, James Boswell, undertook a circular tour of Scotland, beginning and ending in Edinburgh, with the principal purpose of visiting the Highlands and islands of western Scotland. In a period when foreign travel meant the Grand Tour, the notion of traveling not to the Mediterranean, but in the opposite direction to a cold, wet, remote, and barbarous land "to find simplicity and wildness" was as apparently perverse as it was unusual. Yet it gave rise to two great works of travel literature: Johnson's *A Journey to the Western Isles of Scotland* and Boswell's *Journal of a Tour to the Hebrides.*

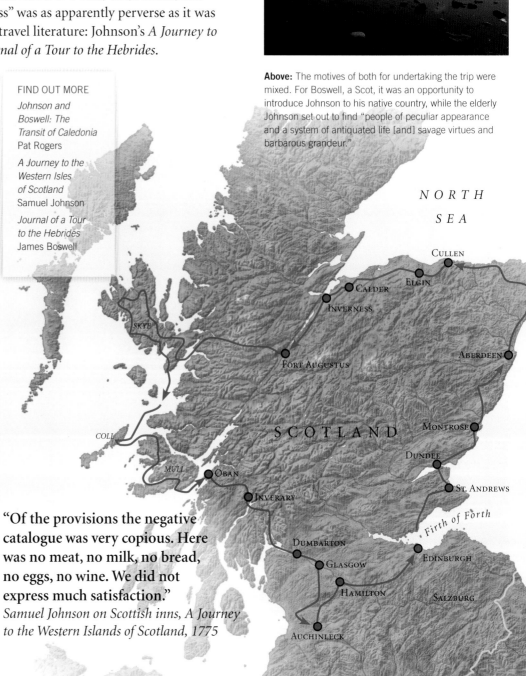

Above: The motives of both for undertaking the trip were mixed. For Boswell, a Scot, it was an opportunity to introduce Johnson to his native country, while the elderly Johnson set out to find "people of peculiar appearance and a system of antiquated life [and] savage virtues and barbarous grandeur."

A Scottish tour

Boswell and Johnson left Edinburgh on August 18, 1773, following the east coast northwards. By August 21 they had reached Aberdeen, where they spent four days, before continuing north to Banff and then to Nairn,

"a town in a state of miserable decay." From there they journeyed to Inverness where they "bid farewell to the luxury of traveling." Until they reached the Lowlands again they would find no more paved roads, and in many instances no roads at all. Now they traveled on horseback or on foot, "climbing crags and treading bogs" as they followed the Great Glen southwest to Fort Augustus

before heading west to Skye. They reached the island on September 2 and left, having been gale-bound for much of the time, on October 3, with autumn closing in rapidly. A series of open boat journeys took them down the coast to Mull, which they reached on October 20. The following day they crossed back to the mainland, to Oban, and continued to Glasgow. By November 12 they were back in Edinburgh, their curious tour at an end.

FIND OUT MORE

Johnson and Boswell: The Transit of Caledonia
Pat Rogers

A Journey to the Western Isles of Scotland
Samuel Johnson

Journal of a Tour to the Hebrides
James Boswell

"Of the provisions the negative catalogue was very copious. Here was no meat, no milk, no bread, no eggs, no wine. We did not express much satisfaction."
Samuel Johnson on Scottish inns, A Journey to the Western Islands of Scotland, 1775

NORTH SEA

CULLEN

ELGIN

CALDER

INVERNESS

SKYE

ABERDEEN

FORT AUGUSTUS

COLL

SCOTLAND

MONTROSE

DUNDEE

MULL

OBAN

INVERARY

St. Andrews

Firth of Forth

DUMBARTON

GLASGOW

EDINBURGH

HAMILTON

SALZBURG

AUCHINLECK

JOHN STEINBECK
California dreaming

John Steinbeck (1902–1968) was born in Salinas, the center of northern California's lettuce industry, southeast of San Francisco. An awkward and gangly loner, he got odd jobs to help him through high school and Stanford University, working on fruit and cattle farms and rubbing shoulders with factory workers, migrant fruit pickers, hobos, dreamers, and drifters. The atmosphere of his fiction is infused with impoverished types from Salinas, Monterey, Carmel, and Big Sur, all near Pacific Grove where his family had a summerhouse. In the 1920s Steinbeck was scratching a living in New York, but returned to California in 1930. Fame came with his 1935 novel, *Tortilla Flat*, which features characters from Salinas, Monterey, and his beloved Pacific Grove. However, he is best known for *Of Mice and Men* (1937), a story that takes place near Soledad, and *The Grapes of Wrath* (1939), written in Los Gatos and featuring the families who had fled Oklahoma to find a better future in California.

The call of home

Although Steinbeck spent the latter part of his life, with his third wife Elaine, back in New York, he wanted to be buried in his home state. After he died on December 20, 1968, his ashes were interred in the family plot back in Salinas, California.

> "It seems to me that if you or I must choose between two courses of thought or action, we should remember our dying and try so to live that our death brings no pleasure on the world."
> *John Steinbeck*

Left: The spirit and landscape of Salinas, California, the place where Steinback was born, was immortalized in many of his stories, including *The Grapes of Wrath* (1939) and *East of Eden* (1952).

The beautiful coastal town of Pacific Grove is just a few miles from Monterey and Cannery Row. It was the setting for Steinbeck's *The Red Pony* (1937) and some scenes from *Cannery Row* (1945).

Above: A still from the 1940 movie, *The Grapes of Wrath*, directed by John Ford. The movie was based on Steinbeck's 1939 novel of sharecroppers fleeing Oklahoma during the Great Depression to seek a better future in California's Central Valley.

Patrick Leigh Fermor
On foot across Europe

In two remarkable books, *A Time of Gifts* and *Between the Woods and the Water*, Patrick Leigh Fermor precisely evoked the spirit of pre-war Mittel Europa. They were based on a journey he made, almost entirely on foot, between Holland and Istanbul in 1933–5. What was exceptional was not just that he undertook it at all; nor even that he was only 18 when he set off. Rather, it was his limitless curiosity. He cast himself with typical romantic zeal as "a pilgrim or a palmer, an errant scholar, a broken knight." Cathedrals and cowsheds alike were to him objects of wonder, the "immeasurably old" as enticing as what, to Leigh Fermor, was a world "totally unknown."

Contrasting worlds

Leigh Fermor described himself as "an affable tramp," his original goal being that he would "only consort with peasants and tramps." Yet a chance encounter in Munich opened an entirely new, aristocratic world to

him. Through the summer of 1935, traveling across Czechoslovakia, Hungary, and Romania, he found himself handed on from one landed family to another, spending days or occasionally weeks in a series of castles, palaces, and country houses. In improbable contrast this high life was periodically studded by days back on the road and nights under the stars on mountainsides; "the haunt of bears, wolves, and eagles."

Left: A taste for adventure ran through Leigh Fermor's life. During the Second World War he spent two years in German-occupied Crete after its fall in 1941, living with shepherds, organizing resistance, and, memorably, capturing the German commandant, General Kreipe, who he smuggled off the island.

Above: Leigh Fermor published the first volume of his journey in 1977. This took his story to the Hungarian border. The second appeared in 1986 and took the author to the Iron Gates on the Danube. A third volume, bringing the story to a conclusion— he reached Istanbul on January 1, 1935—has never appeared.

NETHERLANDS
Rhine
ROTTERDAM
KR
COLOGNE

Left: Holland proved a consistent series of delights for the youthful Leigh Fermor, its canals and widmills a source of almost exotic pleasure. Leigh Fermor had been destined for the army when his plan to walk to Istanbul "unfolded with the speed and completeness of a Japanese paper flower in water."

Rotterdam to Istanbul

Among the many exceptional, not to say eccentric, features of Leigh Fermor's walk was that he began it in mid-winter. He arrived in Rotterdam on December 9, 1933, and for the next three-and-a-half months made his way slowly across Holland, Germany, Austria, and Czechoslovakia through a landscape of ice and snow. Far from deterring him, these apparently unfavorable conditions only added to the appeal of his improbable undertaking. The rhythm of his days was dictated not merely by the pace of his walking, but by frequent halts to gasp at castles and to drink in views. His nights were spent in tiny inns and, on occasion, in barns. He had £1 a week to live on, enough for "bread, cheese, and apples... and an occasional mug of beer."

Above and right: Aside from a rushed side trip by train to Prague, Leigh Fermor stayed largely true to his goal of accepting lifts only if "walking became literally intolerable." There were two major exceptions, however. In Germany he was offered and accepted a lift on a Rhine barge, while in early April he was lent a horse, Malek, on which he rode across the Great Hungarian Plain for a week or more.

"I shudder to think of the scourge I must have been. The idea that they are always welcome is a protective illusion of the young. Dangerously untroubled by doubts, I rejoiced in these changes of fortune with the zest of an Arab beggar clad and feasted by the Caliph."
Patrick Leigh Fermor, A Time of Gifts

FIND OUT MORE
A Time of Gifts
Patrick Leigh Fermor

Between the Woods and the Water
Patrick Leigh Fermor

Words of Mercury
ed. Artemis Cooper

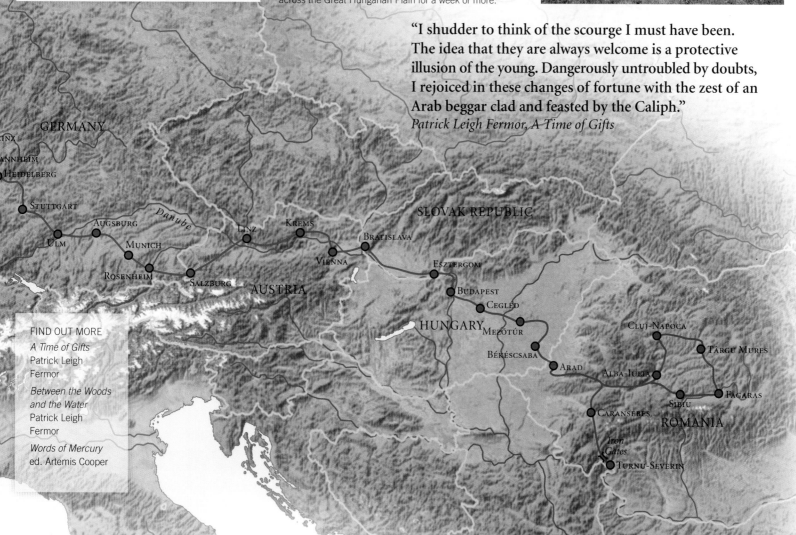

MAINZ
MANNHEIM
HEIDELBERG
STUTTGART
GERMANY
ULM
AUGSBURG
MUNICH
ROSENHEIM
SALZBURG
Danube
LINZ
KREMS
VIENNA
AUSTRIA
BRATISLAVA
SLOVAK REPUBLIC
ESZTERGOM
BUDAPEST
CEGLÉD
HUNGARY
MEZŐTÚR
BÉKÉSCSABA
ARAD
CLUJ-NAPOCA
TÂRGU MUREŞ
ALBA-IULIA
FĂGĂRAŞ
CARANSEBEŞ
SIBIU
ROMANIA
Iron Gates
TURNU-SEVERIN

ERNEST HEMINGWAY
A Spanish affair

Spain for Hemingway was "the last good country left." He revered it as a land of passion, honor, pride, and untouched, wild landscapes. Above all, for Hemingway, it was the land of the bullfight, "an ancient tribal rite" that possessed a kind of purity and nobility—as well as death—that to Hemingway made it an object almost worthy of worship. Spain was the country, perhaps more than any other, where he felt most instinctively and completely at home. It was emphatically not the Spain of the coast that drew him but that of the unchanging, harsh interior, whether Madrid—"mountain city with a mountain climate"—or "the over-foliaged, wet, green Basque country."

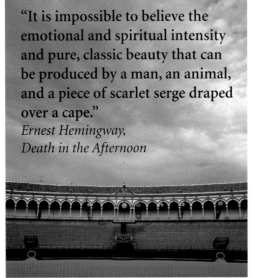

"It is impossible to believe the emotional and spiritual intensity and pure, classic beauty that can be produced by a man, an animal, and a piece of scarlet serge draped over a cape."
Ernest Hemingway,
Death in the Afternoon

Above, right, and below: Before Hemingway, Spain was a country visited by almost no one. When he first went to Pamplona in 1923, he estimated there were no other English-speakers there. Almost literally, Hemingway put this neglected corner of Europe on the map.

Right: In addition to *For Whom the Bell Tolls*, the Spanish Civil War also inspired a play by Hemingway, *The Fifth Column*. He also wrote the script of a documentary film, *The Spanish Earth*. It was to have been narrated by Orson Welles, but Welles took exception to Hemingway's script, with the result that the two found themselves in a fist fight. The dispute was resolved over a bottle of whiskey.

FIND OUT MORE
Hemingway and Spain: A Pursuit
Edward F Stanton

The Dangerous Summer
Ernest Hemingway

For Whom the Bell Tolls
Ernest Hemingway

Death in the Afternoon
Ernest Hemingway

The Sun Also Rises
Ernest Hemingway

ERIC NEWBY
Through the Hindu Kush

By 1956 Eric Newby had spent 10 years in the fashion trade, and while this was an unlikely background for a would-be explorer of "unknown territory," he had already sailed round the world on a four-masted barque before the Second World War. In the summer of '56, Newby and a companion, Hugh Carless, traveled across one of the world's most remote regions—the mountains of Nuristan in northern Afghanistan. It was a country that no Briton had penetrated since the late 19th century, and Newby's account of the journey became an instant travel classic. *A Short Walk in the Hindu Kush* was a vivid, consistently witty account of two Englishman brought up short not just by an alien landscape, but also by an alien culture.

I have nine fingers, you have ten

Newby and Carless's goal was a 20,000-foot (6,096 m) mountain, Mir Shamir. In the truest traditions of the British amateur, Newby, who had never climbed in his life, prepared by spending a "brief weekend in the Welsh hills." Carless was at home in Afghanistan, a country through which he had traveled extensively, but to Newby the "shattered landscapes" they encountered, the all-but-inedible food, the freezing nights at altitude, and the searing temperatures by day rapidly reduced him to prostration. In addition, his boots flayed his feet raw and

both men contracted dysentery. Newby consoled himself by reading a grammar of the Kafir language, published in 1901, which contained such baffling statements as: "I have nine fingers, you have ten" and "A gust of wind came and took away all my clothes." To test if his watch was, as he claimed, waterproof, tribesmen once memorably lowered it into a bubbling goat stew.

FIND OUT MORE
A Short Walk in the Hindu Kush,
Eric Newby

A Traveler's Life
Eric Newby

▲▲ Peak

"Can you travel Nuristan June?"
Telegram from Newby to Carless, 1956

Left: Staggering back from Nuristan, Newby and Carless met another, very different English traveler, Wilfred Thesiger. Their encounter provided a moment of high comedy as, preparing to sleep on ground "like iron with sharp rocks sticking out of it," Newby and Carless inflated air beds. Thesiger declaimed, "God, you must be a couple of pansies."

Religion is one of the great spurs to travel. Visits to shrines and other holy places are one of the most obvious factors common to faiths across the world, a sacred duty for millions of pilgrims whether in search of enlightenment, atonement, or spiritual uplift. Even in the Christian West, the role of pilgrimage, however reduced, remains central.

SACRED ROUTES
The pilgrim paths

The prophet Mohammed enjoined that every Muslim must visit Mecca, the site of his birth, at least once. In fact, many Muslims make multiple visits, with millions from across the globe descending on the city every year. Where once this would have involved a perilous journey of many months, much on foot, today the strain of the journey itself is hardly felt at all. But the logistics of accommodating such vast numbers nonetheless present problems of their own.

For Hindus, Varanasi on the Ganges, a city venerated by Buddhists as well, exerts a similar pull, with the "sacred river" said to cleanse sins following a ritual

immersion. For Buddhists, Lhasa, the holiest city in Tibet, enjoys a unique status. Whatever the deliberate depredations of the communist Chinese and the enforced exile of the Dalai Lama, the city continues to draw the faithful in huge numbers, all braving the inevitable difficulties of travel in a land both mountainous and poor.

It is hard not to be moved by such an obvious outpouring of faith in the face of official persecution, yet in medieval Europe such obvious manifestations of piety were commonplace. Pilgrimage, whether to Rome, the Holy Land itself, or the likes of Canterbury in England and Santiago de Compostela in Spain was a regular feature of life, with journeys of inevitable hardship undertaken not just out of religious duty, but also in the hope of redemption. The pilgrim, dusty and footsore, is a recurring figure of the period, and Rome and the Holy Land continue to draw the faithful in substantial—and increasing—numbers. Since the 1980s, Christian pilgrimage has increasingly reverted to its roots. In 1986, 2,500 pilgrims journeyed to Santiago de Compostela on foot, while in 2006, the figure was 100,000.

In Christ's Footsteps
A Tour of the Holy Land

The historical reality of Christ has long been a matter of contention among scholars. The written records—essentially the four Gospels—not only contradict each other in key respects, but also cannot be verified with any certainty. All are in any case copies of copies written in Greek rather than Aramaic, the language Christ would have spoken. Unsurprisingly, Christ's travels in the Holy Land during his "ministry"—a period of anywhere between one and three years—can only be reconstructed exceptionally tentatively. Nonetheless, whether intended as literal truth, or as metaphor, they highlight certain key features of where Christ traveled.

Left: The 2,900 foot (883 m) high Mount of Olives, located just to the east of Jerusalem, is replete with religious associations. From the 3rd millennium BC it has been one of the city's two most important burial grounds. The Church of the Holy Ascension marks the site where, by tradition, Christ ascended to heaven.

Below: The uncertainty about the locations of Christ's ministry is highlighted by the Church of the Holy Sepulchre in Jerusalem, reputed to be the site of the crucifixion and the burial of Christ. The site is believed to have been used for Christian worship since the 1st century AD.

Above: Nazareth during the time of Christ was a village with a population of about 200. It was where Christ was raised, and its most important Christian site is the Church of the Annunciation, built where the Virgin Mary was visited by an angel and told she would be the mother of Christ.

Christ's ministry

The period in Christian tradition during which Christ revealed himself as the Son of God—preaching, gathering followers, and performing miracles before his crucifixion and resurrection—took placed in two broad areas of the Holy Land. The first was in the north of present-day Israel, in and around

the Sea of Galilee. He spent the first 25 or 30 years of life at Nazareth, a period about which practically nothing is known. It was here that he performed his first miracles: at Cana, where he turned water into wine; and on the Sea of Galilee itself, whose waters he is said to have walked upon. Near Tiberius he gave the Sermon on the Mount and—perhaps at Bethsaida—he is said to have fed 5,000 with no more than five loaves and two fishes.

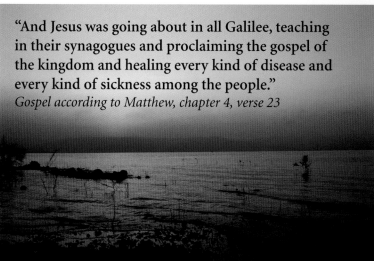

"And Jesus was going about in all Galilee, teaching in their synagogues and proclaiming the gospel of the kingdom and healing every kind of disease and every kind of sickness among the people."
Gospel according to Matthew, chapter 4, verse 23

The Holy City of Jerusalem

Jerusalem, the spiritual center of Judaism and the administrative capital of Roman Palestine during Christ's life, was the second major focus of his ministry. He is said, albeit only in one of the Gospels (Luke), to have first visited it when he was aged 12, when he was found earnestly disputing in the Temple with the high priests. The majority of Christ's ministry was in the north of Palestine, but it was at Bethany, just outside Jerusalem, that he raised Lazarus from the dead. No less important, it was in and around Jerusalem that the Passion—the last supper, his betrayal and trial, the crucifixion, and his resurrection three days later—took place. It was also just outside the city, on the Mount of Olives, that 40 days later he is said to have ascended into heaven.

▲▲ Peak

Left: In Christian tradition, Bethsaida is important not just as the site where Christ is said to have fed the 5,000, but it was also the home of three of the Apostles—Philip, Andrew, and Peter. Some contend that two others—James and John—were also from Bethsaida, a village well known for its fishermen.

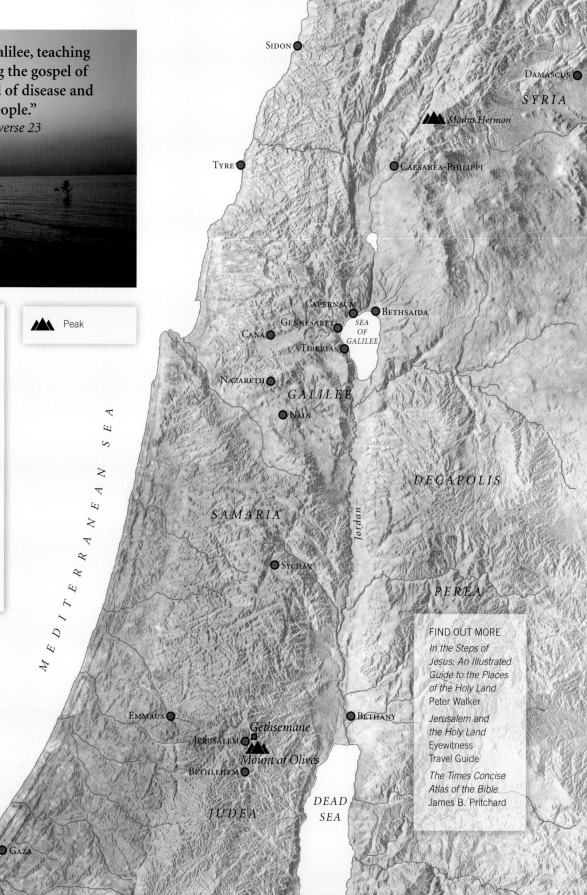

SIDON

DAMASCUS

SYRIA

▲▲ *Mount Hermon*

TYRE

CAESAREA-PHILIPPI

CAPERNAUM
GENNESARET
CANA
TIBERIAS

BETHSAIDA

SEA OF GALILEE

NAZARETH

GALILEE

NAIN

DECAPOLIS

M E D I T E R R A N E A N   S E A

SAMARIA

Jordan

SYCHAR

PEREA

EMMAUS

Gethsemane

JERUSALEM

Mount of Olives

BETHLEHEM

BETHANY

JUDEA

DEAD SEA

GAZA

FIND OUT MORE

In the Steps of Jesus: An Illustrated Guide to the Places of the Holy Land
Peter Walker

Jerusalem and the Holy Land
Eyewitness Travel Guide

The Times Concise Atlas of the Bible
James B. Pritchard

THE HAJJ
The pilgrimage to Mecca

Every able-bodied Muslim that can afford to, must make the pilgrimage to Mecca at least once in their lifetime. Hajj means "to set out for a place," and the rituals followed by the pilgrims were laid down by the Prophet Mohammed in the 7th century, recalling events in the life of the Prophet Ibrahim who made the first Hajj to Mecca many centuries before. Mohammed also decreed that only Muslims could go to the Kaaba, which previously had attracted pilgrims from all religions. Today in Dhu'l-Hijjah, the 12th month of the Islamic calendar, over two million Muslims flock to the Holy places of Saudi Arabia—the largest annual pilgrimage in the world.

Left: In 622 BC (year 1 of the Islamic calendar) Mohammed and his followers fled from Mecca to Medina. The Prophet transformed the town, formerly known as Yathrib, into a model Muslim city, and built a simple mosque. As the Prophet was buried here, Medina is often visited by pilgrims, though it is not part of the Hajj.

Right: Mina becomes "tent city" when the Hajj pilgrims arrive, creating a logistical problem for the Saudi authorities.

Below: God instructed the Prophet Ibrahim and his son Ishmael to build the Kaaba, "House of God," in Mecca. The Angel Gabriel brought the Black Stone from paradise.

Dhu'l-Hijjah and The Hajj

The Hajj starts on the 6th day of *Dhu'l-Hijjah* in Mecca with pilgrims completing *tawaf* at the Haram Mosque. Having donned the simple clothing of ihram, they enter the Holy Sanctuary and walk seven times anti-clockwise round the *Kaaba*, kissing the Black Stone. Then they pass seven times between the hills of Safa and Marwah as Ibrahim's wife Haagar did in search of water for her son Ishmael. The 8th day of *Dhu'l-Hijjah* is spent in prayer at nearby Mina. The spiritual highlight comes the next day at Mount Arafat, where pilgrims commune with God and witness the spot where Mohammed gave his last sermon. In the Muzdalifah valley pilgrims gather 70 pebbles to use back in Mina for the ritual of the stoning of the three pillars. A second *tawaf* in Mecca is followed by a return to Mina for a further stoning ritual, but pilgrims must leave before sunset on the 12th day of *Dhu'l-Hijjah*.

The Prophet Mohammed

Mohammed was the founder of Islam, born in Mecca around 570 CE. His parents both died early, and his uncle trained him as a merchant. In 595 he married Khadijah, a 40-year-old widow, who bore him six children. Mohammed earned a reputation for

trustworthiness, and despised the pagan idols that cluttered the Kaaba. During a sojourn in Hira cave in 610, the Angel Gabriel appeared to him and told him he was the "Messenger of God." These and subsequent revelations of the word

of God to Mohammed were later transcribed in the Holy Qur'an. Two years later he started preaching in Mecca, and attracted a community of followers—but also enemies. Forced to escape to Medina in 622, it was only in 630 that he took control of Mecca, and reconsecrated the Kaaba to the one God. Two years later he died, having established a strong new faith.

Jabal Nur

MECCA

Haram Mosque

The Jamarat

MINA

MUZDALIFAH

Peak

Mosque

"And proclaim the Pilgrimage
Among men: they will come
To thee on foot and (mounted)
On every kind of camel,
Lean on account of journeys
Through deep and distant
Mountain highways."
*Surah Al Hajj 22: 27
from the Holy Qur'an*

Jabal Rahma

PLAIN OF ARAFAT

Namira Mosque

Above: On the return to Mina, pilgrims perform *ramy*, stoning the three pillars that represent the three attempts of the devil to tempt Ibrahim to refuse God's demand that he sacrifice his son Ishmael. Each pillar must be hit seven times. Then an animal must be sacrificed to God, as Ibrahim did after God spared his son.

117

NEOLITHIC LEY LINES
The links to prehistoric landmarks

In 1921, English amateur archaeologist Alfred Watkins noticed that several ancient landmarks in Herefordshire lay along a straight line. So began his quest for ley lines linking the prehistoric sites of Britain, hypothesizing they were Neolithic trading routes. His theories had little in the way of evidence, but the idea of ley lines was gradually popularized around the globe, taking on mystical dimensions, such as their adoption by New Age believers as lines of spiritual or cosmic energy, and even becoming associated with UFOs. Whatever the truth, the journey of discovery will lead you through truly magnificent sites that date back five or six millennia, and are well worth further investigation.

> "Imagine a fairy chain stretched from mountain peak to mountain peak, as far as the eye can see."
> *Alfred Watkins in The Old Straight Track*

Above: Nobody knows why or how Stonehenge was constructed, but it is likely to have been a ceremonial site, dating from well before the time of the Druids. None of Britain's other stone circles have such large stones, or the lintels along the top.

Below: The Uffington White Horse is the largest chalk-etched horse known, and is thought to date back some 3,000 years.

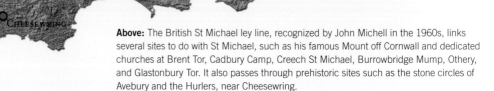

Above: The British St Michael ley line, recognized by John Michell in the 1960s, links several sites to do with St Michael, such as his famous Mount off Cornwall and dedicated churches at Brent Tor, Cadbury Camp, Creech St Michael, Burrowbridge Mump, Othery, and Glastonbury Tor. It also passes through prehistoric sites such as the stone circles of Avebury and the Hurlers, near Cheesewring.

SEEKING BUDDHA
Nepal and the Himalayas

Prince Siddhartha Gautama, born around 623 BC, was brought up by his father, King Suddhodana, to see only luxury and happiness. When he came across sickness and poverty he was appalled by the shallowness of his life, and renounced his riches to go and seek *nirvana* (enlightenment). After seven years of learning, asceticism, and meditation he discovered the "Middle Way" and became Lord Buddha. He spent the remaining 45 years of his life wandering the Gangetic Plains teaching the Four Noble Truths and the Noble Eightfold Path of Buddhism. His disciples heard him tell of pilgrimage to "The Four Great Wonders," and two centuries later, after Emperor Ashoka converted to Buddhism, pilgrims began to come from across Asia to the holy sites of the spreading faith.

Finding nirvana

Start by visiting Prince Siddhartha's birthplace, Lumbini, in southern Nepal, where the sacred garden contains a stone slab marking the exact spot of his birth and Ashoka's pillar, erected in 300 BC. Bodhgaya is where the prince found enlightenment after meditating for 49 days under the bodhi tree, and where Ashoka built a shrine, to be replaced later by the Mahabodhi Temple. The large Buddha inside could be as much as 1700 years old, and there is a project to build the world's biggest Buddha here—a 490 ft (150 m) statue—as a symbol of world peace. The Buddha gave his first sermon in Sarnath, now the site of the Damekh Stupa that dates from around 500 AD. The Mukatanabandhana Stupa and the reclining red Buddha in Kushinagar mark where he "entered parinirvana" at the age of 80.

Above: When tempted by Mara, Buddha pointed downwards and called forth the Earth Goddess, who sent a flood to drown Mara and his demons, symbolizing the triumph of good over evil.

Right: Lumbini is in the foothills of the Himalayas. It is here that the founder of Buddhism was born, and so it is one of the sacred places to visit. It was named as a UNESCO World Heritage Site in 1997.

"It is better to conquer yourself than to win a thousand battles. Then the victory is yours."
Buddha

TO BENARES
On the banks of the Ganges

Varanasi—or Benares as it used to be known—is the 3,000-year-old holy city of Hindus (or 5,000 years according to some legends) on the banks of the sacred Ganges. Lord Shiva is supposed to have resided there, and he is closely associated with the Ganges. Hordes of Hindu pilgrims and sadhus come here for a ritual bath in the river, performing puja (offering) to the rising sun, to wash away their sins. It is said that anyone who dies in Varanasi will be released from the cycle of reincarnation. A seat of great learning and culture, it is famous for its silks and brassware, and is also holy to Buddhists and Jains.

Left: Ghats are a special type of embankment, leading down to the riverside where people can take a holy dip. Of all India's ghats, the most spiritually important are those on the Ganges at Benares. The River Ganges is believed to flow from heaven to wash away human sins, so thousands of pilgrims gather before dawn to cleanse their souls in the first rays of sun.

Above: Venkateshwara Temple is the richest temple in the world, located in Tirumala near Chennai (Madras). It is unusual in that it allows non-Hindus into its inner sanctum. Dating from 300 AD, it is dedicated to Lord Vishnu and is visited by 60,000 pilgrims every day.

Left: An enduring image of India, little can compare with the bustle of activity at the great amphitheater of ghats on the Ganges in Benares. Holy Brahmins (or Pandas) read sacred passages aloud, and ash is dispensed to mark the pilgrims' foreheads. But around all this ritual, daily life continues: washing, bathing, playing, selling, and business. And among it all wander the holy cows of India.

The Vishwanath Temple (**left**) is hidden among the crowded lanes of Varanasi (**right**), and is one of the holiest temples for Hindus. It is supposed to be the place where Shiva established his supremacy over the other gods. Those who come here are believed to achieve liberation and happiness.

PAKISTAN

NEPAL

BHUTAN

HARIDWAR

DELHI

Ganges

PUSHKAR

ALLAHABAD

KHAJURAHO

VARANASI
(BENARES)

Ganges

BANGLADESH

ARABIAN
SEA

UJJAIN

KOLKATA
(CALCUTTA)

INDIA

NASIK

Bay of
Bengal

TIRUMALA

CHENNAI
(MADRAS)

MADURAI

SRI
LANKA

INDIAN
OCEAN

Festivals, fairs, and temples

The Hindu myth of the Churning of the Ocean is celebrated at Kumbh Mela, the largest festival on earth, which attracts millions of pilgrims every three years to one of the four locations where drops of the nectar of immortality fell: Ujjain, Nasik, Haridwar, and Allahabad. Vegan Pushkar, famous for its annual camel fair, has myriad bathing ghats around its holy lake and one of the only temples to Brahma, the divine creator. The erotic temples of Khajuraho include one to Vishnu, the last of whose incarnations was as Buddha. But the holiest city of India is Benares, with the 18th century ghats and funeral pyres on the river and Lord Shiva's Vishwanath Temple with its gold-plated dome.

"Older than history, older than tradition, older even than legend, and looks twice as old as all of them put together."
Mark Twain on Varanasi

FIND OUT MORE

Ram Charit Manas
Tulsi Das

An Introduction to Hinduism
Gavin Flood

River of Gods
Ian McDonald

A Suitable Boy
Vikram Seth

Benaras: A Mystic Love Story (Movie)

THE PATH TO ROME
To the seat of the Pope

When Pope John Paul II died in Rome in April 2005, almost four million people descended on the city for his funeral. It was the largest single gathering of pilgrims the city had ever seen, comfortably exceeding the million or so visitors the city attracts every Easter. But Rome, headquarters of the Catholic church, has been attracting pilgrims ever since the emperor Constantine declared Christianity legal in 313 AD. With the Holy Land under Muslim rule (other than the brief period of the Crusader states), Rome naturally became the focus of intense religious devotion and pilgrimages to it from all parts of Europe were commonplace throughout the Middle Ages.

A medieval backwater

Whatever the pre-eminence of Rome as the seat of the Pope and heart of Catholocism, the medieval city was otherwise squalid and small, a pestilent, ruined backwater of hardly 20,000 people. Given the damage to the standing of the papacy caused by its enforced move to Avignon in southern France in the 14th century, attracting pilgrims to such an uninviting destination became progressively harder. In 1300, in an attempt to reverse what were now several centuries of decline, Pope Boniface VIII instituted the first Jubilee or Holy Year. All pilgrims visiting the city would be granted plenary indulgences—that is, as a reward for their pilgrimage all their sins would be forgiven. It proved a striking success and an important step in the restoration not just of Rome's religious standing, but of its financial health as well. Pilgrims, no less than modern tourists, were an important source of revenue and competition to attract them could be fierce.

The Romieux

Pilgrimages could be undertaken for a variety of reasons: to discharge a religious obligation; as a penance; in the hope of a cure for the sick; or just in search of spiritual uplift. Whatever the motive, two constants dominated. There was first the journey itself. For most, it could mean months on the road, with nights often spent in the open, food hard to come by, and progress painfully slow. Footsore and hungry, the faithful—known as the *Romieux* or "Rome-seekers"—gradually converged on the city from across the continent. Second, once in Rome, the pilgrims had to visit all seven of its major pilgrimage churches. These include the four papal basilicas: St. Peter's, St. Paul's, St. John Lateran, and St. Mary Major, as well as three smaller churches, St. Lawrence, the Church of the Holy Cross and, until it was replaced by the Sanctuary of the Madonna of Divine Love in 2000, that of St. Sebastian.

Left: Pilgrims were among the great constants of medieval Europe, a familiar sight as they trudged (only the rich could afford to ride) wearily to and from their spiritual goal.

Below: St Mary Major is among the oldest churches in Rome, built around 440. Today, the immense church is encased in an 18th-century outer shell.

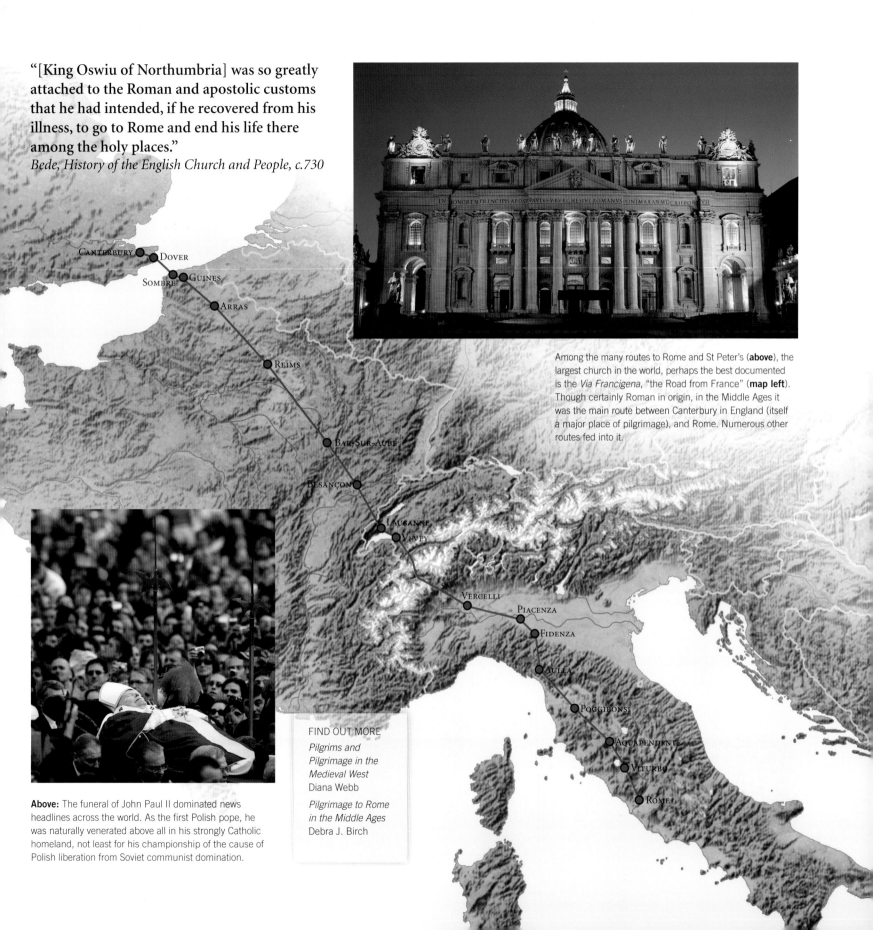

"[King Oswiu of Northumbria] was so greatly attached to the Roman and apostolic customs that he had intended, if he recovered from his illness, to go to Rome and end his life there among the holy places."

Bede, History of the English Church and People, c.730

Among the many routes to Rome and St Peter's (**above**), the largest church in the world, perhaps the best documented is the *Via Francigena*, "the Road from France" (**map left**). Though certainly Roman in origin, in the Middle Ages it was the main route between Canterbury in England (itself a major place of pilgrimage), and Rome. Numerous other routes fed into it.

Above: The funeral of John Paul II dominated news headlines across the world. As the first Polish pope, he was naturally venerated above all in his strongly Catholic homeland, not least for his championship of the cause of Polish liberation from Soviet communist domination.

FIND OUT MORE
Pilgrims and Pilgrimage in the Medieval West
Diana Webb

Pilgrimage to Rome in the Middle Ages
Debra J. Birch

Map labels: Canterbury, Dover, Sombre, Guines, Arras, Reims, Bar-Sur-Aube, Besançon, Lausanne, Vevey, Vercelli, Piacenza, Fidenza, Aulla, Poggibonsi, Aquapendente, Viturbo, Rome

THE ROAD TO LHASA
Nepal to Tibet

The 600 miles (965 km) between Kathmandu in Nepal and Lhasa, capital of Tibet, are among the most dramatic in the world, comprising a five-day journey from the lush greenery of Nepal to the vastness of the windblown Tibetan Plateau. It is a landscape of lunar-like desolation, ringed to the south by the Himalayas, studded by tiny farming communities, and all but impassable in winter when snows choke the passes. Yet this is a journey whose purpose is profoundly spiritual, and its goal is the heart of Tibetan Buddhism: Lhasa. Founded in the 7th century, Lhasa was the seat of the country's temporal and spiritual ruler, the Dalai Lama, until the Chinese invasion in 1950. The Dalai Lama's vast Potala Palace still towers over the city.

"There is an old Tibetan saying: wherever you feel at home, you are at home. If your surroundings are pleasant, you are at home."
Tenzin Gyatso, 14th Dalai Lama

Kathmandu to Lhasa

There are no less than five passes over 16,500 feet (5,030 m) high between Kathmandu and Lhasa, which at an altitude of 12,000 feet (3,657 m) is the world's highest city. The climb begins almost the moment you leave Kathmandu, following the precipitous road along the Sun Kosi River, towards the Tibetan border at Kodari. Beyond it is the 17,000-foot (5,181 m) Lalung La pass, the entrance to the Tibetan Plateau, or the "roof of the world." By day three you have reached Shigatse, Tibet's second-largest city and the site of the Lhunpo monastery, the traditional seat of the Panchen Lama who is the country's next highest-ranking official after the Dalai Lama. From Shigatse, two more days' travel takes you via Gyantse and over two more giant passes: the Karo Lo and the Kamba La, to Lhasa.

FIND OUT MORE

Tibet, Tibet: A Personal History of a Lost Land
Patrick French

The Hotel on the Roof of the World: Five years in Tibet
Alec le Seur

The Power Palaces of Central Tibet: The Pilgrim's Guide
Keith Dowman

Left: Sitting squatly on the Red Hill, and at 13 stories high, the Potala Palace dominates Lhasa. It contains more than 1,000 rooms, 10,000 shrines, and 200,000 statues. At its base, its walls are over 15-feet (4.5 m) thick. Today, it is a museum.

Right: At an altitude of over 14,000 feet (4,265 m), the Yamdrok-Tso Lake is a startling expanse of water in a bleak landscape.

THE PILGRIMS' WAY
To Canterbury cathedral

When Chaucer's pilgrims in *The Canterbury Tales* set out from London, their goal—the shrine of Thomas Becket in Canterbury cathedral—was the most important pilgrimage site in Christendom. They traveled along what today is the A2 road, an unappealing hinterland of south London that gives way to an ugly, semi-urban sprawl along which traffic thunders relentlessly. Yet there is another Pilgrims' Way—an ancient track of prehistoric origins—that runs south of London, across the North Downs between Winchester, Canterbury, and Dover. If much of this now also consists only of roads clogged with traffic, enough remains to convey a potent sense of history, and of timeless landscapes traversed by Celts, Romans, traders, and pilgrims.

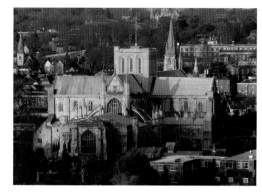

Above: Winchester Cathedral dates from 642, although the present building—entirely rebuilt and substantially extended—dates from a variety of periods in the Middle Ages, from the 11th to the 16th centuries. It has the distinction of being the longest Gothic cathedral in Europe.

"**In England, folks to Canterbury wend: To seek the blissful martye is their will.**"
Geoffrey Chaucer, The Canterbury Tales, c.1380

East from Winchester

Chaucer's pilgrims may have traveled the best known route to Canterbury, but those journeying from Winchester were following a path that was just as old. Since 1978, it has been designated the North Downs Way, leading eastward for 120 miles (193 km) from Winchester to Canterbury before looping south for a further 30 mile (48 km) stretch to Dover. Its glory is the North Downs—chalky uplands where even today you can lose yourself in ancient forests and unchanging landscapes. High ground skirts boggy valleys below it and even in winter it offers an obvious way both east and west.

Appalled by the murder of his archbishop, Henry II, barefoot and whipped by bishops, walked to the cathedral in Canterbury in an attempt to atone for his inadvertent role in the death of his stubborn cleric. Later, the traditional starting point for the pilgrimage was Southwark, its cathedral (**right**) a rare Gothic survival in London.

THE ROAD TO SANTIAGO
From France across northern Spain

Since Pope John Paul II declared 1983 a Holy Year, the Gothic cathedral of Santiago de Compostela, one of the great pilgrimage goals of the Middle Ages, has seen a significant and continuing upsurge of pilgrims. These are not mere tourists traveling by air or car, but pilgrims in the medieval sense, who undertake a long and arduous journey, most traveling on foot, some on horse back or—in a concession to modernity—on bicycles to this otherwise obscure and remote corner of northwest Spain.

Left and below: Anyone walking 60 or more miles (97 km) to Santiago, or cycling at least 120 miles (193 km), who is able to attest their journey has been for spiritual reasons, qualifies for a *Compostela*, a document issued by the diocese confirming that they are true modern pilgrims. They must first obtain a *credencial*, or pilgrim's passport, which has to be stamped en-route as evidence of having made the journey.

The burial site of St. James

It is a measure of the importance of Santiago as a place of pilgrimage that in the Middle Ages it was one of only three Christian destinations—with Rome and Jerusalem—for which pilgrimage earned pilgrims plenary indulgences, the full remission of their sins. Its fame stemmed from the fact that St. James,

the apostle, is said to have been buried here, and by the 12th century it was drawing pilgrims from across Europe, most proudly displaying the traditional emblem of St. James—a scallop shell. Just as the many roads to Santiago converge, so the grooves of the shell meet at a single point, and it's also suggestive of the setting sun towards which many of the pilgrims trudged. Those who reached Santiago would return with a shell itself—proof of the success of their journey.

On the Camino

Technically, there is no one *Camino de Santiago* or "Way of St James," as any route that leads to Santiago, from any starting point, can be a pilgrim route. In the Middle Ages there were no less than four officially recognized routes across France. Today, one trail dominates; that leading across northern Spain from the Pyrenees, and this is the route that the overwhelming majority of today's pilgrims follow. Now the "official" *Camino de Santiago* (or *Camino Francés* as it is commonly known), it leads from St-Jean-Pied-de-Port in the French Pyrenees. Starting with a dramatic and rocky descent from the Pyrenees, the route crosses the high *meseta*, or tableland, of northern Spain, before reaching the mountainous lushness of Galicia and Santiago itself, covering some 500 miles (805 km) in all. The route is exceptionally well marked, with yellow arrows and scallop shells counting off the distance. There is an abundance of places to stay, including *refugios*—hostels open only to pilgrims. Most pilgrims manage the distance in about five weeks of steady walking.

"The 'traditional ways' are those that involve making the journey by one's own motive power, implying an investment of physical effort or sacrifice, an element of physical vulnerability, and a frame of mind that is open to encounter."
Laurie Dennett, former chairman, the Confraternity of St James

Left and right: June to September, remains the popular time to make the pilgrimage to Santiago, but the determined will make the journey even in winter, when snow in the Pyrenees is almost certain. The mountains themselves, however spectacularly beautiful, present a formidable hurdle.

FIND OUT MORE

A Pilgrim's Guide to the Camino de Santiago
John Brierly

Walking the Camino de Santiago
Benjamin Cole and Bethan Davies

Website of the Confraternity of St James:
www.csj.org.uk

127

The brutal realities of conflict and conquest may sometimes have produced remarkable journeys, but in general, they generated only suffering and destruction. That the imperatives of war have led armies, whether bent on subjection or liberation, to foreign fields is a constant of human history. Glorious or sordid, these are stories always worth pursuing.

THE SCENT OF WAR
Classic campaigns and battlefield tours

More Americans—60,000—were killed in the three days of Gettysburg in July 1863, the climatic battle of the American Civil War, than in the whole of the Vietnam War. It was a profoundly traumatic moment in America's story, with Robert E. Lee's Army of Northern Virginia confronted by the inescapable realities of the North's vastly superior resources.

The First World War eclipsed even this slaughter, industrial warfare mocking not just notions of gallantry, but delivering death on a hitherto unimaginable scale. Comparable levels of casualties were produced by the Allied invasion of

Normandy in June 1944, as well as the infinitely more attritional Allied campaign in Italy after 1943—a conflict in which advances were measured in yards.

The contrast with Napoleon 140 years earlier is striking. His were campaigns that ranged from Spain to Russia, in which maximum force was brilliantly brought to bear, so that victories seemed inevitable. His final defeat at Waterloo was by no more than the slimmest of margins.

Medieval warfare in Europe was vastly more ponderous, with tiny armies, almost always plagued by disease, in search of elusive enemies. As a result, the great Anglo-French conflict of the 14th and 15th centuries took almost 120 years to reach its final resolution, while the Reconquista—the Christian re-conquest of Muslim Spain—lasted almost 800 years, resulting in the slow extinction of one of the medieval world's most brilliant cultures. By contrast, Caesar's conquests of Gaul, relentless and implacable, were not merely swift, but overwhelming, as an entire people were brought under an iron rule. Yet as America's ultimate defeat in Vietnam makes clear, overwhelming force is no guarantee of victory.

The Great Wall of China
Defending the state

Snaking over 4,000 miles (6,435 km), the Great Wall of China constitutes perhaps the most remarkable achievement of any Ancient World civilization. Built between 220 BC and 200 BC, partly on the course of a number of earlier walls, it was not just an emphatic statement of China's organizational might, but an overwhelming assertion of its self-belief. Since the emergence of the first Chinese state around 1800 BC, the Chinese never doubted their superiority. If the barbarian nomads who periodically thundered in on their ponies from the wastes of Mongolia could not be contained by force, they could nonetheless be cowed by a structure so vast as to dwarf efforts to overthrow it.

Above: An estimated one million Chinese worked on the Wall over the centuries; peasants, soldiers, and slaves alike. It is impossible to guess the numbers killed during its construction, although 400,000 has been suggested.

The modern wall

Almost none of the original wall remains—the Great Wall as it stands today was built during a vast 200-year construction programme during the Ming dynasty (1368–1644). It followed a new course along the southern border of Mongolia, and was studded with forts and watchtowers along its length. It stood on average 25 feet (7.5 m) high and 18 feet (5.5 m) wide. Its mountainous eastern lengths were built mostly of brick and stone, while its western, desert-like lengths of clay and earth were often reinforced with wood. Little but rubble now remains of the last 300 miles (483 km) of the wall to the west, and the best estimates suggest that about half the Great Wall has disappeared entirely, much in the 20th century as the result of neglect, war and, on occasion, official policy. It is the remaining sections to the east, close to Beijing, that are the best preserved and visited today.

Great Wall (predominately Ming Dynasty build shown)

MONGOLIA

INNER MONGOLIA

Yellow

Jiayu Pass JIAYUGUAN

YINCHUAN

NINGXIA

SHAANXI

XINING

LANZHOU

GANSU

CHINA

Left: Conflict between the Chinese and their nomad Mongol neighbors to the north was endemic. Although the Wall's purpose was clearly defensive, its length made it impossible even for as populous a state as China to man in strength. It could be—and was—breached by enemies mustered in sufficient numbers.

"...to the ancient Chinese rulers, frontiers were the creation of Heaven, not of man... It was only when rude nomads refused to recognize such a profound concept that it was felt necessary to add to Heaven's gift."
The Great Wall of China, Steve Turnball, 2007

Visiting the Wall

The four best-known sections of the Wall are readily accessible from Beijing. May and October are the best months to visit, as crowds are relatively thin and the weather warm.

Badaling: Located 40 miles northwest of Beijing, Badaling is by some way the most well-known and popular stretch of The Great Wall, but complaints about over-commercialization and serious overcrowding are rife. The Wall here is 2.3 miles (3.7 km) long, at an altitude of 3,280 feet (1,000 m).

Mutianyu: There are only 1.4 miles (2.25 km) of wall but it snakes spectacularly over the mountains, making this relatively unvisited stretch many people's favorite.

Simatai: A 12 mile (19 km), unrestored stretch of the Great Wall, located 80 miles (129 km) northeast of Beijing. Some parts are hard to explore, but the location is remarkable.

Jinshanling: A near 7 mile (11 km) stretch, at an altitude of 2,300 feet (700 m), Beijing is just visible on clear days, and this is among the least-visited of the major stretches of wall.

Above: It was only in the 1980s that the Chinese government made serious efforts to preserve the remaining sections of the wall. This was partly recognition that, as a tourist attraction, the Wall was a key source of revenue, and partly that it was a structure of global importance. As late as the 1960s, Mao had urged the Chinese to carry off stone from the Wall for new buildings, claiming they should "Allow the past to serve the present."

FIND OUT MORE

First Pass Under Heaven: One Man's 4,000 Kilometer Trek Along the Great Wall of China
Nathan Gray

The Great Wall: From Beginning to End
Michael Yamashita and William Lindesay

The Great Wall: China Against the World
Julia Lovell

Alone on the Great Wall
William Lindesay

Left and right: There has been a persistent belief that the Great Wall of China is the only man-made object visible from space. However appealing the idea, it is quite untrue. Despite its length, the width and coloring of the Wall—essentially that of the surrounding soil and rock—make it no easier to see than a road.

Julius Caesar
Through Gaul and Britain

In 58 BC Julius Caesar ended his consulship in Rome. To advance his career, pay off debts, and secure the Rhine border for Rome, he started waging military campaigns throughout Gaul; subjugating the rebellious southern Helvetii tribes, and defeating German mercenaries at Vosges. In 57 BC he conquered northern Belgae (modern Belgium), before putting down the Veneti tribe in Armorica (modern Brittany). Seemingly unstoppable, Caesar's Gallic Wars saw him rampage across Gaul, subduing the Eburoni, Belgae, Nervii, Menapii, and Treveri tribes. Gallic resistance solidified under the Arverni warrior, Vercingetorix, but he was soundly defeated by Caesar at the Battle of Alésia. This destroyed the Gallic resistance, allowing Caesar to secure many of Gaul's remaining territories in 51–50 BC.

Into Britain

Although Caesar was largely triumphant in continental Europe, his journeys to Britain were less successful. In July 55 BC, he invaded Britain with two legions on the slim basis that it held quantities of silver and tin. He was met at Dover by blue-painted, heavily bearded warriors, and massed chariots. At first daunted, Caesar's men fought some skirmishes, but a tribal revolt by the Belgae meant they had to return to Gaul. The withdrawal was only temporary, and in the summer of 54 BC, Caesar returned to Britain with a larger force of five legions. He pushed across the Thames, securing tribute from the Catuvellauni before he was required back in Gaul—the harvest had failed and the Belgae were again stoking revolt. Fearing being stranded in Britain during the winter, Caesar sailed back to Gaul once more, the island unconquered, and his British expeditions little more than propaganda victories.

Left: Shortly after taking Bourges in 52 BC, Caesar successfully besieged the hilltop town of Alesia, which was being held by a confederation of Gallic tribes under Vercingetorix. At one point Gauls outnumbered Romans five to one, but the battle decimated the remaining Gallic resistance to Rome.

Left: In 52 BC, Caesar took the strategically vital Gallic stronghold of Bourges (Avaricum) from Vercingetorix, leader of the Averni. In Caesar's own words, this was "perhaps the most beautiful town in the whole of Gaul."

Left: In order to prevent Germanic tribes from crossing the Rhine River into Gaul, Caesar had two bridges built, and crossed over into Germany. Nearly all the Germanic tribes sued for peace, and Caesar spent just 18 days in Germany before returning to Gaul and destroying his bridges behind him.

THE ANGEVIN EMPIRE
The 100 Years' War

When King Henry II, king of England from 1154, was on the throne, he ruled over the largest empire in western Europe—the Angevin Empire—which extended over England, much of Ireland, and the whole of western France, from the Channel to the Pyrenees. However, by 1216 almost all the French lands had been lost. No systematic attempt was made to win them back until, in 1337, Edward III declared himself heir to the throne of France and began what became known as the 100 Years' War. The war saw enormous English gains, although these were lost almost as quickly as they had been won.

Above: Less than 6,000 English and Welsh soldiers faced 36,000 Frenchmen at Agincourt. The longbow won the day for Henry V, scything down the French knights who found their armor handicapping, rather than protecting them.

A century of war

Between 1339 and 1346 Edward III led five major campaigns through northern and eastern France, his armies enjoying near-continuous success, and their hit-and-run techniques more than a match for the much larger and more ponderous French forces. Crécy in 1346 was the highpoint—a dazzling display of English arms, and the first demonstration of the lethal effectiveness of the longbow. This was followed 10 years later by a crushing English victory, from Edward's son—known as the Black Prince—who routed the French at Poitiers. Yet for all these startling successes, the war was intermittent, and lapsed into an uneasy standoff until, in 1415, Henry V—now King—took to the field once more. His victory at Agincourt saw 6,000 French troops dead to only 400 English, and with the whole of northern France now in English hands it looked like there was the prospect of total victory. However, Henry's early death in 1422 coincided with a French revival. Even the capture of Joan of Arc, in 1430, could not halt the gathering pace of French military success. 116 years of warfare ended in 1453 with the absolute defeat of the English.

FIND OUT MORE

The Archer's Tale
Bernard Cornwell

The 100 Years' War
Robin Neillands

The 100 Years' War
Anne Curay

> "With a firing rate of around 1–2 shots every two minutes, they [the French crossbowmen] were no match for the longbowmen, who could fire one shot every five seconds."
> *Froissart's Chronicle. Book 1, 1377, on the battle of Crécy*

ENGLAND

ENGLISH CHANNEL

BRUGES
GHENT
CALAIS
AMIENS
ROUEN
NORMANDY
PARIS
DEPENDENCIES
OF THE
FRENCH
KING
RENNES
MAINE
ORLEANS
BRITTANY
LE MANS
ANGERS
TOURS
NANTES
ANJOU
TOURAINE
DIJON
POITOU
POITIERS
LA MARCHE
ANGOULEME
LIMOGES
CLERMONT
ANGOULEME
LIMOGES
AUVERGNE
PERIGORD
BORDEAUX
SAINTOGNE
COUNTY
OF
TOULOUSE
NIMES
GASCOGNE
AUCHE
TOULOUSE
TARBES

The Reconquista
The reconquest of Muslim Spain

By 716 Spain had fallen victim to a lightning Muslim conquest, part of the blaze of Muslim expansion after 632 that saw Islam surge from its Arabian heartlands to India in the east and Spain in the west. The upsurge of Christian arms that drove the Crusades after 1096 made the reconquest—the *reconquista*—of Spain an urgent Christian necessity. Between about 1000 and 1492, the distinctive Muslim civilization of Spain, tolerant, technically advanced, and intensely cultivated, was gradually driven back until, in 1492, it was finally extinguished. Yet in southern Spain in particular, the impact of almost 800 years of Muslim rule are still obvious.

Muslim expulsion

The reconquista can be said to have begun with the victory of a Visigothic Christian army over the Muslims at Covadonga in northwest Spain in 722, but it would not be until the Caliphate of Cordoba began to splinter after the death of its ruler, al-Mansur, in 1002, that sustained Christian expansion seemed likely.

Within 100 years, Muslim rule was restricted to little more than the southern third of Iberia. Cordoba itself fell in 1235, and Seville in 1248, reducing Muslim rule to Granada, a rump state clinging precariously to the Mediterranean coast.

Anyone visiting the great cities of Muslim Spain—Seville, Granada, Toledo, Cordoba—is made aware of the sophistication and technical accomplishment that underpinned Moorish rule. At the time, these were cities without parallel in a Europe still fitfully emerging from the obscurities of the Dark Ages. For example, The Alhambra in Granada (**above**) is a fantastical palace, with breathtaking, lace-like arches. The Giralda in Seville (**left**) is no less remarkable, but it precisely underscores the reality of Christian victory. On the orders of the Christian conquerors of Spain, Ferdinand and Isabella (**below**), what was originally one of the largest mosques in the Muslim realm became one of Europe's largest cathedrals.

The culture of Islam

There were various centers of Muslim learning across al-Andalus, as the country was known; however none rivalled Cordoba on the banks of the Guadalquivir in southern Spain. With a population approaching 500,000, in the 10th century it was by some measure the largest city in Europe, with 700 mosques and 70 libraries, the largest containing 600,000 books. And it was a mosque—the Mezquita—that was at the heart of the city. Extensively rebuilt and enlarged in the 10th century, it was the second largest in the Muslim world, its echoing roofs carried on 1,000 columns supporting remarkable striped and banded double-arches. It was in Cordoba that the scholar and polymath Averroes was born, in 1126. He was responsible for the recording and transmission of an immense amount of ancient learning. Much of what is known of Aristotle, for example, was due to him. An almost exact contemporary was a Jewish philosopher, Maimonides, as much a polymath as Averroes, and as interested in astronomy as in mathematics, in engineering as in methods of agriculture.

"5,954 years have now passed from the beginning of the world to the era 792 which has now begun, the tenth year of the emperor Constantine, the fourth of the Abd Allah, the Amir Almuminim, the seventh of Yusuf in the land of Spain, and the one hundred and thirty-sixth of the Arabs."
Islamic Chronicle of 754 (written in Spain)

Extent of Muslim held lands circa 790

Extent of Muslim held lands circa 1300

Bay of Biscay

TOULOUSE

GIJÓN

OVIEDO

NARBONNE

SANTIAGO DE COMPOSTELA

PAMPLONA

GERONA

COVADONGA

LÉON

KINGDOM OF ASTURIAS

Ebro

ZAMORA

Duero

SARAGOSSA

BARCELONA

OPPORTO

TARRAGONA

SALAMANCA

GUADALAJARA

COIMBRA

Tagus

TOLEDO

VALENCIA

Balearic Islands

LISBON

BADAJOZ

Guadiana

EVORA

ALICANTE

FIND OUT MORE

Reconquest and Crusade in Medieval Spain
Joseph F. O'Callaghan

Moorish Spain
R.A. Fletcher

The Spanish and Portuguese Reconquest, 1095–1492
Charles Julian Bishko

CÓRDOBA

Guadalquivir

SEVILLE

GRANADA

ALMERIA

MÁLAGA

ATLANTIC OCEAN

JABAL TARIQ (GIBRALTAR)

MEDITERRANEAN SEA

NAPOLEON'S BATTLES
A Journey through the Heart of Europe

Born in Corsica in 1769, Napoleon was a General during the French Revolution of 1788-1799, but it was his later conquests on the battlefields of Europe that history remembers best. Like Caesar before him, Napoleon's objectives were both grand in scale and brilliant in their execution, as he set out to expand his empire across the continent—from France in the west, to the Russian frontier in the east. Covering a distance of over 1,000 miles (1,600 km) Napoleon's progress was a display of military might and prowess on an epic scale, which saw entire nations bow before the Emperor and his armies.

The Rise to Power

During 1796–97 Napoleon (**center left**) fought battles in northern Italy, gaining a reputation as a tactical genius who inspired immense loyalty in his troops. He drove the Austrian Army out of Lombardy, routed the army of the Papal States, and led his armies into Austria in early 1797, forcing it to sign the Treaty of Campo Formio in October, and giving him control of northern Italy.

Hoping to destabilize British influence, and bolster French trade, he waged an Egyptian campaign in 1798–99, but after Horatio Nelson defeated his fleet at the Nile in 1798 he had to attend to French reverses in Europe, where Austria had reclaimed Italy.

Following a coup d'état in 1799—when he installed himself as First Consul—he returned to Italy in 1800, routing the Austrians at Marengo (1800), before solidifying his gains with a Concordat with Rome (1801), and the Peace of Amiens with Britain (1802).

However, the peace did not stand for long. What were to be later known as the "Napoleonic Wars" commenced around 1803, with Napoleon proclaiming himself Emperor the following year and setting out to expand his empire.

Above: Arthur Wellesley (1769–1852) was made Duke of Wellington after his triumphs over Napoleon's armies in Portugal and Spain during the Peninsular War. He also commanded British, German, and Dutch forces in his victory over Napoleon at the Battle of Waterloo.

Above: Horatio Nelson (1758–1805) was made a viscount after winning the Battle of Copenhagen in 1801. On board HMS Victory, he joined the blockade of Toulon, but the French escaped in 1805. The ensuing chase culminated in Nelson's triumph—and death—at the Battle of Trafalgar.

NORTH SEA

WATERLOO

Rhine

PARIS

Above: The Arc de Triomphe was commissioned by Napoleon between 1806 and 1808 to be a triumphal arch commemorating France's military victories in 1805. Its model was the Arch of Septimius Severus in Rome.

Right: The Battle of Waterloo was fought on 18 June 1815. Blücher's Prussian troops arrived at the battle's climax to lend vital support to the Duke of Wellington's forces. The battle was especially significant as it effectively ended the Napoleonic Wars.

BALTIC SEA

FRIEDLAND

EYLAU

Vistula

BERLIN

Warta

Oder

Elbe

AUERSTÄDT

JENA

Left: The city of Jena sits on the Saale River in central Germany. Dating back to the 12th century it is now a thriving center of industry, but during the Napoleonic Wars set the scene for one of Napoleon's earliest Fourth Coalition battles, when he crushed Prussian forces on the way to Berlin.

The Fourth Coalition

It was during the Fourth Coalition that Napoleon made some of his most dramatic gains, and delivered some of his most devastating victories. One of his earliest triumphs came in Jena, Germany, on October 14, 1806, where he personally took to the field against the Prussians, crushing their forces and opening the road to Berlin, capturing the city on October 25.

Napoleon continued east, pursuing a retreating Russian army and meeting little resistance as he crossed into Poland. The Russian retreat stopped on the snowy plains at Eylau, in February, 1807, in what was to become one of the bloodiest battles of the war. Historians estimate that between 25,000—50,000 men were killed or maimed at Eylau, but despite a Russian retreat, neither side could claim victory.

However, four months later, at the Battle of Friedland, the result was far more decisive, with Napoleon's troops crushing the Russian army and forcing the Tzar of Russia into a reluctant alliance at the Treaty of Tilsit (1807). In a year, Napoleon had humiliated both Russia and Prussia, with only Britain continuing to defy France.

HADRIAN'S WALL
Britain's dividing line

Today, 1,900 years after it was built, Hadrian's Wall remains an audacious monument to Roman military and administrative might, and a stern reminder of the reach of one of the greatest of the ancient world's empires. It was built on the orders of the Emperor Hadrian from AD 122 and was largely complete about seven years later. It is 73.5 miles (118 km) long and once formed a continuous and precise northern demarcation of Roman Britannia, from the Solway Firth in the west, to Wallsend in the east. The wall was not purely defensive though, as it was intended to regulate the movements of the native Britons on both sides "to separate the barbarians from the Romans."

"And so, having reformed the army quite in the manner of a monarch, he [Hadrian] set out for Britain, and there he corrected many abuses and was the first to construct a wall, eighty miles in length, which was to separate the barbarians from the Romans."
Historia Augusta

Route of wall
Standing section

BELLINGHAM

Chesters (Cilurnum) · Carrawburgh (Brocolitia) · Rudchester (Vindobala) · Wallsend (Segedunum) · TYNEMOUTH

Housesteads (Vercovicium) · Great Chesters (Aesica) · Birdoswald (Banna) · Haltonchesters (Onnum) · SOUTH SHIELDS

Carvoran (Magnis) · Chesterholm (Vindolanda) · HAYDON BRIDGE · Benwell (Condercum) · Newcastle (Pons Aelius)

Bowness-on-Solway (Maia) · Burgh by Sands (Aballava) · Castlesteads (Camboglanna) · HEXHAM · Tyne

Solway Firth · Drumburgh (Concavata) · Stanwix (Uxelodunum) · CARLISLE

Forts and Milecastles

Though plundered for centuries after the Romans left Britain in 410, with stones still being carried off for use as late as the early 20th century, significant sections of the wall remain, particularly along the central stretch. None is now higher than about 10 feet (3 m), whereas the original averaged about 15 feet (4.5 m), with parapets extending upwards a further 5 feet (1.5 m). Eighty milecastles, one every Roman mile, each housing a few dozen troops, were also built, as were smaller turrets, manned by just a handful of men, at regular intervals between them. Deep ditches were dug on both sides of the wall, clear evidence that the continued subjection of the tribes to the south remained as much a priority for the Romans as repulsing the Caledonians to the north. A series of substantial forts, perhaps as many as 17, were added some years after the main body of the wall had been completed.

Above: Hadrian's Wall was more than an attempt to fix the northern limits of Rome's rule in Britain: it was part of an initiative to rationalize the empire's borders (**above right**), which Hadrian felt had become unmanageably large.

Left: Housesteads Fort is the best-preserved Roman fort in Britain. The Romans called it *Vercovicium*, which translates as "The Place of the Fighters."

FIND OUT MORE
A Walk Along the Wall
Hunter Davies

Hadrian's Wall Path
Anthony Burton

hadrians-wall.org

nationaltrail.co.uk

ALONG THE FOSSE WAY
Following Roman footsteps

The Fosse Way was the first great Roman Road in Britain, constructed in the 1st century AD and for several decades marking the western boundary of the Roman empire. Its name comes from *fossa* meaning "ditch," but it is not known whether the ditch was filled in to make the road, or whether the Romans built the road alongside the ditch. It runs from Exeter to Lincoln, both important Roman trading settlements that now boast two of England's finest medieval cathedrals. Nowadays a mix of bridle path, country lane, and busy highway, its near-straight route can easily be divined on a modern road atlas.

> "... the whole sweep of country to the south was safe in our hands. The enemy had been pushed into what was virtually another island."
> *Tacitus in Agricola*

Above: Chesterton Windmill, built in 1632, is a striking landmark on the Fosse Way near Warwick. It was possibly designed by John Stone, pupil of Inigo Jones.

Below: Lincoln Cathedral was the tallest building in the world from 1300 until 1549 when the 525 ft (160 m) spire collapsed. It was nearly twice as tall as it is today.

Left: Chedworth is one of the largest Roman villas in Britain, accidentally rediscovered in 1864 when a gamekeeper was digging for a ferret and found pieces of pottery and paving on a bank of soil. Originally, 11 of its main rooms were decorated with mosaics, although only five of these remain today. In more recent years, hypostyle underfloor heating systems, baths, and a sauna have also been unearthed.

Lincoln to Exeter

The Bishop of Lincoln was a signatory of the Magna Carta, and one of the four original copies is kept in the city's castle. Leicester has Roman remains at Jewry Wall, while placenames further on, like Stretton-under-Fosse, are a reminder of the road's former importance. In Roman times, Cirencester was second only to London, and traces of an amphitheatre can still be seen. Bath's Roman baths saw their glory days restored in the 18th century, as the city turned into a center of fashionable life, much associated with England's best-loved author, Jane Austen. Finally pass through the pretty village of Ilchester and the carpet-making town of Axminster before reaching Exeter.

LINCOLN (LINDUM)

LEICESTER (RATAE DUBUNNORUM)

HIGH CROSS (VENONIS)

COTSWOLD HILLS

GLOUCESTER (GLEVUM)

MORETON-IN-MARSH

Chedworth Villa

CIRENCESTER (CORINIUM)

BATH (AQUAE SULIS)

SHEPTON MALLET

Bristol Channel

EXMOOR

ILCHESTER (LINDINIS)

AXMINSTER

EXETER (ISCA DUMNONIORUM)

Ruin

SIMÓN BOLÍVAR
Through Latin America

The freeing of Central and South America from three centuries of colonial rule, by Portugal in Brazil, and by Spain across most of the rest of the continent, was an epic undertaking, comparable to the ending of British colonial rule in North America. With the exception of Brazil, it was a protracted, brutal struggle that lasted 20 years or more and saw a series of major set-piece battles, frequent reversals of fortune, and acts of great daring and heroism. Its leading figure was Simón Bolívar— *El Liberator*—high-born (and even more high-minded) and directly responsible for the liberation of six countries—Panama, Colombia, Ecuador, Peru, Venezuela, and Bolivia.

Champion of South America

Bolívar was very precisely a product of his period and class, born in Venezuela in 1783 in what was then the Viceroyalty of New Grenada, one of three such colonies across the Americas directly ruled from Spain. Quite apart from the obvious example of the newly independent Unites States, the more recent revolution in France provided a direct stimulus to those in South America who increasingly saw Spain's rule as tyrannical and an obvious denial of liberty to the peoples of South America, whether natives

or, like Bolívar, of Spanish origin but still excluded from a government reserved exclusively for Spaniards born in Spain. Visits to Europe in 1799 and 1804 exposed Bolivar to Enlightenment writers—Voltaire and Locke above all—and as his political philosophy developed, it became clear he was no democrat. He believed that new states with no history of self-government needed strong leaders, a role he naturally saw himself occupying. Yet as a champion of South American liberty and independence, Bolívar has no peer.

El Liberator

The decisive moment in the struggle for independence came in August 1819 at the Battle of Boyacá in Colombia. It followed a daring march by Bolívar's tiny army, only 2,500 strong, westward across the Andes to Colombia. Here he surprised a royalist army, complacently thinking itself impregnable to attack from the east. It was a stunning feat of arms that reversed the repeated defeats that characterized the first years of the campaign against Spain, and in a typically bold gesture, Bolívar had already pronounced the existence of the Republic of Gran Colombia the previous February, a state that spanned modern-day Venezuela, Panama, Colombia, and Ecuador. The last royalist troops would not be driven from Ecuador until 1822, but the pro-independence tide had clearly turned in Bolívar's favour. Over the following two years, Bolívar secured the independence of Peru, with "Upper Peru" declared the independent state of Bolivia in honor of *El Liberator* in August 1825.

Bolívar may have posed as a national "liberator;" a "New World" Napoleon determined to drive through a startling popular nationalism, but he was always confronted by the reality of harsh landscapes (**left and below**) and inadequate forces. His eventual triumph was a spectacular vindication of goals that, measured rationally, should surely have been unobtainable.

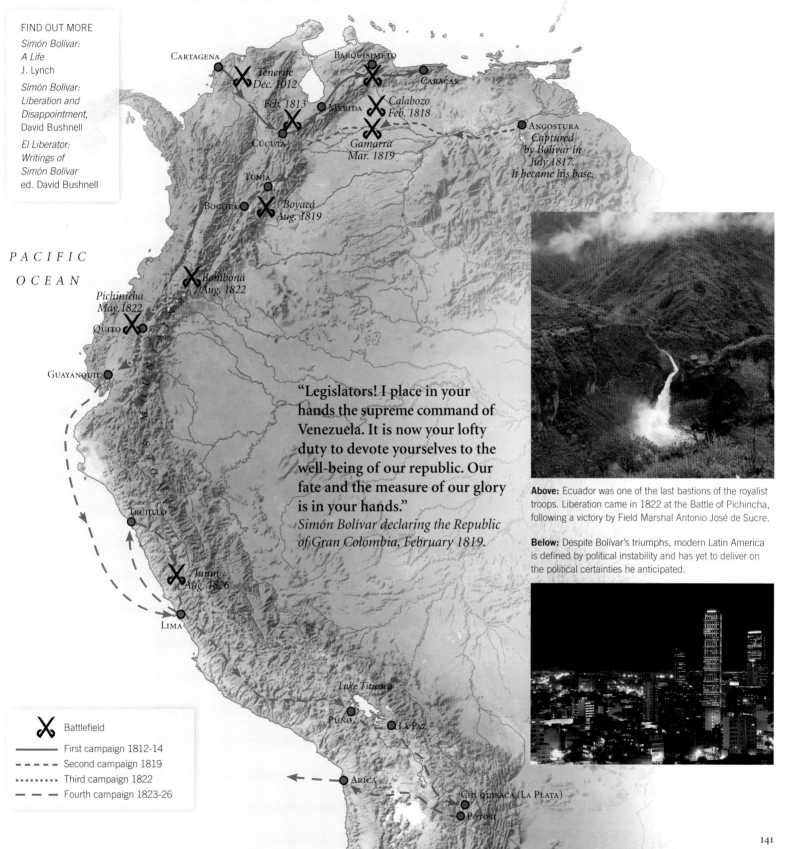

CARIBBEAN SEA

FIND OUT MORE
*Simón Bolívar:
A Life*
J. Lynch

*Simón Bolívar:
Liberation and
Disappointment,*
David Bushnell

*El Liberator:
Writings of
Simón Bolívar*
ed. David Bushnell

PACIFIC

OCEAN

CARTAGENA

*Tenerife
Dec. 1012*

Feb. 1813

CÚCUTA

MÉRIDA

BARQUISIMETO

CARACAS

*Calabozo
Feb. 1818*

*Gamarra
Mar. 1819*

ANGOSTURA
*Captured
by Bolívar in
July 1817.
It became his base.*

TUNJA

BOGOTÁ

*Boyacá
Aug. 1819*

*Bomboná
Aug. 1822*

*Pichincha
May 1822*

QUITO

GUAYANQUIL

A N D E S   M O U N T A I N S

"Legislators! I place in your
hands the supreme command of
Venezuela. It is now your lofty
duty to devote yourselves to the
well-being of our republic. Our
fate and the measure of our glory
is in your hands."
*Simón Bolívar declaring the Republic
of Gran Colombia, February 1819.*

TRUJILLO

*Junín
Aug. 1826*

LIMA

Lake Titicaca

PUNO

LA PAZ

Above: Ecuador was one of the last bastions of the royalist
troops. Liberation came in 1822 at the Battle of Pichincha,
following a victory by Field Marshal Antonio José de Sucre.

Below: Despite Bolívar's triumphs, modern Latin America
is defined by political instability and has yet to deliver on
the political certainties he anticipated.

✗ Battlefield

——— First campaign 1812-14
- - - - Second campaign 1819
········· Third campaign 1822
— — — Fourth campaign 1823-26

ARICA

CHUQUISACA (LA PLATA)

POTOSÍ

AMERICAN CIVIL WAR BATTLEFIELDS
North against South, 1861–1865

On 12 April, 1861, Confederate artillery opened fire on the Union garrison of Fort Sumter, South Carolina, in what was to become the opening engagement of the American Civil War. The war continued for almost four years, with Union generals attempting to capture the Confederate capital in Richmond, Virginia, while the Confederates took the war north to Maryland, Pennsylvania, and even Washington D.C.

Key western battlefields, 1861–63

Hatteras Inlet and Port Royal Sound, North and South Carolina, August 27–29, November 7, 1861:
Union forces employ superior naval power to seize forts and blockade Southern ships.

Forts Henry and Donelson Campaign, Tennessee, February 6–16, 1862:
Ulysses S. Grant wins Union victories by seizing control of the Tennessee and Cumberland rivers.

Shiloh, Tennessee, April 6–7, 1862:
Albert Johnston and Pierre Beauregard's Confederate army attacks Grant's unprepared troops at Shiloh on the Tennessee river, but Grant prevails.

Stones River, Tennessee, December 31, 1862:
Confederates under Braxton Bragg are narrowly defeated by Union troops under William Rosecrans.

Vicksburg, May 19–July 4, 1863:
The last Confederate stronghold on the Mississippi surrenders to Grant after a six-week siege. This was a key turning point in the war, as it split the Confederacy in two.

Chickamauga, Georgia, 18–20 September, 1863:
In one clear Confederate victory in the West, Bragg defeats Rosecrans' Union troops.

Chattanooga, Tennessee, November 23–25, 1863:
Bragg is defeated, forcing Confederate forces out of Tennessee and opening a Union route to Atlanta, Georgia.

Above: The former Confederate capital of Richmond, Virginia, lies almost 100 miles (160 km) south of Washington D.C., on the banks of the James River. In 1865, retreating Confederate soldiers set fire to the city, destroying roughly a quarter of its buildings.

The final year, 1864–65

On March 9, 1864, President Lincoln appointed Ulysses S. Grant commander of all Union armies. Grant engaged Lee's Confederate forces in the east at Wilderness (May 5–6), Spotsylvania (May 8–21), and Cold Harbor (June 1–12), before pinning

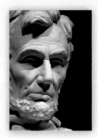

him down in the Siege of Petersburg. Lee broke the siege in 1865, but was forced to evacuate the city. Richmond was evacuated the same day, and on April 9, 1865, Lee surrendered the east.

In the west, Sherman's Union forces faced Confederates under Joe Johnston and John Hood, meeting at Resaca (May 13–15), Kennesaw Mountain (June 27), and Atlanta (July 22) in 1834. Hood was crushed at Franklin (November 30) and Nashville (December 15-16), and in early 1865, Johnston was defeated at Bentonville (March 19–21), surrendering the west on April 26.

KENTUCKY

Fort Henry
Fort Donelson
Nashville
NASHVILLE
Franklin
Stones River
TENNESSEE

Shiloh

Chattanooga

Chickamauga

Resaca

Kennesaw Mountain

Atlanta

MISSISSIPPI
ALABAMA
GEORGIA

Vicksburg

Left: This photograph by Timothy O'Sullivan, *The Harvest of Death, Gettysburg, Pennsylvania*, taken in July 1863, was described by the publisher of Gardner's *Photographic Sketchbook of the Civil War* as showing "...the blank horror and reality of war, in opposition to the pageantry."

Key eastern battlefields, 1861–63

First Manassas (First Bull Run), Northern Virginia, July 21, 1861:
A weak Union Army is defeated, partly due to Confederate General Thomas Jonathan "Stonewall" Jackson.

Ball's Bluff, Virginia, October 21, 1861:
Confederates defeat the small Union force of George McClellan.

Seven Pines, Central Virginia, May 31–June 1, 1862:
McClellan attacks Joe Johnston's Confederates at Seven Pines. There are many casualties, Johnston is badly wounded, but the result is inconclusive.

Seven Days' Battles, Richmond, Virginia, June 25–July 1, 1862:
Robert E. Lee takes over command of the Confederate Army from Johnston to defend Richmond. He outmaneuvers McClellan, who withdraws to Washington.

Second Manassas (Second Bull Run), Northern Virginia, August 29–30, 1862:
Lee's Confederates drive Union forces back to Washington. In two months Lee has transferred the war from Richmond to Washington.

Antietam (Sharpsburg), Washington County, September 16–18, 1862:
McClellan's troops pierce the Confederate center, but he is too cautious. Vastly outnumbered, Lee fights to a standstill then withdraws, inconclusively.

Fredericksburg I, Northern Virginia, December 13, 1862:
Lee's forces, in fourteen frontal assaults, massacre Burnside's Union army.

Gettysburg, Pennsylvania, July 1–3, 1863:
Lee's "Pickett's Charge" pierces George Meade's Union line, but is repulsed. Lee withdraws to Virginia, ending hopes of pressuring Washington.

Bristoe Station, October 14, 1863:
After several months recuperating in Virginia, Lee is defeated again by Meade.

✕ Battlefield

BATTLEFIELDS OF THE WESTERN FRONT
A poignant tour from World War I

The statistics are starkly sobering. 1.4 million French dead, 1.9 million German dead, 700,000 British dead—to say nothing of the 1.7 million Russians who lost their lives on the Eastern Front. And this was a conflict—a stirring call to arms—that almost everyone thought would be "over by Christmas." Yet it lasted more than four years and dealt out death on a scale that defied comprehension and numbed the world. Visit any First World War cemetery and the rows of precisely maintained graves tell their own tale; they need no commentary. But while visiting the battlefields of this 20th century Armageddon is easy, understanding what it meant for its victims is much harder.

Above: None of the remaining World War I battlefields comes close to conveying the horrors of the fighting. Today, grassy indentations in placid landscapes, such as this trench from the Battle of the Somme, are all that remain.

A journey of memories

With Ypres as a base, a series of major First World War battlefields and memorials are easily reached. In four days, you can comfortably visit all of the most important ones, but only specialists are likely to be able to make sense of the battlefields themselves as the vast, sprawling sites are now mostly marked only by gentle indentations in countryside that is otherwise largely indistinguishable from other parts of Belgium and northern France.

This is why the memorials and cemeteries, being so much more easily understood, remain the focus of most visits, especially for those in search of family members. That said, the trench system at the Canadian National Vimy Memorial outside Arras is exceptionally well preserved, with a visit to them in the rain a peculiarly poignant experience.

Limit of German advance, 1914
Line of prolonged trench warfare
Hindenburg line
Line of German armistice, 1918

Left: The Neuville St Vaast German military cemetery contains 44,533 graves marked with black crosses.

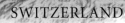

Right: The Tyne Cot war memorial and cemetery outside Ypres commemorates the British and Commonwealth dead. Of the 11,908 graves, some 70% of the bodies were never identified, their graves marked with the inscription "A Soldier of the Great War—Known unto God."

FIND OUT MORE

The Battlefields of the Western Front
Peter Barton and Richard Holmes

The Fallen: A Photographic Journey Through the War Cemeteries and Memorials of the Great War, 1914–1918
John Garfield

THE ITALIAN CAMPAIGN
World War II: A diversionary invasion

Following the Allied victories in North Africa in 1942–3, an invasion of Italy promised the most likely way, at least in the short term, to take the land war to the Germans. It was never intended to be the major land campaign against Germany as that was always going to be across northern France following D-Day, but it was hoped it might at least divert German troops from what would become the major front. In the event, even after Italy withdrew from the war in September 1943, it proved a brutal, 30-month slogging match, with gains won painfully slowly, and with a great loss of life.

Above: The Allied campaign was inspired and bedevilled in equal measure by its leaders. Montgomery (nearest blackboard), Britain's premier general, was consumed by the need to demonstrate his infallibility. The American Patton (right), was no less obssesed by his reputation.

Into Italy

While the British landings at Reggio di Calabria and Taranto were unopposed, the American landing at Salerno saw a desperate three-week struggle to hold the beachhead. The German tactics were clear: to harrass the invaders, before falling back to a series of prepared defensive positions. By November the Germans had established their most formidable defensive stronghold—the Gustav Line—and for six months the Allied advance stalled, despite an attempted outflanking maneuver with a landing at Anzio. Once the Gustav Line was broken, the Allied advance regathered momentum until, in August, it reached the last German position—the Gothic Line. For eight months, a stalemate ensued. The breakthrough in April 1945 was as much the result of the imminent German defeat in Germany as the fighting in Italy.

FIND OUT MORE
Fatal Decision: Anzio and the Battle for Rome
Carlo d'Este

Monte Cassino: The Hardest-Fought Battle of World War II
Matthew Parker

Tug of War: The Battle for Italy 1943–45
Dominick Graham and Shelford Bidwell

Cassino: The Hollow Victory
John Ellis

Above: In February 1944, in two days of bombing raids, the Allies obliterated Monte Cassino. One of the great treasures of Europe—a monastery founded by St Benedict in 524 AD—was destroyed. It was a disturbingly precise expression of the priorities of "total war."

✝ Church
━━ Allied advances
╌╌ Allied frontlines

SWITZERLAND
AUSTRIA
May 1945
MILAN
TRIESTE
VENICE
TURIN
BOLOGNA
Jan. 14, 1945
GENOA
"Gothic" line Aug. 4, 1944
FLORENCE
June 17, 1944
ITALY
"Gustav" line Jan. 15, 1944
Corsica
ROME
Monte Cassino
Sept. 8, 1943
ANZIO
Oct. 8, 1944 NAPLES
BARI
SALERNO
Sardinia
TARANTO
MEDITERRANEAN SEA
PALERMO
CALABRIA
Sicily
TUNIS
MALTA
TUNISIA

FROM NORMANDY TO BERLIN
World War II: D-Day to the heart of Germany

It took seven weeks of bitter attritional fighting for the Allies to break out of Normandy after D-Day on June 6, 1944. But when it came, the breakout was spectacular. Operation Cobra, begun on July 25, saw the American Third Army smash through now brittle German defences and, outflanking them, speed eastward. Paris was reached on August 25, and by early September, Brussels had been liberated. The prospect of imminent German capitulation was real, but the very success of the Allied breakthrough was its downfall. It proved impossible to resupply the forward forces and the winter promised—and delivered—more grim slogging. Yet by March the Allies were across the Rhine, and on May 8, a prostrate Germany surrendered unconditionally.

The collapse of the Third Reich

The Western Allies never reached Berlin before the German surrender—it was the Soviets who captured the German capital, on May 2, 1945—but the overall campaign was a triumphant success. It divided neatly in four stages; the initial Normandy campaign, bloody, brutal, and apparently stalled; the breakout and headlong rush across France to Belgium; the increasingly dour fighting of the autumn and winter, as the Germans, defying every reasonable expectation, stemmed the Allied advance; and the final, utter collapse of the Third Reich, reduced in the end to rubble, its leader dead, its armies crushed, its cities and industries destroyed, and its peoples destitute. Whatever the overwhelming material advantages of the Allies, there was nothing inevitable about their victory, or at least not until the Rhine had been crossed. It was a triumph of logistics, organization, and, ultimately, of fighting spirit.

The Allied troops who surged ashore on the beaches of Normandy were part of the largest amphibious operation ever launched (**below**). Yet however meticulously planned, this was still nothing less than a knife-edge gamble. Hitler's Germany may have been down, but it was a long way from being out. If Arnhem (**left**), in September, was a bridge too far for the Allies, the Ardennes (**above**), site of the Battle of the Bulge, underlined that Nazi resistance would be desperate to the last.

FIND OUT MORE

Normandy to Berlin: Into the Heart of the Third Reich
Karen Farrington

Road to Berlin: Allied Drive from Normandy
George Forty

Accidental Warrior: In the Front Line from Normandy till Victory
Geoffrey Picot

Overlord: D-Day and the Battle for Normandy, 1944
Max Hastings

"The German Seventh Army is now in full retreat. You can state this tremendous news as simply as that... the Germans here are defeated."
Alexander Clifford, The Daily Mail, August 19, 1944

THE HO CHI MINH TRAIL
In the jungles of Vietnam

The Ho Chi Minh Trail was fundamental to the victory of the communist North Vietnamese in the Vietnam War. It wasn't a single trail though, rather a vast network of jungle paths, tracks, crude roads, and some stretches of river that extended north to south across Vietnam, and through the neighboring kingdoms of Laos and Cambodia. In all, the "trail" covered almost 10,000 miles (16,093 km), and acted as the principal means of supply for the Viet Cong. At its peak, around 20,000 soldiers a month and 65 tons (60 tonnes) of supplies a day were reaching the South using the Ho Chi Minh Trail.

Above: When the Trail was opened in 1959, it took almost six months to traverse. At its peak, soldiers traveling on foot could do the same journey in six weeks.

The indestructible trail

In a conflict that the Americans sought to win by ever more technologically sophisticated means, the Ho Chi Minh Trail embodied the low-tech way in which the Viet Cong fought. Despite repeated and increasingly savage attempts to bomb it out of existence, the Ho Chi Minh Trail was little more than simple paths hacked from the jungle, so was almost impossible to destroy. Additionally, up to 300,000 Vietnamese were employed to maintain it, so almost any damage could quickly be made good. As the war intensified, so the trail became more sophisticated. Underground base camps were gradually built at regular intervals, providing a network of subterranean tunnels that was almost as intricate as the paths above ground.

FIND OUT MORE

A History of the Ho Chi Minh Trail: The Road to Freedom
Virginia Morris

The Blood Road: The Ho Chi Minh Trail and the Vietnam War
John Prodos

Mission of the Ho Chi Minh Trail: Nature, Myth and War in Vietnam
Richard L. Stevens

—— Main trackways
----- Footpaths

"We have to win our independence at any cost, even if the Truong Song mountains burn." *Ho Chi Minh.*

Left: The Vietnamese victory precisely refutes the belief that in war GDP (Gross Domestic Product) will always prevail. America, infinitely richer than North Vietnam, was unable to impose itself on an impoverished opponent whatever the resources—in men and arms—it threw into the conflict. The dollar fell foul of an opponent that it could never defeat.

CHINA

NORTH VIETNAM

HAIPHONG
HANOI

Gulf of Tonkin

LAOS

TO VINH

HA TINH

DONG HOI

19th Parallel

HUE

DA NANG

THAILAND

DAK SUI

SOUTH CHINA SEA

KONTUM

SOUTH VIETNAM

CAMBODIA

BUON ME THUOT

NHA TRANG

Gulf of Thailand

SIHANOUKVILLE (KAMPONG SAOM)

SAIGON (HO CHI MINH CITY)

Mekong delta

The sea has been a highway to new worlds since the beginning of recorded history. Greeks and Phoenicians, heirs to the mythical voyages of Odysseus, regularly bisected the Mediterranean. Much later, Europeans pioneered sea routes that revealed almost the entire globe, and the oceans—however hostile and remote—have proved the consistent factor in the opening up of the world.

CRUISING
The romance of the sea

It is a striking fact that almost every one of the world's great historic cities is either on the sea or a navigable river. It was the silt-rich Nile that gave birth to ancient Egypt, its abundance enabling the development of settled agriculture, the foundation on which the first civilizations depended. A Nile cruise remains one of the great journeys into the past.

The Danube, the only major European river to flow eastward, likewise nurtured societies along its 1,800-mile length and today, four capital cities stand astride it. The great, almost inland sea that is the Mediterranean saw societies established all around its rim to create a distinctive world

that was simultaneously African, Asian, and European.

Homer's *Odyssey*, however fantastical, underlines a central truth of the ancient Greek world: the sea was its lifeblood. The Baltic, a more northern sea, acted as a similar facilitator of trade and travel for the peoples on its shores, and in the age of European global exploration, it was also a hugely important source of hemp, tar, and timber, without which Europe's maritime adventuring would have been impossible.

One of the most dramatic moments in the opening up of the world occurred when Ferdinand Magellan led an expedition to attempt the first circumnavigation, revealing the true vastness of the Pacific, which Columbus believed could be sailed in days. It was the Pacific that was also the site of one of the most enduring maritime dramas—the mutiny on the Bounty in 1789. And it was across this same sea that the young Charles Darwin sailed in 1835, on a voyage that would detonate belief in a divinely created Earth. Joshua Slocum's single-handed circumnavigation in 1895–8 underlines a further aspect of the sea: as a source of personal fulfilment and adventure.

ODYSSEUS
Homer's Odyssey

Composed around 800 BC as part of a bardic oral tradition, and traditionally said to be the work of the blind poet Homer, the sprawling 12,100-line epic that is the *Odyssey* recounts the 10-year journey home of Odysseus, king of Ithaca, at the end of the Trojan War around 1,200 BC. No less than Homer's *Iliad*, which tells the story of the war itself, it is an extraordinary confection of Dark Age Greek myth and legend, deeply human, and filled with acute psychological insight, whose dramas are played out against a background of gods and monsters. It is a world that is simultaneously cruel and noble, filled with suffering, betrayal, heroism, and benevolence.

Above: Whether the Straits of Messina were the location of the terrifying Scylla and Charybdis or not, monsters and ogres, no less than gods and goddesses, loomed exceedingly large in the lives of the ancient Greeks.

The voyage of Odysseus

Odysseus's wanderings begin with a raid by him and his men on the island of Isomer. They escape the island's inhabitants, the Ciconians, only to be swept to the land of the Lotus-Eaters where they encounter the one-eyed son of Poseidon, the sea-god Polyphemus. Odysseus tricks and blinds Polyphemus, earning him Poseidon's implacable enmity. Continuing their journey, they arrive in Aeolia, whose ruler, Aeolus, promises Odysseus a fair wind home, giving him a bag in which he has imprisoned all contrary winds. Odysseus's men open it and are blown to Telepylos, the home of the Laestrygonians, a race of cannibal giants. Only Odysseus's ship escapes, sailing on to a further island, Aeaea, home of the enchantress Circe with whom Odysseus fathers a son. Leaving Aeaea, Odysseus and his crew voyage to Hades, the Underworld, and from there past the Sirens, the crew blocking their ears with wax to protect themselves against the Sirens' bewitching songs. Skirting the six-headed Scylla and the whirlpool Charybdis, their next landfall is Thrinacia, home of the sun god Helios, whose sacred cattle Odysseus's starving crew slaughter. They are punished by shipwreck, with all but Odysseus perishing. He is washed up on the shores of Ogygia, staying here for seven years with Calypso, the daughter of Atlas. When she allows him to leave he is carried to Scheria, from where he is finally permitted to return to his kingdom of Ithaca.

> "Grant, father, that if my enemy Odysseus ever returns home, he may arrive late, in evil plight, from a foreign ship, having lost all his comrades."
> *Prayer by Polyphemus to Poseidon from the Odyssey, Homer*

FIND OUT MORE
The World of Odysseus
M.I. Finley

The Jason Voyage: The Search for the Golden Fleece
Tim Severin

The Odyssey
Homer (trans. Walter Shewring)

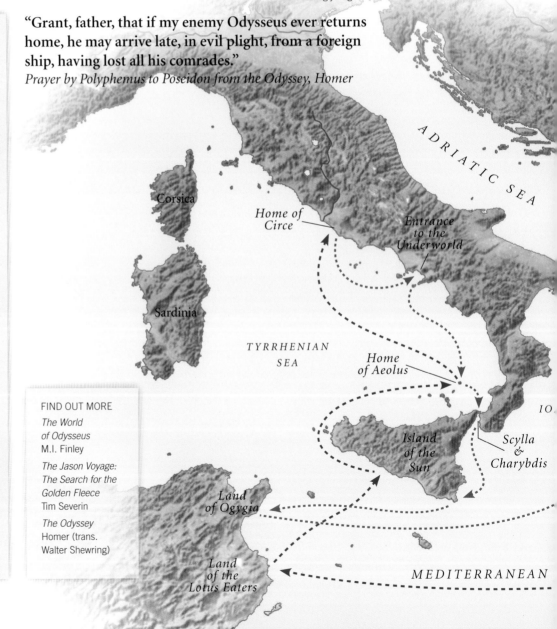

ADRIATIC SEA

Corsica

Home of Circe

Entrance to the Underworld

Sardinia

TYRRHENIAN SEA

Home of Aeolus

IO

Island of the Sun

Scylla & Charybdis

Land of Ogygia

Land of the Lotus Eaters

MEDITERRANEAN

The true source of the Odyssey

The extent to which Odysseus's journey is based on actual places is almost impossible to say: as has been repeatedly pointed out, the *Odyssey* is a poem, not a guidebook, yet it is still a question that has exercised scholars for 2,000 years. There is more or less a general agreement that the Straits of Messina between Sicily and Italy may be the location of Scylla and Charybdis. Sicily has also been fairly convincingly identified as the home of the Polyphemous and the Laestrygonians, Corfu as Scheria, and North Africa is widely accepted as the site of the Lotus-Eaters. Yet there is so much confusion and speculation as to just where Odysseus journeyed (much of it amounting to nothing more than guesswork), that some contend that his voyage was in the Atlantic—to Madeira and the Azores. Others have him venturing even further—to the Carribean, Mexico, and South America— while a further school of thought contends that Troy was in England and that the Atlantic coasts of the British Isles, France, and Iberia are the setting of the poem.

Above: The rocky shores of Sardinia, typical of the Mediterranean's bleached and scented beauty. When Odysseus returned to his island home, Ithaca, he had long since been given up for dead and his presumed widow, Penelope, was under siege by no less from 108 suitors. Odysseus, disguised as a beggar, slayed them all.

- – – Journey to war with Troy
- - - - Return voyage (to home of Circe)
- · · · · Return voyage (from home of Circe)
(All routes conjectural)

ISMAROS

Scheria

AEGEAN SEA

○ Troy

PYLOS

Ithaca

Crete

Above: Whether he lived or not, Homer's influence on Western literature cannot be overstated. The *Illiad* and the *Odyssey* are the bedrock on which it rests, as influential in the Classical world as in later ages. Their influence and impact have reverberated down the centuries, no less than the works of William Shakespeare.

CRADLE OF CIVILIZATION
The Mediterranean

In strictly geographical terms, the notion of "Europe" has always been spurious, as Europe as a landmass is clearly no more than the western extension of Asia. To single it out as a separate geographical entity is to invite hair-splitting at best. Yet as a cultural entity, Europe has long asserted its own identity. To a crucial extent, this was the result of the colonization of the Mediterranean by two states, shaped by Asian models, but newly "European" in outlook. They were Greece and Phoenicia, and together, between the 9th and the 6th centuries BC, they implanted colonies across the Mediterranean that would transform an emerging continent: that of Europe.

Above: The Valley of the Temples in Agrigento in Sicily contains the most important collection of Greek temples outside the Greek mainland. Of them, the Temple of Concordia, built c. 430 BC, is the best preserved.

The culture of Ancient Greece

For the Greeks, seafaring came naturally. Greece, other than its few coastal plains, is a land of imposing mountains that is bitter in winter and arid in summer. Its immense, shattered coastline and numerous islands give such immediate access to the sea that it was inevitable the sea would shape the country's destiny. Establishing more distant colonies meant little more than an extension of this maritime tradition, with the impetus provided by several reasons. As the growing population competed for scarce productive land, official policy actively encouraged emigration, while trade, and competition between the emerging city-states (driven as much by prestige as by the prospect of trade-generated wealth) were further factors that drove the Greek people from Greece. The consequence was the export of Greek culture—the arts and sciences as much as political culture—at precisely the moment when it was evolving towards its most distinctive and sophisticated form.

FIND OUT MORE

Carthage
Ross Leckie

The Hellenistic Settlements in Europe, the Islands and Asia Minor
G. M. Cohen

The Heritage of Hellenism
J. Ferguson

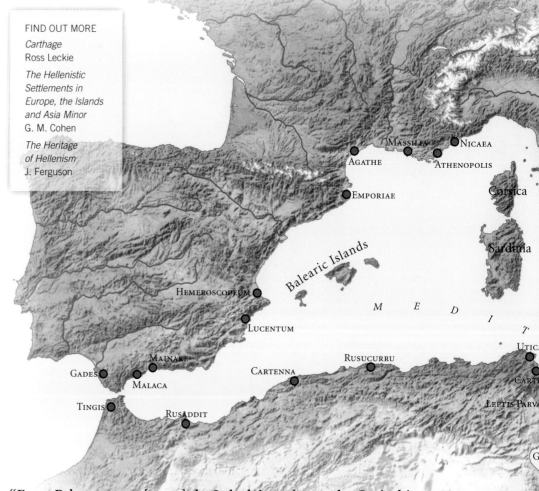

Left: When the Phoenicians ventured across the Mediterranean to Spain, they encountered a highly developed "Iberian" culture. The Lady of Elche is the most celebrated example, speaking volumes for the wealth of the world that produced her.

"From Peloponnesos [came] the Lakedaimonians... the Corinthians... the Sikyonians... the Epidaurians... the Troiezenians... All these... belong to the Dorian and Macedonian nation [and] had emigrated last from Erineus and Pindos and Dryopis."
History, Herodotus, book 8, chapter 43

Ascendancy of the Phoenecians

The impetus behind the Phoenician colonization was direct and simple. The rapid rise of the Assyrian empire in the 9th century left the Phoenicians with little option but to seek new lands away from their smallholdings in the Levant. Reputedly founded in 814 BC, but in reality rather later, Carthage in Tunisia formed the heart of what by the 4th century had become by some way the dominant power in the western Mediterranean, spreading across much of north Africa and southern Spain, as well as the Balearics, Corsica, and Sardinia. Following its final conquest by Rome in 146 BC, its values would be extended across most of Europe.

Right: Though progressively squeezed out of the western Mediterranean by the Carthaginians, there were important Greek emporia in France and Spain, of which the best-known example is Marseilles in southern France, or *Massilia* to the Greeks. It was the first Greek colony in western Europe and subsequently became the first Greek settlement to be granted official status as a city.

OLBIA
TANAIS
TYRAS
KALAS LIMEN
PANTICAPAEUM
PHANAGORIA
ISTRUS
CHERSONESUS
THEODOSIA
TOMI
CALLATIS
ODESSUS
BLACK SEA
PITYUS
MESEMBRIA
DIOSCURIAS
APOLLONIA
CYTORUS
SYNOPE
PHASIS
EPIDAMNUS
AMISUS
COTYORA
TRAPEZUS
APOLLONIA
BYZANTIUM
HERACLEIA
ABDERA
MARONEA
PERINTHUS
POLIS
METHONE
ACANTHUS
SESTUS
CYZICUS
POSIDONIA
LAUS
SYBARIS
CORCYRA
PHOCAEA
SARDIS
CROTON
AMBRACIA
CHALCIS
ERETRIA
ORMUS
CORINTH
SAMOS
HIMERA
RHEGIUM
ARGOS
ATHENS
MILETUS
Sicily
SPARTA
HALICARNASSUS
AGRIGENTO
SYRACUSE
SIDE
SOLOI
THERA
PHASELIS
R
RHODES
NAGIDOS
KELENDERIS
Malta
Crete
SALAMIS
A
N
E
GORTYN
A
N
S
E
A
OEA
APOLLONIA
LEPTIS MAGNA
CYRENE
KINYPS

Phoenician colonization, from 9th century BC
Main areas of Greek city-states, end of 9th century BC
Greek colonization, from 8th to 6th centuries BC

UP THE NILE
Through the land of the pharaohs

Africa's longest river is not only the best means of gaining an insight into the 3,000 year existence of the world's greatest civilization, but also the reason that the Egyptians rose to such heights. The annual flooding of the Nile provided a plentiful water supply, natural irrigation of the parched land, and left Egyptians with an enforced period of "leisure time" to devote to literature, the arts, and the building of amazing memorials for their pharaohs. Early cities of the Old Kingdom at Memphis and Saqqara display the stepped overground tombs that were perfected in the iconic pyramids at Giza. The underground chambers in the Valley of the Kings opposite Thebes protected the mortal remains of later pharaohs in the after-life. Ancient Greeks and Romans were the first tourists to this historical wonderland, admiring a culture that was as old to them as theirs are to us today.

Left: Queen Hatshepsut, the only woman to be crowned as the ruler of Egypt, is thought to have been in power from 1479-1458 BC. Her mortuary temple stands on the West Bank of the Nile at Luxor, near the entrance of what is now known as the Valley of the Kings.

Below: Nile cruises are a classic holiday, and the perfect way to tour the amazing monuments of the ancient Egyptians. Sailing in a traditional *felucca* is the best way to get up close to the river and its pretty islands, especially around Aswan's cataracts.

Cruising from Luxor

All Nile journeys will include a visit to bustling Cairo, its treasure-filled Museum, and the nearby pyramids, but cruises begin in Luxor, site of the ancient capital of Thebes. The imposing Temple of Karnak is a 100 acre complex around the huge hypostyle hall with its forest of 134 pillars, covered in ancient hieroglyphics. An avenue of sphinxes leads all the way to Luxor Temple, which holds one of the rare statues of Tutankhamun. Across the river is the famed West Bank with the world's richest concentration of archaeological sights. Cruise ships then glide up the Nile, stopping at more temples, such as Edfu, Esna, and Kom Ombo to reach Aswan, where Egypt meets Nubia. Here you can ride a *felucca* (sailing boat) along the Nile's myriad cataracts, enjoy the sights and smells of the town's spice market, and take trips to the vast modern dam, the ancient granite quarries, and the Temple of Philae. Further up the Nile stands Abu Simbel, faced by four colossal statues of Ramses II. Here the Nile widens into Lake Nasser, and then crosses the Sudanese border.

Above: Commonly believed to have been built over 4,500 years ago, the pyramids at Giza remain one of the true wonders of the ancient world, and demonstrate the capabilities of the ancient Egyptian culture. Even from present-day Cairo, their presence dominates the skyline.

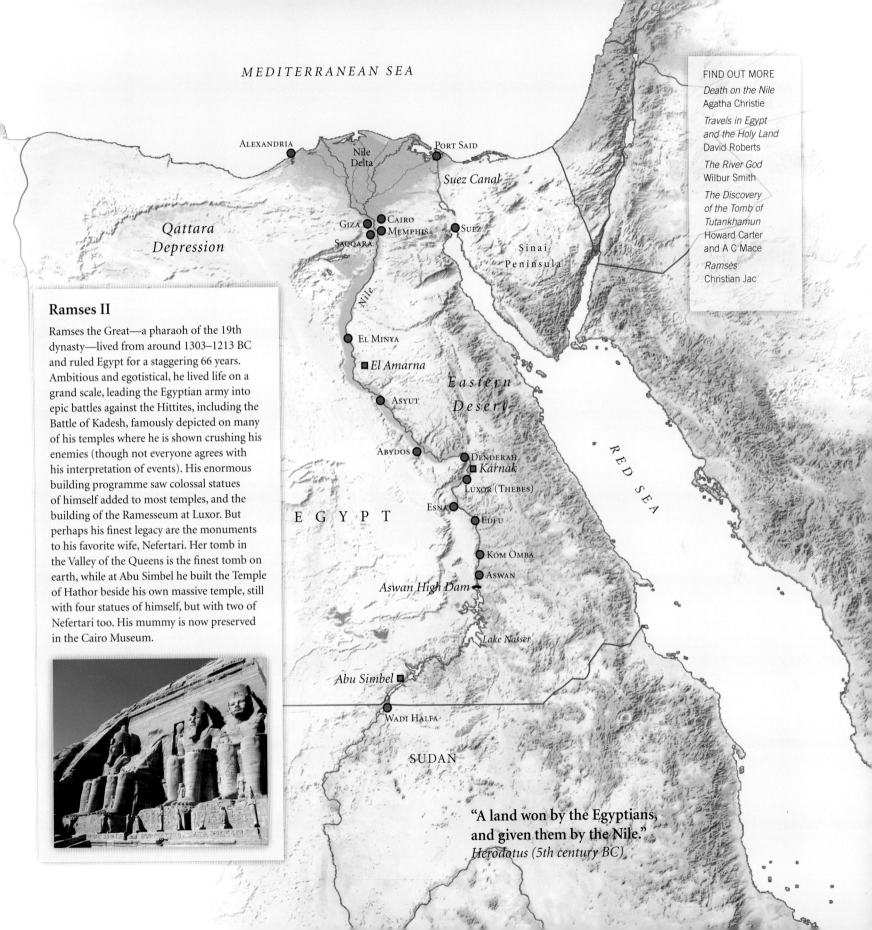

MEDITERRANEAN SEA

ALEXANDRIA

Nile Delta

PORT SAID

Suez Canal

Qattara Depression

GIZA • CAIRO
MEMPHIS
SAQQARA
SUEZ

Sinai Peninsula

Nile

EL MINYA

■ *El Amarna*

Eastern Desert

ASYUT

ABYDOS

DENDERAH
■ *Karnak*
LUXOR (THEBES)

ESNA
EDFU

KOM OMBA

ASWAN

Aswan High Dam

RED SEA

Lake Nasser

E G Y P T

Abu Simbel ■

WADI HALFA

SUDAN

FIND OUT MORE

Death on the Nile
Agatha Christie

Travels in Egypt and the Holy Land
David Roberts

The River God
Wilbur Smith

The Discovery of the Tomb of Tutankhamun
Howard Carter and A C Mace

Ramsès
Christian Jac

Ramses II

Ramses the Great—a pharaoh of the 19th dynasty—lived from around 1303–1213 BC and ruled Egypt for a staggering 66 years. Ambitious and egotistical, he lived life on a grand scale, leading the Egyptian army into epic battles against the Hittites, including the Battle of Kadesh, famously depicted on many of his temples where he is shown crushing his enemies (though not everyone agrees with his interpretation of events). His enormous building programme saw colossal statues of himself added to most temples, and the building of the Ramesseum at Luxor. But perhaps his finest legacy are the monuments to his favorite wife, Nefertari. Her tomb in the Valley of the Queens is the finest tomb on earth, while at Abu Simbel he built the Temple of Hathor beside his own massive temple, still with four statues of himself, but with two of Nefertari too. His mummy is now preserved in the Cairo Museum.

"A land won by the Egyptians, and given them by the Nile."
Herodotus (5th century BC)

DOWN THE DANUBE
Through Eastern Europe

The "Blue" Danube flows halfway across Europe, covering 1,800 miles (2,895 km) from the heart of Germany to the Black Sea. Already a major river by the time it reaches Vienna, it traverses diverse landscapes, from the wide Hungarian plains to dramatic Iron Gates canyons in the Carpathian foothills, before disgorging in the maze of channels at its delta. The ebb and flow of history and empire in central and Eastern Europe has glided on its waters—the conquering Romans, the imperial Hapsburgs, and the upstream invasions of the Turkish Ottomans. The river ports along its banks provide glimpses of these past glories, and introduce countries that have emerged from the yoke of communism.

Vienna to the Black Sea

Leaving intellectual Vienna, the river flows through Bratislava to Budapest—the "Paris of the East." The next stop could be Kalocsa for its paprika museum, or a horse-breeding farm in the Hungarian *puszta* before heading on to Belgrade. Passing the imposing Baba Vida fortress in Vidin, the great river forms the Romanian/Bulgarian border for much of the rest of its route, and detours either side can reach the fantastic red sandstone formations of Belogradchick, the epic Russo-Turkish War battle site at Pleven, or Bucharest, known as "Little Paris," for its French-style boulevards. Finally, you reach the delta at the Black Sea, a perfect chance to track down one of the many resorts for a few days of sun.

Above: The magnificent Glorietta gatehouse overlooks Schönbrunn Palace and the city of Vienna. For centuries the Austrian capital was the intellectual heart of Europe and is still world famous for its musical tradition.

Below: In Budapest, the Danube divides the old town houses of Buda from cosmopolitan Pest. This new EU city has a fascinating past, from the splendors of the imperial Hapsburgs to the tragedy of its Jewish community.

Johann Strauss

In the Vienna of the 1840s the two Johann Strausses—father and son—each had an esteemed orchestra greatly sought after for concerts and balls. The elder Johann, whose father had drowned himself in the Danube while he was just a boy, wrote graceful waltzes and rousing marches, including the Radetzky March. But he was eclipsed by the younger Johann, "the Waltz King," who is forever linked with the great river for his sentimental Blue Danube waltz. It was originally composed for the Vienna Men's Choral Association in 1867, while Johann was sailing down the river. Soon adapted into an orchestral version, it is now played annually at Vienna's New Year's Concert and famously featured in the classic Stanley Kubrick film *2001: A Space Odyssey*.

Above: Belgrade's many Serbian Orthodox churches are noted for their distinctive architecture. None is finer than the Cathedral of St Sava, the largest Orthodox church in use in the world.

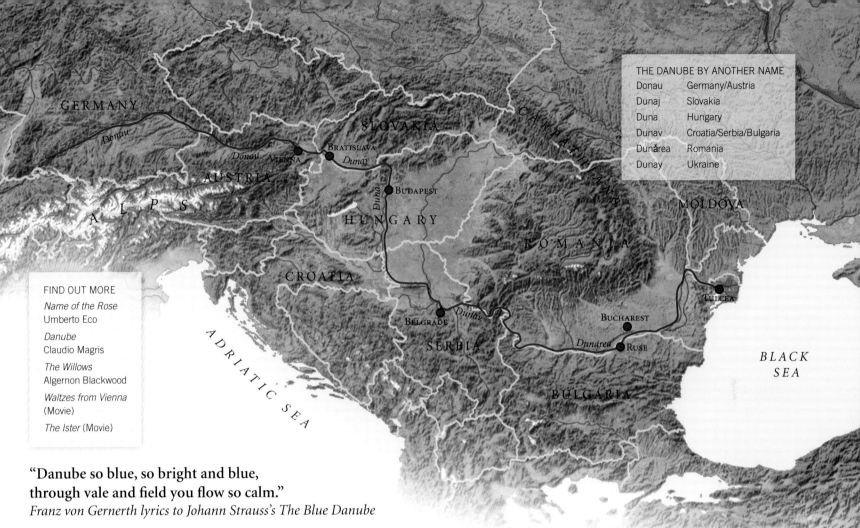

FIND OUT MORE

Name of the Rose
Umberto Eco

Danube
Claudio Magris

The Willows
Algernon Blackwood

Waltzes from Vienna
(Movie)

The Ister (Movie)

"Danube so blue, so bright and blue,
through vale and field you flow so calm."
Franz von Gernerth lyrics to Johann Strauss's The Blue Danube

Above: The People's House in Bucharest, begun in 1984 by President Ceaucescu, was unfinished at his death and only slowly completed afterwards. It holds three world records—the largest and most expensive civilian administrative building, and the heaviest building.

Right: The Danube Delta, which flows into the Black Sea, is the second largest delta in Europe (the Volga is larger). It is one of Romania's seven UNESCO World Heritage sites, hosting over 300 species of bird and 45 species of fish in this important wetland ecosystem.

Around the Baltic
A voyage through Northern Europe

A rich maritime heritage links the lands that shore the Baltic Sea. Over the centuries, ships have brought invaders and pirates to the coastal ports—the name of Estonia's capital Tallinn means "Danish town"—as well as trade and riches. In the medieval era, many Baltic cities joined the Hanseatic League, which dominated European trade for 400 years. The wealth of this era can be seen in the rich merchants' houses of Visby, Gdansk, and Riga. In later years it was Sweden, Russia, and the Grand Duchy of Lithuania that held sway, creating the opulent palaces that can be seen today in Stockholm and St. Petersburg. In the 20th century Communism cast its shadow over the eastern shores, but now the small Baltic republics of Latvia, Estonia, and Lithuania have once again regained their independence.

Above: Stockholm has been the political and economic heart of Sweden for 800 years. Today's visitors can wander the medieval streets of Gamla Stan (the old town), enjoy the city's fine museums, see the 17th-century Vasa battleship, and explore the royal palaces.

FIND OUT MORE

Peter the Great: His Life and World
Robert Massie

God's Playground: A History of Poland
Norman Davies

The Baltic
Alan Palmer

Baltic Storm
(Movie)

Left: Catherine's Palace, at Tsarskoe Selo just outside St. Petersburg, was Catherine I's 18th century masterpiece and became the summer palace of Russia's imperial tsars.

Above right: "The Little Mermaid" fairy story by Hans Christian Andersen tells of a mermaid who is prepared to give up her life in the sea for the love of a prince. This graceful statue—now a tourist attraction— sits on a rock at Langelinie, Copenhagen

Right: Winter in Finland.

Clockwise around the Baltic

From Copenhagen, head for Gotland's medieval Visby, known as the "city of roses and ruins" since its destruction in 1525 by Lübeck. Carry on to Stockholm, and then Helsinki, with its Modernist buildings and Russian-influenced churches, and Sibelius monument. The furthest point east is St Petersburg, where communist Russia meets the splendors of the tsars. From charming medieval Tallinn and Art Nouveau Riga, head along the Latvian/Lithuanian coast to Russia's European exclave of Kaliningrad, before finally taking in the historic shipyards of Gdansk, birthplace of the Solidarity movement.

ALONE AROUND THE WORLD
Joshua Slocum

Joshua Slocum was born in Novia Scotia in 1844, and naturalized an American in 1865. He was a precise product of the final years of the age of sail: a consummate seaman, endlessly resourceful, and limitlessly hardy, who for over 30 years crisscrossed the globe, working his way up to command a variety of vessels. But there was another side to this sturdy personality. A semi-mystical streak tinged his life, which found expression in 1895 when he decided on the apparently impossible—to undertake a single-handed voyage around the world. His ship, Spray, was sturdy, but small at only 36 feet long, yet on this frail wooden boat Slocum defied every rational expectation: Between April 1895 and June 1898, alone, he sailed around the world.

Above: Spray may not have been a beautiful boat, but she proved to be wonderfully seaworthy.

FIND OUT MORE

Sailing Alone Around the World
Joshua Slocum

Sailing Around the World: A Family Retraces Joshua Slocum's Voyage
Guy Bernardin

Alone at Sea: The Adventures of Joshua Slocum
Ann Spencer

The lure of the ocean

The reasons behind Slocum's decision came in the early 1890s, when the onset of middle age, the loss of his first wife, and the rise of the steamship put him at a crossroads in his life. His response was unusual; having been given "a very antiquated sloop," the Spray, he rebuilt her, then determined not just to sail around the world, but to do so singlehanded. It was an extraordinary decision, yet Spray proved an exceptional sea-boat. Weatherly and fast,

her rig was so well balanced that she could steer herself, with Slocum covering 2,000 miles (3,220 km) as he crossed the Pacific, without once touching the helm.

After more than three years, Slocum and Spray returned to Newport, Rhode Island, having successfully circled the globe. That an otherwise obscure American sea captain should have achieved such a feat is a testimony to seamanship of the highest order and for a largely self-taught man whose formal education ended when he was 14, Slocum also proved a gifted writer. His account of his circumnavigation, *Sailing Alone Around the World,* became an instant classic, but life on shore never suited him. In November, 1909, he sailed for the West Indies on the Spray and was never seen again.

Slocum's unorthodox route worked in his favor, as it meant his journey consisted of a series of short stages with frequent halts, including Fuerto de Ventura (**left**) and Rio De Janeiro (**above**). This perhaps explains the leisurely nature of his voyage, which lasted over three years and covered some 46,000 miles (74,000 km)—almost double the distance of a direct circumnavigation.

"I had resolved on a voyage around the world, and as the wind on the morning of April 24, 1895 was fair, at noon I weighed anchor, set sail, and filled away from Boston... I felt there could be no turning back, and that I was engaging in an adventure the meaning of which I thoroughly understood."
Joshua Slocum, Sailing Alone Around the World, 1899

GIRDLING THE GLOBE
Ferdinand Magellan

After Columbus crossed the Atlantic in 1492, the pace of European exploration increased at breakneck speed. By 1520, the outlines of the east coast of America—north and south—were known, and these exhilarating discoveries fed what was becoming an insatiable appetite for exploration and adventure. But if the circumnavigation of the globe—and hence a navigable route to the riches of the Orient—now seemed to be only a matter of time, it would prove a vastly more arduous undertaking than anyone imagined. It was eventually achieved, between 1519 and 1522, by a Spanish expedition led by the Portuguese explorer, Ferdinand Magellan.

Across the Pacific

Even if, however imperfectly, the size of the globe itself was known, no one had imagined that an ocean as immense as the Pacific could exist. Magellan and his men sailed across what seemed a limitless expanse and, missing every single one of the numerous volcanic islands that stud its southern half, they began to starve. On March 6, 1521 they finally reached land; it was Guam. A week later they had reached Samar in the Philippines, and Magellan had successfully circled the Earth.

Left: Magellan's landfall at Guam was on March 6, 1521 after a crossing of the Pacific that took 99 days. By then, every rat on board had been eaten and the crew were reduced to chewing the leather that prevented the sails from chaffing on the masts. Some ate straw dust and "drank yellow water, already many days putrid."

— Outward journey
- - - - Return journey, under command of Juan Sebastián de Elcano

The voyage home

Although Magellan had crossed all the meridians on the globe—and therefore circumnavigated the Earth—he didn't complete the final westward voyage home to truly make it around the world. In April 1521,

a little over a month after arriving in the Philippines, he was killed during the Battle of Mactan, and command of his intrepid endeavor passed to Juan Sebastián de Elcano. In September 1522, de Elcano returned to Spain with a single ship, one of five that Magellan left with, and of the 241 men who set out, only 18 made it home. Yet despite the high losses, Magellan's voyage was a breathtaking accomplishment.

FIND OUT MORE

Over the Edge of the World: Magellan's Terrifying Circumnavigation of the Globe
Laurence Bergreen

The Great Explorers
Samuel Eliot Morison

The Voyage of Magellan: The Journal of Antonio Pigafetta
tran. Paul Spurling Page

Azores

SPAIN
SEVILLE

NORTH ATLANTIC OCEAN

Canary Islands

Cape Verde Islands

SOUTH AMERICA

PACIFIC OCEAN

RIO DE JANEIRO

Río de la Plata

SOUTH ATLANTIC OCEAN

Strait of All Saints (Strait of Magellan)
TIERRA DEL FUEGO

Magellan's death came about because he got involved in a local dispute on the island of Mactan (**above**) in the Philippines, where he was set on and hacked to death. That he was a man of immense resource and iron will, and a charismatic leader, is clear. The Cape of Good Hope (**left**) was doubled on May 1522 by the handful of remaining crew members.

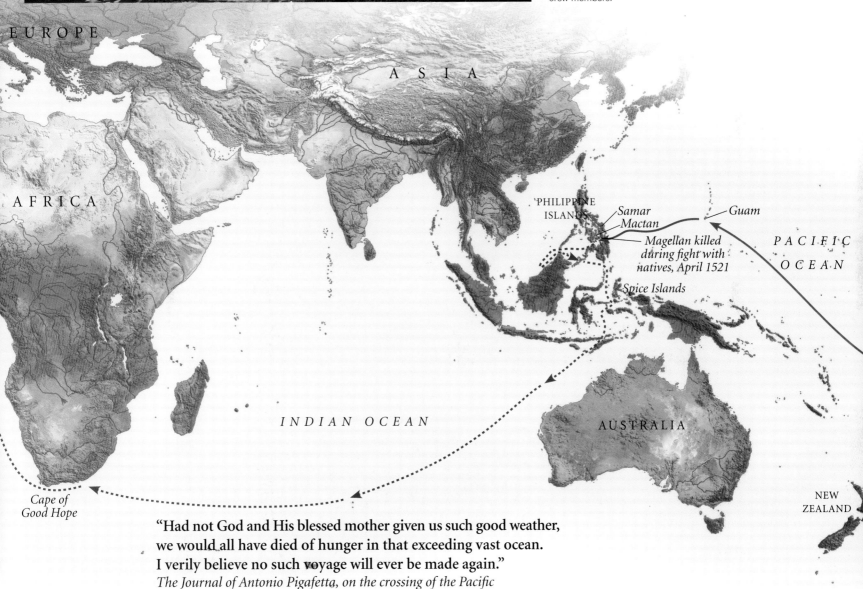

EUROPE

ASIA

AFRICA

PHILIPPINE
ISLANDS
Samar
Mactan
Guam
Magellan killed
during fight with
natives, April 1521
PACIFIC
OCEAN
Spice Islands

INDIAN OCEAN

AUSTRALIA

NEW
ZEALAND

Cape of
Good Hope

"Had not God and His blessed mother given us such good weather,
we would all have died of hunger in that exceeding vast ocean.
I verily believe no such voyage will ever be made again."
The Journal of Antonio Pigafetta, on the crossing of the Pacific

161

Horizons North
The West Coast to Alaska

Cruise from Canada's favorite city, Vancouver, with its glass towers set against beautiful peaks, to one of the remotest places on earth—Alaska, the land of ice and mountains. Rugged islands along the coastline of British Columbia and southern Alaska give way to a stark landscape of calving glaciers, ethereal icebergs, and steep granite cliffs. The remote Indian and Western communities eke out a hard existence in this unconnected corner of the Americas, though the clamor for oil exploration in Alaska's mineral-rich earth threatens to open it up to "civilization."

FIND OUT MORE

▲▲ Peak

Passage to Juneau
Jonathan Raban

The Call of the Wild
Jack London

*Alaska: A History
of the 49th State*
C. Naske and
H. Slotnick

The Story of Alaska
C. L. Andrews

The land of the Tlingit

The Tlingit are a matrilineal people, today numbering about 11,000, living primarily along the stretch of islands and coast known as the Alaskan Panhandle. The abundant supply of food provided by receding tides left them time to develop arts and crafts, as can be seen in their totem poles in Ketchikan, as well as woven baskets, masks, and other carvings in museums around the world. Many converted to Orthodox Christianity in the 19th century as they found their shamans could not cure European-borne diseases, but they have managed to balance Western values with retaining some of their traditions and mythology, such as the raven's role in the world's creation. However, there are now only 140 native speakers of the unique Tlingit language.

Left: A brown bear fishes in the rapid rivers of Alaska. Salmon spawn in rivers, mature in the sea, and then swim back upriver to breed, reputedly going back to the exact location where they were born.

Below: Mt. McKinley is North America's tallest mountain, reaching an altitude of 20,321 feet (6,194 m). Also known as Denali, it is one of the main attractions in Denali National Park in Alaska.

> **"A small five-mile indent in a gigantic glacier."**
> *Captain George Vancouver describing Glacier Bay*

North from Vancouver

Before the cruise starts, take time in Vancouver to enjoy some of Canada's finest museums, and catch the ferry to Pacific Rim National Park and Victoria—so English that Kipling described it as "Brighton Pavilion with the Himalayas as a backdrop." The coastal voyage sails out of Vancouver's Lion Gate Bridge and heads north to the Queen Charlotte Islands, an "Arctic Galapagos." From Ketchikan, which has the world's largest collection of totem poles, you enter the meandering straits off the Alaskan shore. Frederick Sound, a great place to see humpback whales, orcas, and bald eagles, and Stephen's Pass lead to the Alaskan capital Juneau, which is only accessible by sea. Sitka, the capital of the region until Russia sold the whole area to the United States in 1867, still has its striking Russian Orthodox St Michael's Cathedral. Then sail past the mighty Glacier Bay, Prince William Sound, and Kenai Fjords National Park to reach Alaska's largest city, Anchorage, which was mostly destroyed in the 1964 Good Friday earthquake. The cruise ends here, but once ashore take a trip to Mt McKinley, towering over Denali National Park, to spot moose, caribou, or grizzly bears fishing for salmon.

ALASKA (U.S.A.)

Denali National Park
▲▲ *Mt. McKinley*

● ANCHORAGE   ● VALDEZ

● SEWARD

Kenai Fjords National Park

Prince William Sound

Yakutat Bay

GULF OF ALASKA

Kodiak Island

PACIFIC OCEAN

SKAGWAY

Glacier Bay

JUNEAU

SITKA

Alexander Archipelago

Frederick Sound

KETCHIKAN

Queen Charlotte Islands

BRITISH COLUMBIA

Vancouver Island

VANCOUVER

VICTORIA

Left: The West Coast of Alaska is one of the best places to experience glaciers. The most dramatic views are from the sea, either from cruise ships or smaller boats that can sail up closer. For those not on a cruise, there are still many places you can drive to for a short walk to the foot of a glacier.

Right: Cruises to Alaska leave Vancouver before heading up the Canadian coast to the northern wildernesses. However, harbor cruises are well worth taking to see the sights of Vancouver such as Stanley Park, the Lookout Tower, and the Lion's Gate Bridge.

TRACKING DARWIN'S BEAGLE
A voyage to the unknown

Charles Darwin was a theology student at Cambridge with a lively interest in the natural world, when, in December 1831, at the age of 22, he set sail on HMS Beagle on what would prove to be a five year voyage around the world. Darwin had been asked to accompany the vessel as a "gentleman's companion" to the captain, Robert FitzRoy, but he would return and become a naturalist of world renown. It was during the Beagle's voyage that Darwin began to formulate his theory of natural selection, a theory that would shake the thunderous religious certainties of the Victorian world to their very foundations, revealing a world evolved over eons rather than one created by God.

Above: The Beagle spent only 10 days in the Cocos Islands on her return home in 1836, but it was long enough for Darwin to confirm another idea: if landmasses such as the Andes were being squeezed upwards, then coral atolls such as the Cocos Islands were sinking.

To South America

Above all, the goal of the Beagle's journey was to survey the coasts of newly independent South America. Apart from the purely scientific satisfaction for the Admiralty in London of better charts, there was also a potential increase in trade. But for a naturalist, the voyage was heaven-sent, involving long periods on what by definition were little-known coasts with ample opportunity for

exploration ashore. The voyage had a further purpose too—to return three Fuegians, natives of Tierra del Fuego, to their home in the remote and hostile far south of South America, where they were to form the kernel of a Christian mission.

The Beagle arrived in Brazil on February 28, 1832. It was the overture to a stay of two years and four months on the east coast of South America, which the ship repeatedly traversed. Darwin made a series of extended journeys into the interior, collecting specimens (which he would periodically dispatch to England) and writing his notes and journal. He was increasingly puzzled by fossils of what he knew were extinct animals, just as he was by apparent evidence of great if infinitely slow changes in the landscape.

> "The natural history of this archipelago [The Galapagos] is very remarkable: it seems to be a little world within itself; the greater number of its inhabitants, both vegetable and animal, being found nowhere else."
> *Charles Darwin, Journal of the Beagle*

NORTH ATLANTIC OCEAN

Azores

Canary Islands

EUROP

Cape Verde Islands

AFRIC

Galapagos Islands

SOUTH AMERICA

Ascension Island

CALLAO

BAHIA

St. Helena

RIO DE JANEIRO

VALPARAISO

MONTEVIDEO

SOUTH PACIFIC OCEAN

SOUTH ATLANTIC OCEAN

CAPE TOWN

Falkland Islands

Strait of Magellan TIERRA DEL FUEGO

FIND OUT MORE

Journal of Researches into the Natural History and Geology of the Countries Visited During the Voyage of HMS Beagle
Charles Darwin

Inside the Beagle with Charles Darwin
Fiona MacDonald

Fossils, Finches, and Fuegians: Darwin's Adventures and Discoveries on the Beagle
Richard D. Keynes

Above: When Darwin's *Origin of the Species* was published in 1859, God-fearing Victorian opinion was outraged by the idea that men might share their ancestry with apes.

Above: Tierra del Feugo and the Straits of Magellan made a forceful impression on the young Darwin. This was not merely the result of its isolation, bitter climate, and savage grandeur. Rather, he was fascinated and appalled by its natives, "miserable savages" in his words. "Could our progenitors have been men like these?" he asked. "Could civilized men have evolved from such brutish backgrounds?"

The voyage home

On June 11 the Beagle entered the Pacific and headed north to Valparaiso. Over a 15 month period Darwin mounted three major sorties into the Andes, finding clear evidence that these lofty heights had once been at the bottom of the sea.

On September 7, 1835, the ship began its voyage home, calling first at the Galapagos, then Tahiti, New Zealand, and Australia, before heading north to the coral atolls of the Cocos Islands in the Indian Ocean, which Darwin correctly identified as having once been volcanoes. May 31 saw the expedition at Cape Town. Falmouth, and home, was reached on October 2, 1836 after brief halts at St Helena, Ascension Island, and Brazil.

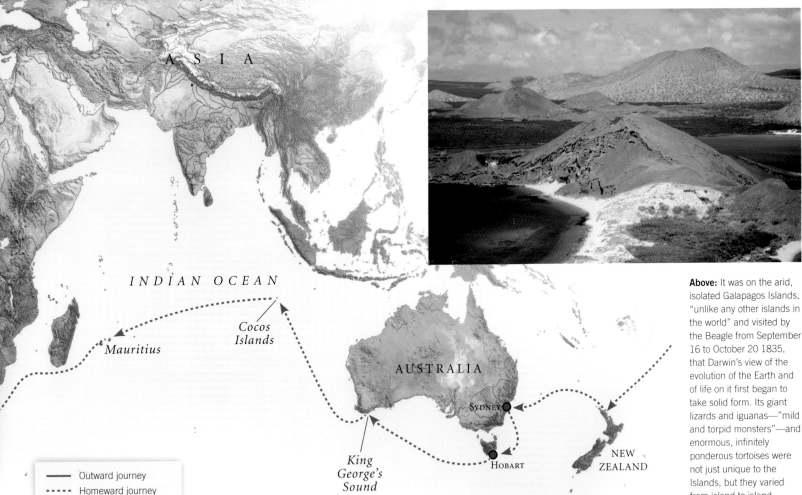

A S I A

INDIAN OCEAN

Cocos Islands

Mauritius

AUSTRALIA

SYDNEY

King George's Sound

HOBART

NEW ZEALAND

—— Outward journey
---- Homeward journey

Above: It was on the arid, isolated Galapagos Islands, "unlike any other islands in the world" and visited by the Beagle from September 16 to October 20 1835, that Darwin's view of the evolution of the Earth and of life on it first began to take solid form. Its giant lizards and iguanas—"mild and torpid monsters"—and enormous, infinitely ponderous tortoises were not just unique to the Islands, but they varied from island to island.

ACROSS THE PACIFIC
Mutiny on the Bounty

Second-in-command on the Bounty, Fletcher Christian was only 24 years of age when he overthrew his suddenly tyrannical captain, William Bligh. Three weeks out from Tahiti, Christian was tormented by the need to choose between his professional duties, or to end his humiliation at Bligh's hands. On April 28, 1789, he chose a criminal act of desperation that could end only with life-long exile or the hangman's noose. Mutiny required a degree of moral courage that effectively destroyed him, while Bligh, bent on revenge, suffered no such qualms. This was a human drama played out against the improbable background of a voyage to the Pacific to collect food to feed West Indian slaves.

Above: Bligh's 47-day, 3,620-mile (5,825 km) journey to Timor in the overloaded launch into which he and 18 loyal crew members had been hastily forced, was a feat of seamanship, navigation, and endurance that is almost without equal.

The Voyage of the Bounty

At the start of the voyage in December 1787, the mood on board was optimistic, and Bligh and Christian, who had sailed together before, were unusually close. Yet Tahiti, reached 10 months later, was their undoing. The ship was there for almost six months, collecting 1,015 breadfruit plants. The island was a tropical idyll, its people childlike in their innocence and lavish with sexual favors. The return to sea and reality lowered spirits all round and almost at once, Bligh began to pick on Christian, rounding on him on the flimsiest of pretexts and frequently humiliating him in front of the ship's company. Christian was well liked, but given to black moods, and when Bligh accused him of stealing some coconuts—an accusation that is said to have reduced Christian to tears—the younger man snapped. He intended at first to build a raft and take his chances on his own, risking sharks and shipwreck. Instead, muttering all the while, "I am in hell, I am in hell," and egged on by similarly disaffected members of the crew, he decided on mutiny. At 5:30 the following morning, Bligh, incredulous and outraged, was bundled from his cabin. The die was cast.

Above: The mutiny on the Bounty has inspired three major Hollywood movies: in 1935, with Clark Gable as Fletcher Christian and Charles Laughton weighing in as Bligh; in 1962, with an unusually languid Marlon Brando pitting himself against Trevor Howard's permanently angry Bligh; and in 1985, with Mel Gibson and Anthony Hopkins.

—— Route of the Bounty before the mutiny
—— Route of the Bounty after the mutiny
----- Route of Bligh in an open boat

NEW GUINEA

Timor

Torres Strait

CORAL SE

AUSTRALIA

TASMANIA

Left: Tahiti loomed large in European imaginations ever since the first European landing there in 1767. Its climate was gentle, its soil fertile, and its seas teeming. The people were also unspoiled, and so the image of the "noble savage," untainted by contact with civilization and living in harmony with a benign nature, was born.

"There never was such a set of damned thieving rascals under any man's command before. God damn you, you scoundrels... You may all go to hell!"
William Bligh, to the crew of the Bounty, April 27, 1789

Pitcairn

Knowing the Royal Navy would hunt them down, the mutineers spent nine months voyaging across the South Pacific without purpose. They eventually arrived—by chance—at Pitcairn Island in January 1790. Realizing that Pitcairn had been mis-charted by the Navy, and was hence a fairly safe refuge, the island gave them the promise of salvation. However, life on Pitcairn was less than idyllic. Nine mutineers, including Christian, arrived at Pitcairn, along with six Tahitian men, 11

Tahitian women, and a baby. There were tensions from the start and in September 1793, five of the mutineers, Christian among them, were killed fighting the Tahitian men, all of whom were also killed. Of the remaining four mutineers, one subsequently fell off a cliff when drunk, a second was "executed" in 1799, and a third died naturally the next year. This left only John Adams—the "patriarch of Pitcairn"—who died in 1825 at the age of 62.

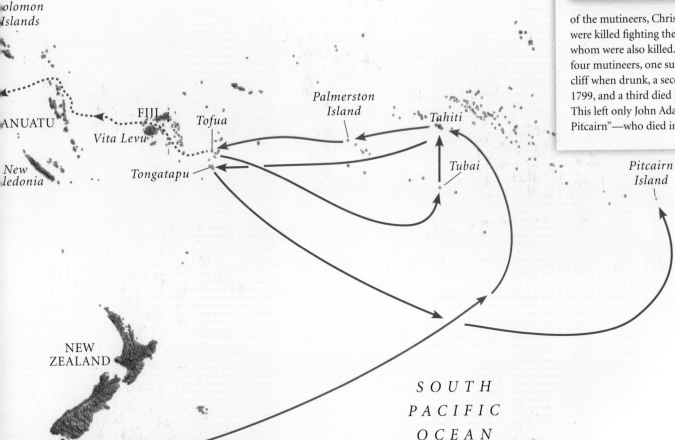

olomon
Islands

ANUATU

FIJI

Vita Levu

Tofua

Palmerston
Island

Tahiti

New
ledonia

Tongatapu

Tubai

Pitcairn
Island

NEW
ZEALAND

SOUTH
PACIFIC
OCEAN

FIND OUT MORE

A Narrative of the Mutiny on Board His Majesty's Ship Bounty
William Bligh

The Bounty: The True Story of the Mutiny on the Bounty
Caroline Alexander

Captain Bligh and Mr Christian: The Men and the Mutiny
Richard Hough

Even as the population of the world grows to 6.6 billion, substantial areas of unspoilt wilderness and grandeur remain. Mountains, deserts, and jungles across the globe retain their pristine glory. The icy wastes of the Arctic and Antarctic alike necessarily remain almost entirely aloof from human activity. Elsewhere, deliberately preserved national parks allow anyone to experience nature in the full.

NATURAL SPLENDORS
Wonders of the modern world

Whatever the rate of deforestation in South America, huge areas of tropical jungle remain, such as Venezuela's Mount Roraima, the "lost world" of popular imagination and an area of natural beauty that is utterly remote from the modern world. The vast open spaces of the American west boast a series of magnificent national parks that serve as stark reminders that little more than a century ago these magnificent landscapes were still genuinely a frontier. Even as apparently domesticated a country as New Zealand offers a series of impressive natural attractions: the Southern Alps in the South Island, and a chain of volcanoes

in the North Island. To its south lies Antarctica, a magnificently desolate wasteland of snow, ice, and mountains.

At the opposite end of the Earth is the fjord-fractured coastline of Norway, site of tiny fishing communities, medieval "stave" churches, teeming bird life, and immense views. An entirely different experience is offered by Timbuktu in the arid and empty expanses of the bleakly beautiful southern Sahara, and once one of the major entrepôts of an elaborate trans-Saharan trade network. It is a land of heat, dust, and history. Africa was the birthplace of humanity, mankind's earliest ancestors emerging perhaps 4.5 million years ago. The extraordinary landscapes where they took their first tentative steps lie in the shadow of Mount Kilimanjaro, its peak permanently snow-capped despite its proximity to the Equator and the fact that it is a volcano. As the highest mountain in Africa, it is also one of the "seven summits"—the highest mountains in each continent. Together, they make a unique challenge to mountaineers, but towering over them all is Everest, the world's highest mountain and still the ultimate climbing experience.

THE AMERICAN WEST
National Parks

The scenic wonderland of national parks in the American West are a geologist's paradise. As well as the vast Grand Canyon, carved out by the mighty Colorado River, other canyon landscapes provide a kaleidoscope of colors. Amazing rock formations of arches, natural bridges, pinnacles, and needles defy gravity—some, such as Rainbow Bridge, the largest natural bridge in the world, are not even technically within national parks, so rich is this region in natural treasures. Ancient Pueblo cultures that flourished around 1000 years ago built huge villages and cliff dwellings, while traces of pre-human life are now fossilized in the rocks. And finally there are fantastic sand dunes, huge caves, and the drama of the Rockies. Where else on Earth can you see such variety?

Above: Carlsbad Caverns is best known for its "Big Room," but one of the most exciting caves here is the Lechuguilla Cave, a very deep cave in pristine condition that is being studied by scientists for possible cures for cancer.

A tour of the parks

Begin your journey in the great red desert landscapes: the towering buttes and mesas of Monument Valley; the perfectly framed sandstone Arches; and the fragile flaming orange pinnacles of Bryce Canyon. For more fantastical rock formations head to Canyonlands. You reach the continental divide in the high peaks of Rocky Mountain National Park, and follow the range south to Great Sand Dunes. Now head into New Mexico, to the underground landscape of Carlsbad Caverns, and the gypsum emptiness of White Sands. Finally it's back into Arizona to the Petrified Forest and on to the Grand Canyon.

Left: Monument Valley was made famous by John Ford's 1939 *Stagecoach*, starring John Wayne. Since then it has been used as a typical Wild West backdrop in many other movies.

Below: At Mesa Verde, the Puebloan people built 500 dwellings in the sandstone cliff, including a 200-room palace. This, and other centers, were abandoned around 1300 AD.

Grand Canyon

One of the world's greatest wonders, the Grand Canyon is 280 miles (450 km) long, on average 10 miles (16 km) wide, and around 1 mile (1.5 km) deep—and getting deeper as the Colorado river continues to carve out the rock. It is not the deepest canyon in the world, nor the longest, but its immense volume earns it its name. Over four million visitors flock to the South Rim each year to gape at the 7,380 foot (2,250 m) drop from Grandview Point. The popular Bright Angel Trail descends to Phantom Ranch in the canyon bottom, where summer temperatures can be 61°F (16°C) hotter than on the North Rim.

CANADA

North Cascades

WASHINGTON

Olympus

Mount Rainier

ROCKY MOUNTAINS

Glacier

MONTANA

NORTH DAKOTA

T. Roosevelt

SOUTH DAKOTA

OREGON

IDAHO

Crater Lake

Yellowstone

Grand Teton

WYOMING

Wind Cave

Badlands

Redwood

NEVADA

Dinosaur National Monument

UTAH

Rocky Mountain

COLORADO

Great Basin

Capitol Reef

Arches

Yosemite

King's Canyon

Bryce Canyon

Canyonlands

Zion

Mesa Verde

PACIFIC OCEAN

Sequoia

Death Valley

Monument Valley

Grand Canyon

CALIFORNIA

Petrified Forest

ARIZONA

NEW MEXICO

Channel Islands

White Sands National Monument

Carlsbad Caverns

TEXAS

MEXICO

Big Bend

FIND OUT MORE

Down the Grand Canyon: John Wesley Powell's 1869 Journey of Discovery and Tragedy Through the Grand Canyon Edward Dolnick

Pueblos: Prehistoric Indian Cultures of the Southwest Bruggmann, Maximilien, and Sylvio Acatos

Photographs of the Southwest Ansel Adams

www.npr.gov

Left: The fantastic orange, red, and white-colored rock formations of Bryce Canyon make it one of the highlights of the American West. It is not actually a canyon, but a giant picture-perfect amphitheater of hundreds of eroded pinnacles known as *hoodoos*, a few of which form natural arches.

"The one great sight that every American should see."
Theodore Roosevelt after visiting the Grand Canyon.

VIKING VOYAGES
Iceland to Newfoundland

That the Vikings had reached and settled Newfoundland was long assumed little more than myth, known only from sagas, their own origins lost in impenetrable Dark Age obscurity and only written down many centuries later. Even the much better attested Portuguese and English voyages of the late 15th and early 16th centuries to North America are themselves only dimly known from fragmentary sources. There is no documentary evidence at all of the Viking voyages—the record is purely archaeological. Yet it unambiguously confirms that around 1000 AD, possibly blown off course during an attempted voyage from Greenland, Leif Eriksson, son of Eric the Red, who himself established two settlements in Greenland, reached and briefly settled Newfoundland.

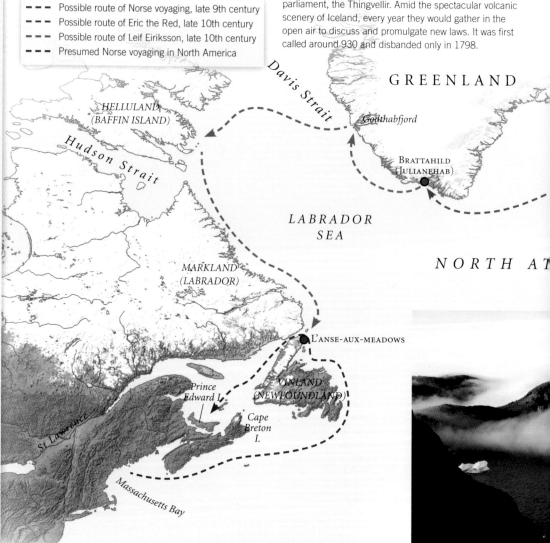

Above: As the Vikings gradually colonized Iceland in the 9th century, so they imported their own distinctive forms of administration. Among the most important was a parliament, the Thingvellir. Amid the spectacular volcanic scenery of Iceland, every year they would gather in the open air to discuss and promulgate new laws. It was first called around 930 and disbanded only in 1798.

Following the Vikings

Reconstructing the process where the Vikings ventured west into the Atlantic is a matter of conjecture at best. That they had ocean-going vessels is certain. There is equally little doubt that the perils of ocean voyaging were familiar to them, even if this inevitably raises questions about how reliably they could navigate over long distances. It is equally the case that the climate between about 800 to 1300 was substantially warmer than today, this "medieval warm period" making even such northerly outposts as Iceland and Greenland viable places of settlement and, no less important, reducing the risks of ice swept south from the Arctic. By the late 9th century, Vikings had established themselves in Iceland and by the late 10th century in Greenland. Brattahlid—the "Eastern Settlement"—was founded in 986, while today's Godthåbfjord—the "Western Settlement"—was established some years later.

- - - Possible route of Norse voyaging, late 9th century
- - - Possible route of Eric the Red, late 10th century
- - - Possible route of Leif Eiriksson, late 10th century
- - - Presumed Norse voyaging in North America

Davis Strait

GREENLAND

Godthabfjord

HELLULAND (BAFFIN ISLAND)

Hudson Strait

BRATTAHILD (JULIANEHAB)

LABRADOR SEA

NORTH AT

MARKLAND (LABRADOR)

L'ANSE-AUX-MEADOWS

Prince Edward I.

VINLAND (NEWFOUNDLAND)

Cape Breton I.

St Lawrence

Massachusetts Bay

Left: The frigid, mountainous landscape of Baffin Island highlights the hostility of the new lands the Vikings sought out. Yet they could never have been reached at all had the Vikings not been supreme shipbuilders, their vessels swift and sturdy. In fact the reality of long voyages on an undecked ship, at the mercy of winds and currents, almost always cold and wet, explains why regular voyages to Newfoundland could not be sustained.

Leif Eriksson

Swept west from Greenland across the Davis Strait, Leif Eriksson subsequently turned south, skirting the coasts of Baffin Island, which he called Helluland (or "Rock Island"), and Labrador, which he called Markland (or

"Woodland"). When he reached it, he called Newfoundland "Vinland," a reference to the grapes he claims to have found there. He reported that it was plentifully stocked with fish, salmon especially, and well grassed. A settlement was subsequently established at L'Anse-aux-Meadows. It lasted a matter of years only and was abandoned at some point between 1010 and 1025, the settlers driven away both by natives and, it is thought, the realization that it was simply too distant to support. Nonetheless, it has been conjectured that exploratory voyages to the south, perhaps as far as Massachusetts, were made. All that can be said with certainty is that the remains of 15 dwellings have been excavated at L'Anse-aux-Meadows, but there is little evidence of long-term settlement. The Vikings may have reached America, but it was a discovery with no consequences, unreported elsewhere, and never followed up. However remarkable, it became, in effect, unknown.

Left: The fog-shrouded coast of Newfoundland. The Vikings were not the only Dark Age sailors believed to have crossed the Atlantic. In the 6th century, St. Brendan is said to have journeyed to the New World in a leather-built boat. His voyage was recreated by English adventurer, Tim Severin, in 1976–7. In 1998, an American expedition sailed a reconstruction of a Viking ship from Greenland to Newfoundland, a journey that took 87 days.

> **FIND OUT MORE**
>
> *The Viking Discovery of America: The Excavation of a Norse Settlement* Helge Ingstad and Anne Stine Ingstad
>
> *Viking Voyagers* Alan Lawrie Binns
>
> *Viking America: The Norse Crossings and Their Legacy* James Robert Enterline

Left: These reconstructions of the Viking dwellings at L'Anse-aux-Meadows highlight the lonely, windswept nature of the site: remote and isolated, perched on the lip of a vast and threatening sea, and accessible only by a tortuous voyage. They are an eloquent witness to the hardiness of these early pioneers.

Map labels

Denmark Strait

ICELAND

NORWEGIAN SEA

Faeroe Is.

Shetland Is.

NORWAY

IC OCEAN

NORTH SEA

IRELAND

FJORDLAND AND THE NORTHERN LIGHTS
Along the Norwegian coast

Norway's six-day cruise from Bergen to Kirkenes, along a thousand miles of mountainous coastline riven with sinuous fjords, is the "World's Most Beautiful Voyage." Once north of the Arctic Circle, the summer nights are non-existent as the sun never dips below the horizon, while in winter the dark skies are illuminated by the glimmering green glow of the Aurora Borealis (Northern Lights). Painted wooden houses line the waterfronts of the towns that nestle in the rocky landscape, which is home to flocks of puffins, guillemots, and other seabirds. You may also spot reindeer around the cliffs, and whales can often be sighted north of the rugged Lofoten Islands towards Tromso.

"Hammerfest… is on the edge of the world, the northernmost town in Europe, as far from London as London is from Tunis, a place of dark and brutal winters, where the sun sinks into the Arctic Ocean in November and does not rise again for ten weeks."
Bill Bryson, Neither Here Nor There

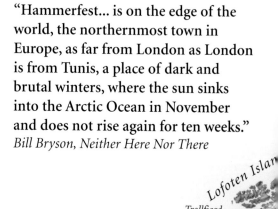

Crusing the north coast

Cruises start from Bergen, calling first at Sognefjord—the longest fjord—which contains some of the finest stave churches at Urnes and Hopperstad, and the precipitous Flam railway. You can learn about ice at the museum near Jostedalsbreen, the largest glacier in mainland Europe. Most famous of the fjords is majestic Geirangerfjord, with waterfalls tumbling from its steep cliffs and the Art Nouveau town of Alesund perched at its entrance. Trondheim, the country's first capital, still stages the coronations of Norway's kings in its medieval cathedral. Crossing the Arctic Circle, you'll reach Tromso, the starting point for many polar explorers, including Amundsen and Nansen. After Hammerfest, the world's northernmost town, you finally round Nordkapp (North Cape) with its sheer cliffs, before finding safe harbor in Kirkenes on the Russian border.

Above: The Northern Lights (or Aurora Borealis) is a natural light display seen in the polar regions, caused by the collision of charged particles with the Earth's magnetosphere.

Below: Geirangerfjord, known for its outstanding beauty, is almost 10 miles (15 km) long.

Nordkapp

Hammerfest

Tromso

Varangerfjord

Kirkenes

FINLAND

RUSSIA

SWEDEN

Edvard Grieg

Edvard Grieg (1843-1907) is Norway's foremost composer, pianist, and conductor. Born in Bergen, he enrolled at the Leipzig Conservatory of Music at the age of 15. In  1867 he married soprano singer Nina Hagerup, and the couple lived at Troldhaugen (Troll's Hill) just outside Bergen. Much of his music was inspired by Norway's folk music and legends, and best known are his Piano Concerto, Peer Gynt Suites, and Holberg Suite. He once wrote, "I make no pretensions of being in the class with Bach, Mozart, and Beethoven. Their works are eternal, while I wrote for my day and generation."

FIND OUT MORE

An Enemy of the People
Henrik Ibsen

A History of the Vikings
Gwyn Jones

Neither Here Nor There
Bill Bryson

Insomnia
(Movie)

Right: Bergen, known as the "capital of the fjords," is noted for its stunning scenery, but also for its 260 days of rain each year. The town has attractive painted buildings, as well as a castle dating from 1261 and the 11th century St Mary's Church. It was European City of Culture in 2000, and boasts the famed Greighallen (concert hall), as well as a national theater formerly directed by Ibsen.

SCOTT, SHACKLETON, AND AMUNDSEN
The Antarctic

Antarctica is the world's largest desert; 5.44 million square miles (14 million km²) of snow and vast ice sheets whose average depth is over 6,000 feet (1,828 m). It contains the world's seven largest glaciers and boasts the record for the lowest temperature ever recorded, -121°F (-84.9°C). It has been called the world's "coldest, driest, windiest, and highest place," and unsurprisingly, its population is officially zero. It was first sighted in 1820 and first landed on only in 1899. It was this pristine wilderness, its interior entirely unknown, that from the turn of the 20th century lured European explorers, their ultimate object to reach the South Pole itself, the "world's last great geographical goal."

Both Scott's expeditions to the Antarctic (**below**) were concerned with much more than than reaching the Pole itself, although this was the most conspicuous and easily understood goal. Rather, these were properly scientific expeditions. On his second expedition, Scott took no less than eight scientists and two doctors, among them three geologists, a physicist, and a meterologist. Whether studying the infinite variety of sea life (**above** and **left**), meticulously recording the weather, or merely measuring and charting, the foundations for the scientific study of the region were being laid—a tradition that continues to this day.

Robert Scott

The first systematic attempt to open the interior of Antarctica was led by a British naval officer, Robert Scott, between 1901–4. On the whole, it was a discouraging effort. Scott had no experience of polar travel and, inhibited by his rigid naval background, proved a slow learner. He understood neither skis nor dogs, the two essential prerequisites for polar travel, relying instead on man hauling, which ensured minimum progress and maximum effort. Among his expedition was an Irishman, Ernest Shackleton (who developed a cordial loathing for Scott), who in 1907–9 led a second assault on the Pole. Though suffering from the same technical limitations as Scott, he was a strikingly better leader. He not only pioneered a route up the 11,000-foot (3,352 m) Beardmore Glacier to the polar plateau, but also came within 97 miles (156 km) of the Pole before dwindling supplies forced him to turn back. However, the race to the South Pole was unambiguously on.

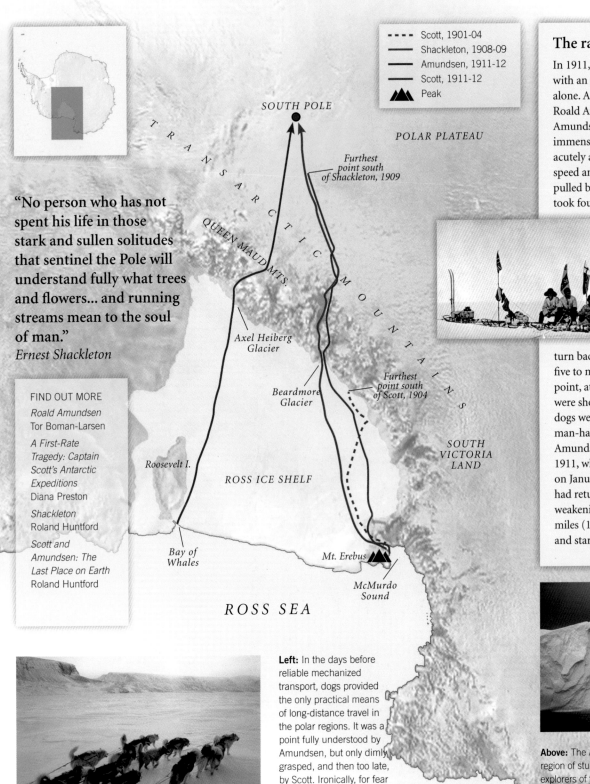

Scott, 1901-04
Shackleton, 1908-09
Amundsen, 1911-12
Scott, 1911-12
▲▲ Peak

SOUTH POLE

POLAR PLATEAU

Furthest point south of Shackleton, 1909

T R A N S A R C T I C   M O U N T A I N S

QUEEN MAUD MTS.

"No person who has not spent his life in those stark and sullen solitudes that sentinel the Pole will understand fully what trees and flowers... and running streams mean to the soul of man."
Ernest Shackleton

Axel Heiberg Glacier

Beardmore Glacier

Furthest point south of Scott, 1904

SOUTH VICTORIA LAND

FIND OUT MORE
Roald Amundsen
Tor Boman-Larsen

A First-Rate Tragedy: Captain Scott's Antarctic Expeditions
Diana Preston

Shackleton
Roland Huntford

Scott and Amundsen: The Last Place on Earth
Roland Huntford

Roosevelt I.

ROSS ICE SHELF

Bay of Whales

Mt. Erebus

McMurdo Sound

ROSS SEA

The race to the Pole

In 1911, Scott returned to the Antarctic with an even larger party, but he was not alone. A Norwegian expedition led by Roald Amundsen had also journeyed there. Amundsen was everything Scott was not: immensely experienced in snow and ice, acutely aware that polar travel depended on speed and mobility, which meant small parties pulled by large numbers of dogs. Amundsen took four men and 52 dogs to the Pole, while Scott took 16 men, 10 ponies, 23 dogs (added almost as an afterthought), and two tractors. Where Amundsen planned to take all his men to the Pole, Scott's were scheduled to turn back at regular intervals, leaving only five to make the final push. Even more to the point, at the foot of Beardmore, the ponies were shot for food. Shortly afterwards, the dogs were returned to base. Thereafter, Scott man-hauled. It was, literally, killing work. Amundsen reached the Pole on December 14, 1911, while Scott got there over a month later, on January 17, 1912. By the time Amundsen had returned to his base, Scott's party, rapidly weakening, were still on the polar plateau, 645 miles (1,038 km) behind. All died, exhausted and starving, on the forlorn journey.

Left: In the days before reliable mechanized transport, dogs provided the only practical means of long-distance travel in the polar regions. It was a point fully understood by Amundsen, but only dimly grasped, and then too late, by Scott. Ironically, for fear that they would spread disease, dogs were banned from Antarctica in 1994.

Above: The Antarctic, fearsomely hostile though it is, is a region of stunning natural beauty. Every one of the early explorers of the region left remarkable accounts of their first sight of its seemingly limitless variety of ice, whether the vast pack-ice that surrounds the continent or the cathedral-like icebergs that plough their stately way through its frozen seas.

To Timbuktu
Into Africa

The fabled city of Timbuktu was an important medieval trading-center, where North African Arabs could swap salt for West African gold brought down the Niger River. Europeans heard tales of untold riches in this exotic city "at the end of the world," and it is still a dreamed-of destination—though most of the excitement is in the intrepid journey, by foot and *pinasse* (boat), through magical Mali. It is inhabited by amazing peoples, from the indigo-clad Tuareg on their camels, the Bozo fishermen of the Niger Delta, to the colorful-masked Dogon performing fantastical ritual dances.

Above: Timbuktu became a great center of trade and learning, in spite of its location in one of the harshest deserts on earth.

Below: Djenné Mosque's mud brick construction, rebuilt in 1906, requires constant maintenance to ensure its survival.

FIND OUT MORE
Sahara
Michael Palin

Cruellest journey: 600 miles to Timbuktu
Kira Salak

"Salt comes from the north, gold from the south, and silver from the country of the white men, but the word of God and the treasures of wisdom are only to be found in Timbuktu."
West African proverb

Bamako to Timbuktu

Mali's capital, Bamako, has one of Africa's finest museums, with fascinating cultural and archeological displays, including a stunning collection of Dogon masks. Head north to Ségou, a French colonial town with bags of atmosphere, before moving on to Djenné, world-renowned for its mosque—the largest mud-brick structure in the world—and its colorful market. The Bandiagara Escarpment is a 1,640-foot (500 m) sandstone cliff that runs for some 93 miles (150 km). It is superb for trekking, and the only way to get to the many inaccessible Dogon villages on the way. Then sail downriver to Timbuktu to see its mosques and soak up its history. If it doesn't feel like you've reached the end of the world yet, join one of the huge camel caravans for the 17-day journey into the Sahara heading north to the salt-pans at Taoudenni, and then on to Tangier, or east through Algeria.

Above: The Dogon people live in the central plateaus of Mali. They follow animist beliefs, in particular worshipping their ancestors. Rituals known as *damas* involve masked dancers portraying animals, people, and objects. There are around 80 styles of mask, decorated with beads, shells, and animal skin.

THE GREAT WALKS OF NEW ZEALAND
Eight walks and a river ride

The Great Walks of New Zealand are eight magnificent walking routes plus, somewhat strangely, a river journey. Take your pick of jaw-dropping scenery: glacial mountains, crystal-clear lakes, mossy rainforests and majestic fjords. Some of the tracks follow old Maori trails, or routes made by pioneer explorers, while others are modern trails laid by the Department of Conservation, who maintain all paths and facilities—indeed, the main challenge may be booking early enough to get in. The most popular are the Routeburn Track, the Tongariro Crossing, and the Milford Track.

Left: Tongariro was New Zealand's first national park, and the fourth oldest in the world. Noted for much volcanic activity, it is also a traditional area for the Maori. Its highest peak, Mt. Tongariro, reaches 6,490 feet (1,978 m).

South Island

Six of the routes are on the South Island, including "the finest walk in the world," the Milford Track. The Routeburn Track is close by, through high passes and rich forested valleys teeming with wildlife. The Kepler Track near Te Anau is another alpine trek, which becomes the annual Kepler Challenge when people run the 37 mile (60 km) distance in under 5 hours! Rakiura Track is a shorter trail on Stewart Island, south of the mainland, which only opened in 2001. Abel Tasman Coast Track and the Heaphy Track—the longest route—follow the impressive scenery along the coastline.

"A land of stupendous mountains, roaring cataracts, silvery cascades, fantastic volcanic formations, magnificent landscapes, noble forests, and picturesque lakes."
Thomas Bracken, The New Zealand Tourist (1879)

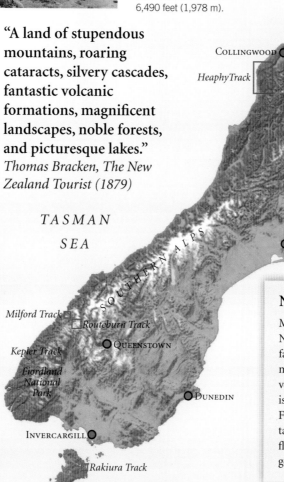

Above: Over half a million visitors come each year to Milford Sound, described by Rudyard Kipling as the eighth wonder of the world. The inlet is named after Milford Haven in Wales and runs inland for over 9 miles (15 km).

North Island

Moving to the North Island, the Tongariro Northern Circuit is an extension of the famous Tongariro Crossing, taking in a moonscape of thermal vents around an active volcano, while Lake Waikaremoana Track is located in the Te Urewera National Park. Finally, once your boots have worn through, take the 5-day Whanganui River Journey, floating by kayak or raft through spectacular gorges and exciting rapids.

THE SEVEN SUMMITS
Climbing the world's peaks

The Seven Summits are the highest mountains on each of the world's seven continents. As a mountaineering goal, tackling them is a relatively recent idea, first put forward in the 1980s by an American, Dick Bass, who completed all seven in 1985. But the list has never been without controversy. Because a mountain is the highest in any given continent, it is not necessarily significant in mountaineering terms, and many claim that the rise of guided climbing has put undue pressure on guides to "deliver" summits to climbers who lack the experience to tackle them. Above all, there is debate about precisely which mountains to include on the list, yet the lure of the Seven Summits persists.

Messner's Seven Summits

Name	Height (ft. / m)	Continent
Everest	29,021 / 8,845	Asia
Aconcagua	22,835 / 6,960	S. America
McKinley	20,316 / 6,192	N. America
Kilimanjaro	19,335 / 5,893	Africa
Elbrus	18,505 / 5,640	Europe
Mount Vinson	16,045 / 4,890	Antarctica
Carstensz Pyramid	16,019 / 4,882	Australasia

 Peak

Seven peaks

Five of the peaks—Everest, Aconcagua, McKinley, Kilimanjaro, and Mount Vinson—are not disputed, but some people argue that Mount Elbrus is not properly in Europe, and that Mont Blanc, at 15,770 feet (4,807 m) should be included in its place. More contentiously, Bass's list also includes Kosciuszko in Australia, which, at 7,307 feet (2,227 m), is not merely the baby of the list, but technically hardly a challenge at all. In 1986 the Italian climber Reinhold Messner (**below**), produced a revised list, with Carstensz Pyramid in Indonesia, taking the place of Kosciuszko. The first man to climb Messner's Seven Summits was a Canadian, Pat Morrow, in 1986, and later that year, Messner himself completed all seven.

Right: The more challenging Messner list, which includes Indonesia's Carstensz Pyramid, is generally accepted as the more authentic of the Seven Summits. The second highest mountain on the list, Aconcagua in the Andes, is not even among the world's 100 highest mountains, all of which are in central Asia, chiefly in the Himalayas and Karkorum mountains.

FIND OUT MORE

Seven Summits: The Quest to Reach the Highest Point on Every Continent Steve Bell, Dick Bass, and Pat Morrow

Beyond Everest, Quest for the Seven Summits Pat Morrow

Seven Summits Dick Bass, Frank Wells, and Rick Ridgeway

www.7summits.com

CLIMBING EVEREST
The world's highest mountain

By 1973, 20 years after the first successful ascent, Everest had been climbed 38 times. Twenty years later it had been climbed a further 576 times, yet by 2003, 10 years later again, it had been climbed a further 1,304 times, taking the total number of successful climbs to 1,918. Over the following four years, this number almost doubled: between 2004 and 2007 there were 1,857 successful ascents of Everest, and 627 in 2007. By the end of the year the mountain had been climbed a total of 3,679 times, but there is still nothing routine about the ascent—to date, 210 people have lost their lives on Everest.

Left: The first successful ascent of Everest was made by a British expedition in May, 1953. Britain had pioneered attempts on the mountain between the wars, but in 1952 a Swiss expedition was the most successful to date, coming within 1,000 feet (305 m) of the summit. The 1953 British expedition, when Edmund Hillary (**right**) and Tenzing Norgay (**left**) reached the summit, was the result of a military-style operation.

Conquering Everest

The figures highlight an evident problem: that Everest, known as Chomolungma or Qomolangma, ("Mother of the Universe") to the Tibetans, and Sagarmatha ("Goddess of the Sky") to the Nepalese, has fallen victim to the kind of status-driven tourism that is rapidly despoiling one of the world's most desolately beautiful and remote regions. Yet whatever the numbers plodding to the summit, or, in the case of French pilot Didier Delsalle in 2005, arriving by helicopter, Everest remains profoundly hostile, its combination of mind-numbing altitude and rapidly changing weather potentially lethal even to the most experienced. In 1996, 15 people died on the mountain, 11 of them in May alone. This makes the achievements of Reinhold Messner, who in 1978 climbed the mountain without oxygen, all the more remarkable. No less extraordinary, in 1999 a Sherpa, Babu, spent 22 hours on the summit without oxygen. Other astonishing firsts were the ascents in 2001 by a blind American, Erik Weihenmayer; by the 15-year-old Temba Tsheri; and, in 2007, by 71-year-old Katsusuke Yanagisawa.

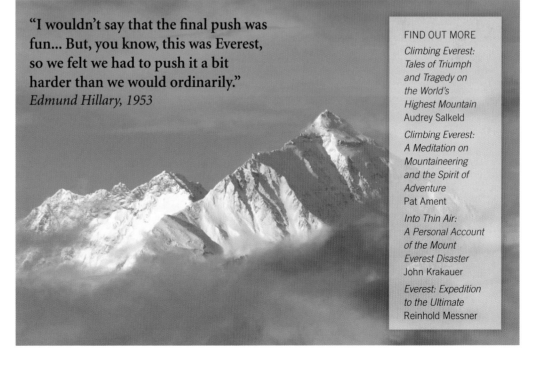

"I wouldn't say that the final push was fun... But, you know, this was Everest, so we felt we had to push it a bit harder than we would ordinarily."
Edmund Hillary, 1953

Above and Right: Everest may not be the most technically demanding mountain to scale, but the simple fact that it is the highest mountain in the world has always made it the ultimate challenge for any climber. It possesses a mystic that no other mountain can claim.

FIND OUT MORE

Climbing Everest: Tales of Triumph and Tragedy on the World's Highest Mountain
Audrey Salkeld

Climbing Everest: A Meditation on Mountaineering and the Spirit of Adventure
Pat Ament

Into Thin Air: A Personal Account of the Mount Everest Disaster
John Krakauer

Everest: Expedition to the Ultimate
Reinhold Messner

KILIMANJARO SAFARI
The peak of Africa

Africa's tallest mountain at 5,895 meters, "Kili" has many titles—the world's tallest freestanding mountain, the world's tallest walkable mountain, and one of the world's tallest volcanoes. Recent evidence suggests it is not inactive but merely dormant—could it be the next Mt St Helens? Kilimanjaro is Swahili for "mountain of greatness" and the Masai nomads know its summit as the "Home of God." Climbing it—a beautiful walk to the roof of Africa—can be combined with a safari on the Serengeti Plains and Ngorongoro Crater, set in the Great Rift Valley (the great gash in Africa from Mozambique up to Syria), or with a relaxing week on the spice island of Zanzibar.

The trek to Kilimanjaro

Start in the rolling grasslands of the Serengeti, dotted with herds of zebra and antelope and Masai tending their cattle, and depending on the time of year enjoy the spectacular annual wildebeest migration, which can only be fully appreciated from the air. Next, on to Olduvai Gorge, the "Cradle of Humankind," where in 1959 Louis and Mary Leakey discovered the skull of the 1.7-million-year-old "nutcracker man." The extinct Ngorongoro Crater has some of the densest populations of game in the world, and at night animals will sniff round your tents on the crater's rim. Finally, a five or six day trek will take you to the summit of Kilimanjaro itself. An army of porters will carry backpacks, supplies, and even the kitchen table on their heads—quite a sight trekking up the mountain, but everything that is needed for the journey has to be carried up.

Above: The "Big Five"—lion, leopard, elephant, rhino and buffalo—are the safari addict's targets. However, sightings of a dashing, rare cheetah or a dangerous, mud-loving, hippo are just as special.

Disappearing glacier

The vast icecap that covered Kilimanjaro's summit a century ago has dwindled by 80% (**below**), and many people now believe it will be gone entirely by 2020. Al Gore, among others, highlighted the ice-melt as a direct result of climate change, although he was condemned for this in court due to a lack of evidence.

In reality it is very hard to say whether the ice-melt is due to increased temperatures, decreased precipitation, a reduction of the forests in surrounding areas, or other factors not caused by humans. But what is clear is that many of the world's tropical glaciers are retreating, and several are predicted to vanish in the near future.

Left: The great plains of Tanzania and Kenya have the greatest concentrations of wildlife anywhere on the planet. Most people have seen these animals in zoos or on TV, but nothing compares with seeing them in the wild. It is the thrill of not knowing what the day has in store—elegant antelope, a majestic pride of lions, flocks of brilliant pink flamingoes—each experience fills you with the awe of nature.

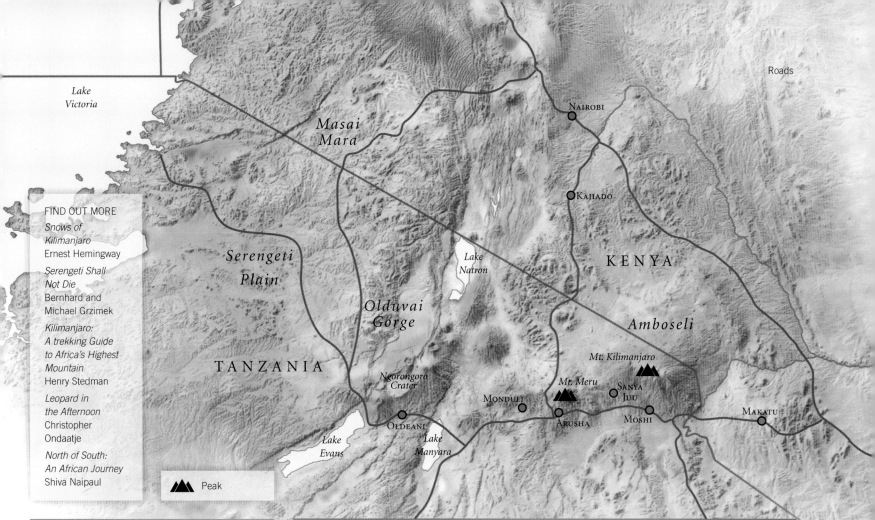

Roads

Lake
Victoria

NAIROBI

*Masai
Mara*

KAJIADO

*Serengeti
Plain*

Lake
Natron

K E N Y A

Amboseli

*Olduvai
Gorge*

Mt. Kilimanjaro

T A N Z A N I A

*Ngorongoro
Crater*

Mt. Meru

SANYA
JUU

MONDULI

MAKATU

OLDEANI

ARUSHA

MOSHI

*Lake
Evans*

*Lake
Manyara*

Peak

"As wide as all the world, great, high,
and unbelievably white in the sun,
was the top of Kilimanjaro."
Ernest Hemingway, Snows of Kilimanjaro

Above and Right: After several days of walking, gaining
height and adapting to the altitude, you are ready for the
final ascent to the top of Kilimanjaro. Starting at around
midnight it is a long, hard and steady slog to reach the
flattish summit, just in time to see a well-earned sunrise
glinting on the icecap.

THE LOST WORLD
The land that time forgot

Deep in Venezuela's remote jungle, the majestic Mount Roraima rises through the clouds. This vast table mountain, 9,219 feet (2,810 m) tall, straddles the border with Guyana and Brazil. European explorers first scaled its immense cliffs in 1874, discovering a unique ecosystem including carnivorous plants, rare orchids, giant rodents, and colorful frogs. Tales of this "lost world" have been the inspiration for many writers from Sir Arthur Conan Doyle to Michael Crichton, whose novel was turned into a sequel to the film *Jurassic Park*. But this is not Venezuela's sole natural wonder. Spectacular waterfalls plummet from the cliffs—including the world's tallest, the 3,212 ft (979 m) Angel Falls—and the Orinoco River has rocky cataracts and a labyrinthine delta of islands and mangroves.

Exploring the Lost World

Orinoco means "a place to paddle," and canoeing at Boca de Uracoa is a great start to a trip. Upstream are the great cataracts, which forced 16th-century explorer Sir Walter Raleigh to turn back from his quest for El Dorado. The road then heads for the gold-mining town of El Callao, and on to the Indian village of Paraitepui, where if you are lucky you may see a poison-arrow frog. From here the trek begins, past waterfalls (Kukenán Falls are the world's second-tallest single drop), across rivers (using ropes if there have

been heavy rains), and sleeping in sandy "hotels" under rocky overhangs. Roraima looms ahead—a sandstone cliff nearly 3,280 feet (1,000 m) high, with a "ramp" path leading to its sky-top plateau.

Three days of walking will bring you to the summit, where you'll explore the crystal valley, see the endemic wildlife, and enjoy the awesome views across the jungle far below. For a much longer trek, descend past two more picturesque waterfalls—Jasper and Chinak Meru—and head for the tallest fall of all, Angel Falls, although easier ways to see it are by taking a boat ride or scenic flight.

Canaima National Park (**above**), covering an area the size of Belgium, was established in 1962. It is home to the Pemon Indians, who believe its fabulous table-top mountains (*tepuis*) are sacred. The area became a UNESCO World Heritage Site in 1994. The most famous tepuis are Mount Roraima (**below**) and Auyantepui, from whose height plummets the graceful Angel Falls (**right**).

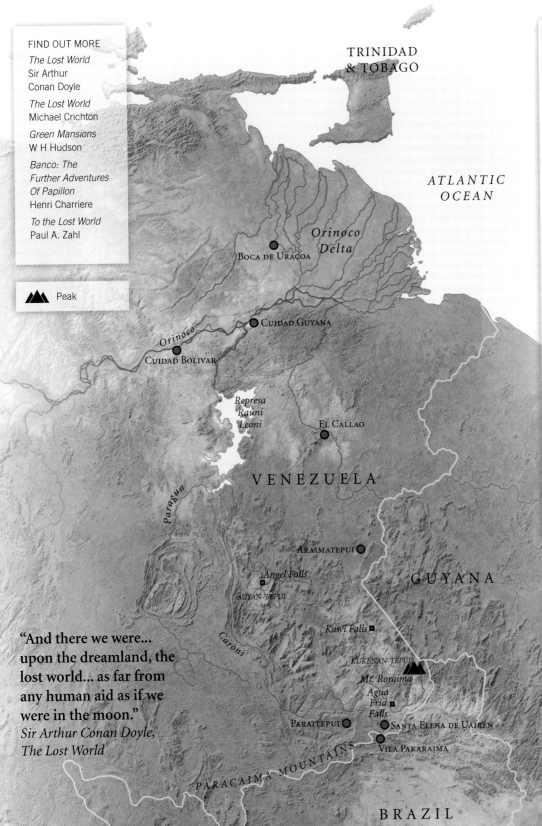

▲▲ Peak

TRINIDAD & TOBAGO

ATLANTIC OCEAN

Orinoco Delta

Boca de Uracoa

Cuidad Guyana

Orinoco

Cuidad Bolivar

Represa Rauni Leoni

El Callao

VENEZUELA

Paragua

Araimatepui

GUYANA

Angel Falls

AUYAN-TEPUI

Caroni

Kawi Falls

KUKENAN-TEPUI

Mt. Roraima

Agua Fria Falls

Paraitepui

Santa Elena de Uairén

Vila Pakaraima

PARACAIMA MOUNTAINS

BRAZIL

"And there we were...
upon the dreamland, the
lost world... as far from
any human aid as if we
were in the moon."
*Sir Arthur Conan Doyle,
The Lost World*

Sir Arthur Conan Doyle

Arthur Conan Doyle (1859-1930) was born in Edinburgh, studying medicine before he turned to writing fiction due to a lack of patients. His first major work was the Sherlock Holmes story *A Study in Scarlet* written in 1887, but it was four years later that his popularity really took off, when he contributed short stories to the *Strand Magazine*. Later in life he somewhat resented being identified solely as the creator of Sherlock Holmes: his second most famous character was Professor Challenger, whose exploits first appeared in *The Lost World* in 1912, in which the hero discovers a plateau cut off from the rest of the world, where dinosaurs still roam.

Above: The Orinoco Delta is a chance to experience the way of life of the indigenous Warao people, while practicing your canoeing skills. It is also where Christopher Columbus is supposed to have set foot on the New World, only realizing it was a continent because of the vast flow of fresh water he found here.

PICTURE CREDITS

ACKNOWLEDGMENTS

No book is produced in isolation, and the publishers would like to thank the following team for their commitment, hard work, and for ensuring the "Great" was kept in *100 Great Journeys.*

Keith Lye, Consultant Editor, for overseeing the maps, retracing the great routes, and lending us his geographical genius.

The writers—**Thomas Cussans, Catherine Jagger,** and **Richard Mason**—for painstakingly researching the journeys (in many cases undertaking them), and bringing their travels to life through words.

Nick Rowland, for the hours spent in front of the computer, meticulously rendering the maps and applying the routes with pinpoint precision.

Rosie Barratt, Tamsan Barratt, and **Mike Croft** for searching through thousands of images to find stunning photographs of the sublime and the obscure, and **James Mollison** for kindly allowing us to use his image of the Khyber Pass.

And last, but by no means least, **Graham Davis,** for taking all of the component parts and piecing them together on the page—the book looks great.

Thank you all for making this happen.

INDEX